Personal narratives of Irish and Scottish migration, 1921–65

MANCHESTER
1824

Manchester University Press

Personal narratives of Irish and Scottish migration, 1921–65

'For spirit and adventure'

Angela McCarthy

Manchester University Press
Manchester and New York

distributed exclusively in the USA by Palgrave

Published by Manchester University Press
Oxford Road, Manchester M13 9NR, UK
and Room 400, 175 Fifth Avenue, New York, NY 10010, USA
www.manchesteruniversitypress.co.uk

Distributed in the United States exclusively by
Palgrave Macmillan, 175 Fifth Avenue,
New York, NY 10010, USA

Distributed in Canada exclusively by
UBC Press, University of British Columbia, 2029 West Mall,
Vancouver, BC, Canada V6T 1Z2

British Library Cataloguing-in-Publication Data is available

Library of Congress Cataloging-in-Publication Data is available

ISBN 978 0 7190 7353 3 paperback

First published by Manchester University Press in hardback 2007

This paperback edition first published 2012

Printed by Lightning Source

Contents

List of figures

Acknowledgements

In 1938 Gerard McCarthy, my grandfather, left his home in Millstreet, County Cork, and voyaged on the *Rangitane*, arriving at Wellington, New Zealand. The passenger register recorded him as a 22-year-old carpenter from the Irish Free State. Accompanying him was his pal, 25-year-old carpenter David Ronayne, listed as originating from Eire. Throughout the next few years Gerard plied his trade as a carpenter and in 1942 was arrested by the police for failing to report to the Army for a medical examination. This would not be his last appearance in the *Police Gazette*! In 1948 he was charged with theft from a boarding house he temporarily managed. His defence, as recounted by *Truth* newspaper, was that he needed to get his wife and sick child to Auckland for medical attention. By 1951 and with four children he disappeared, a warrant having been issued for his failure to provide maintenance. Police and social agency searches were futile. In the late 1990s I discovered Gerard had died two decades earlier in Christchurch. Hospital records revealed that in 1974 a Catholic priest found him unconscious in the street. Admitted to hospital, Gerard underwent surgery to relieve pressure in his cranial area. He had suffered a stroke and was placed in residential care. He was evasive, refusing to answer questions asked by social workers. He even supplied a false name – Patrick Gray – and was listed under both names on his death certificate in 1978, having seemingly divulged his true identity to his carer. Upon receiving the various documents that enabled the reconstruction of the last years of his life, contact was made with the daughter of his carer. She had kept his crucifix and located a photograph of him. Gerard McCarthy's remains lie in an unmarked grave at Ruru Lawn Cemetery in Christchurch.

Stories such as my grandfather's are rarely recounted in studies of migration and this book is no different. Its source materials are based predominantly on migrant testimonies such as letters, shipboard journals, diaries, and interviews. They are the output of those who achieved a measure of success in migrating, or were at least willing to recount their experience as a migrant. Alas, there is little in these pages that recount disturbing and alarming life histories. Yet there is in what follows many frightening aspects of the migrant experience: the terror of events in Ireland during the Revolution; emotional farewells; the dislocation accompanying the voyage out; the trauma at Ellis Island; and the puzzling nature of initial impressions of new societies. But so too is there excitement surrounding packing, the warmth of personal and institutional networks, the vibrant expressions of ethnic identities, and the ongoing ties with home that led some to return to their place of birth. All these themes and more are captured through the lens of personal testimonies.

Among those who generously supplied copies of documents relating either to themselves or their kin who undertook migration experiences were Joan Leonard (Brigid Dawson's daughter), May Tapp (Mary Gibson's daughter), Melanie King (of the Robertson family), and Lorna Ross (née Carter). The latter not only vividly related her experience of migration to me, but also generously supplied me with the original letters she sent home from New Zealand, together with an array of ephemera. I am especially indebted to all. Aonghas MacConnich was also enormously helpful, not only bringing to my attention several Gaelic memoirs held at Comann Eachraidh Nis, but transcribing them into English for me as well.

The bulk of material incorporated throughout this book was obtained from two main sources. First, it draws upon the Oral History collection at the Ellis Island Immigration Museum, where I am grateful to Janet Levine for handling numerous queries and providing permission to publish. Second, it utilises written questionnaires completed by Irish and Scottish migrants who were part of a broader project on assisted migration to New Zealand after the Second World War. This project was conducted by Megan Hutching of the Ministry for Culture and Heritage, New Zealand, and I am enormously grateful to Megan for generously making these questionnaires available to me and to the Ministry for providing permission to publish extracts.

I would also like to acknowledge the assistance of Linda Bevan Smith and Vicki Hughes at the Alexander Turnbull Library's oral history section and Diane Gordon at the Auckland War Memorial Museum Library for facilitating my listening to numerous local and institutional oral history interviews in New Zealand. Permission to quote from these interviews was generously granted by Jacqui Foley, Judith Fyfe, Rosie Little, Trudie Lloyd, Sister Mary McAleese Laboure, Sister Madeline McAleese, Nelson Provincial Museum, Joyce Paton, the New Zealand Society for the Intellectually Handicapped, Ian and Elayne Robertson, Walter Solly, Trade Union History Project, and the Women's Division of Federated Farmers.

Other individuals and institutions were similarly helpful. I am grateful to Doreen Wilkinson and Hamilton City Libraries for granting permission to reproduce interview extracts and to Kate DeCourcy of Special Collections at Auckland City Libraries for providing me with a copy of the Sydney Samuels recording. Source materials were also acquired and are reproduced with permission from the Alexander Turnbull Library, the Oral History Collection, National Library of Australia, the National Library of Scotland, the National

Maritime Museum, Greenwich, and Orkney Archives. I am also grateful to Sean Ladd from the Department of Labour for providing me with permission to consult immigration files at National Archives Wellington.

Examining this material was facilitated by my time as Research Fellow at the AHRC Centre for Irish and Scottish Studies at the University of Aberdeen, while the bulk of it was written during my stint as the 2005 J. D. Stout Research Fellow in New Zealand Studies at Victoria University of Wellington, New Zealand. I am especially indebted to my colleagues at the Stout Research Centre for their support and to the Friday night Bodega crowd for their conviviality and friendship. I would also like to thank Nick Evans, Lyndon Fraser, Chris Harvie, and Don MacRaild who all gave generously of their time to comment on specific chapters. Marjory Harper, John MacKenzie and Eric Richards have been constantly supportive and I would like to thank them for their encouragement and advice.

Research for this book was substantially facilitated by the National Maritime Museum at Greenwich who awarded me the Caird Senior Research Fellowship to undertake research on their maritime ephemera collections which forms a major part of the analysis in Chapters 3 and 4. The National Maritime Museum also provided a number of images for reproduction, as did Glenbow Archives and the National Park Service: Statue of Liberty National Museum. Several repositories generously waived their reproduction fees for the images incorporated in this book and I would especially like to thank: National Archives of New Zealand, Alexander Turnbull Library, Wellington, State Library of Queensland, State Library of South Australia, and the National Library of Scotland. I am grateful to the AHRC Centre for Irish and Scottish Studies for supplying funds for the acquisition and/or reproduction of these images.

Finally, I would like to thank the team at MUP who brought the final product to fruition.

Angela McCarthy
Hull

List of abbreviations

ACL	Special Collections, Auckland City Libraries
AJHR	*Appendices to the Journals of the House of Representatives*
ATL	Alexander Turnbull Library
ATL OHC	Alexander Turnbull Library Oral History Centre
BAIQ	British Assisted Immigrants Questionnaire, Ministry of Culture and Heritage
CEN	Comann Eachraidh Nis
EIOHP	Ellis Island Oral History Programme, Statue of Liberty/Ellis Island National Monument
HCL	Hamilton City Libraries
NAW	Archives New Zealand/Te Whare Tohu Tuhituhinga O Aotearoa, Head Office, Wellington
NLS	National Library of Scotland
NMM	National Maritime Museum
NZMM	New Zealand Maritime Museum
OA	Orkney Archives
OHC NLA	Oral History Collection, National Library of Australia

Editorial notes

Where Ireland is used throughout this book it encompasses the 32 counties. Irish is likewise used to embrace migrants from both states, in light of their own self-identification as Irish.

The spelling and grammar contained in the original documents reproduced in this book remains unaltered, though sentence and paragraph breaks have been incorporated. Editorial excisions have been kept to a minimum but are as follows:

Clarifications:	abal kilt [*about killed*] me
Authentic oddities:	el*e*tist
Illegible words:	[*word illegible*]
Illegible words with suggestions:	[?*oft*]
Words deleted or omitted:	[*erased:* and]

The transcription of interviews is likewise faithful except for the removal of stuttering and fillers such as 'ums' and 'ahs'.

Introduction

Methods, approaches, sources

In April 1929 Annabella Sinclair left Orkney with her young family bound for Sydney, Australia, on board the *Baradine*. During her passage she maintained a journal, noting that 'Loneliness never seems to visit any of our family here at all. I dream many a time of home for all that only to wake up and find myself still in the Red Sea and soaking with sweat. I sweated more here surely than ever I did in my life'. Annabella went on to describe the minimal clothing worn and passengers suffering from swollen legs, including her own.[1] Six months later Ernest Younger returned from Toronto to Tillicoultry, east of Stirling, on board the *Athenia*. He wrote jauntily to his parents while at sea: 'Again Johnnie was among the prizes. A lady rigged him up in one of my rugs (the cheaper one) & he had a little glengarry that someone had given him to take to a friend & with a water bottle under his arm he led the parade round the lounge. He got the prize for the most original costume. He was done up as a billie, & little whisk brush for a sporran & the water bottle was supposed to be bagpipes. The prize was a little camera.'[2] By 1935 13–year-old Mary Jo Lenney accompanied her family on the *Manhattan* to New York from Ballina, County Mayo. Reconstructing that journey 60 years later in an oral interview, Mary Jo mused vividly, 'if you walked down the corridor you couldn't walk a straight line and I remember one night when we were out in the middle of the ocean all the dishes and the food and everything went flying off the table. It was exciting.' Her mother, on the other hand, 'was saying the rosary every day, she was scared to death'.[3] Fifteen years later Thomas Brown, a Presbyterian from Belfast, migrated to New Zealand, and retrospectively recorded his recollections in a written questionnaire:

On the good ship 'Atlantis' we had a number of lectures to explain about life in N.Z. and one piece of advice which made a strong impression on me was 'There

1 Shipboard journal of Annabella Sinclair, 1929, OA, D1/118. Extract dated [28] April 1929.
2 Ernest Younger (*Athenia*) to his parents (Tillicoultry), 5 October 1929, NLS, Acc. 9407/2. Extract dated 10 October 1929.
3 Interview with Mary Jo Lenney by Paul Sigrist, recorded 21 August 1996, EIOHP, EI Series 793.

are 2½ million people in NZ and there is only one of you, so it would be much easier for you to change your ways' good advice which I followed, I refused to join the Irish Club, Settlers Club or the R.S.A. and I never once mentioned 'Back-Ome'.[4]

These brief accounts encompass many aspects contained in this book. Though focusing on a particular element of the migration process – the voyage – they reveal the diverse personal testimonies charting that undertaking. Shipboard journals, private letters, oral interviews, and written questionnaires are all deployed to penetrate the inner worlds of migrants. Such snippets also illuminate the range of destinations covered: Australia, Canada, the United States, and New Zealand, as well as documenting change across time – from the 1920s through to the mid-1960s, reflecting in 1921 the partition of Ireland and gathering of dominion governments to establish the Empire Settlement Act, and the introduction of the United States Immigration and Nationality Services Act of 1965. Likewise, these extracts encapsulate the myriad thoughts and feelings of individual migrants contained in this book: men and women, boys and girls, single and married, Irish and Scots. Among the captivating themes explored, hinted at only briefly in the above snapshots, are loneliness, fear, physical hardship, expressions of identities, and adjustment. The reasons people left, why they chose the destinations they did, their initial impressions of the new worlds in which they settled, their daily adjustments, their ongoing contact with fellow expatriates and home ties, and in some cases their return, are all scrutinised.

This book fills a major gap in the historiography of migration from two of Europe's most striking migrant groups. It makes an original contribution in two respects. First, it adopts a comparative perspective, analysing countries of origin as well as four destinations. The second contribution is methodological, using raw migrant narratives to convey a sense of migration as a story. Before examining the broader context of this outflow from Ireland and Scotland, issues relating to transnationalism, comparison, and history and memory are surveyed.

Transnationalism and comparison

In recent years transnationalism has emerged as a major concept in considering historical and contemporary migrations. Developed initially by anthropologists and sociologists, transnationalism in a broad sense seeks to examine 'the processes by which immigrants build social fields that link together their

4 Thomas Brown, 028, BAIQ.

country of origin and their country of settlement'.[5] These transnational 'social spaces' include familial, economic, political, and religious ties that transcend the borders of nation states. Communication exchanges, flows of information and remittances, and the role of social networks are all fundamental areas of analysis.[6] A transnational approach is important for it 'posits the existence of modes of understanding and of behavior that span homelands and destinations and defy conventional time and space, especially national boundaries'.[7] Shaping and sustaining such transnational ties are informal and formal networks. Composed of family and friends at a social level, or political, cultural, and business contacts in a formal setting, intending migrants could secure a range of information about their proposed destinations and utilise networks to assist their adjustment after arrival. The operation of such networks before, during, and after the move abroad is specifically examined throughout this book.

In an article on the Irish in the United States, Kevin Kenny calls for 'a migration history that combines the disaporic or transnational with the comparative or cross-national'. Such an approach would investigate the contact between the homeland and a number of destinations and 'integrate those transnational inquiries with comparative study'. Both approaches need to be combined, Kenny advocates, as only then can 'immigration and ethnicity be integrated into its wider global context'.[8] Kenny's plea is a sound one, and he grapples with the contested term 'disapora', problematic in part because it is historically associated with forced dispersal, and posits that migrants maintained a collective memory or myth about their homeland based on exile. The term also implies that there was a singular diaspora for various ethnic groups, rather than many diasporas, as Donna Gabaccia has formulated for Italian migration.[9] So too can diasporas move beyond the ethnic group, with Robin Cohen suggesting, among others, trade, labour, and cultural diasporas.[10] Yet using the term diaspora is perhaps more useful as a process rather than descrip-

5 Nina Glick Schiller, Linda Basch and Cristina Blanc-Szanton, 'Transnationalism: a new analytic framework for understanding migration', in Nina Glick Schiller, Linda Basch and Cristina Blanc-Szanton (eds), *Towards a Transnational Perspective on Migration: Race, Class, Ethnicity, and Nationalism Reconsidered. Annals of the New York Academy of Sciences*, 645 (New York: New York Academy of Sciences, 1992), p. 1.
6 Steven Vertovec, 'Conceiving and researching transnationalism', *Ethnic and Racial Studies*, 22:2 (1999), p. 456.
7 David A. Gerber, 'Forming a transnational narrative: new perspectives on European migrations to the United States', *History Teacher*, 35:1 (2001), on line at http://www. historycooperative.org/journals/ht/35.1/gerber.html, paragraph 1.
8 Kevin Kenny, 'Diaspora and comparison: the global Irish as a case study', *Journal of American History*, 90:1 (2003), pp. 135, 150.
9 Donna R. Gabaccia, *Italy's Many Diasporas* (Seattle: University of Washington Press, 2000).
10 Robin Cohen, *Global Diasporas: An Introduction* (London: UCL Press, 1997).

tive tool, denoting 'ideas about belonging, about place and about the way in which people live their lives'.[11] As Rogers Brubaker has recently summarised, the term diaspora has met with wide disagreement surrounding its meaning, essentially encompassing 'every nameable population category that is to some extent dispersed in space'.[12] Despite this seeming impasse Brubaker summarises a number of central elements for the term: dispersal in space, orientation to the homeland, and boundary-maintenance, eventually conceptualising diaspora 'as a category of practice' involving 'stances, projects, claims, idioms, practices, and so on'.[13] Perhaps the most crucial aspect of the term is that 'it forces us to look simultaneously at the many places to which migrants traveled, and at the connections among them.'[14]

This book goes beyond traditional transnational and diasporic approaches, usually focused on two countries, and considers instead a range of destinations in which two migrant groups settled. The book is therefore comparative not only in contrasting the Irish and Scots, but also in evaluating their experiences in different countries of settlement. There are a number of considerable benefits to a comparative approach. First, it exposes similarities and differences in order to identify what is general and specific. It also prevents allegations of exceptionalism. Comparison furthermore enables the formulation of new research problems and questions. There are, however, drawbacks, including the necessity of mastering more than one national historiography. Such are the obstacles that few scholars of Irish and Scottish migration have undertaken such a task.[15]

11 Virinder S. Kalra, Raminder Kaur and John Hutnyk, *Diaspora and Hybridity* (London: Sage Publications, 2005), pp. 3, 29.
12 Rogers Brubaker, 'The "diaspora" diaspora', *Ethnic and Racial Studies*, 28:1 (2005), p. 3.
13 *Ibid.*, pp. 5, 12–13.
14 Gabaccia, *Italy's Many Diasporas*, p. 9.
15 Among those who have taken up the challenge, primarily for the nineteenth century and focused on destinations rather than groups, are Malcolm Campbell in a number of articles: 'Emigrant responses to war and revolution, 1914–21: Irish opinion in the United States and Australia', *Irish Historical Studies*, 32:125 (2000), pp. 75–92; 'The other immigrants: comparing the Irish in Australia and the United States', *Journal of American Ethnic History*, 14:3 (1995), pp. 3–22; 'Ireland's furthest shores: Irish immigrant settlement in nineteenth-century California and Eastern Australia', *Pacific Historical Review*, 71:1 (2002), pp. 59–90; 'Immigrants on the land: a comparative study of Irish rural settlement in nineteenth-century Minnesota and New South Wales', in Andy Bielenberg (ed.), *The Irish Diaspora* (Harlow: Longman, 2000), pp. 176–94; David Noel Doyle, 'The Irish in Australia and the United States: some comparisons, 1800–1939', *Irish Economic and Social History*, 16 (1989), pp. 73–94; J. Matthew Gallman, *Receiving Erin's Children: Philadelphia, Liverpool, and the Irish Famine Migration, 1845–1855* (Chapel Hill: University of North Carolina Press, 2000); Donald Harman Akenson, *The Irish Diaspora: A Primer* (Toronto and Belfast: P. D. Meany Company, Inc. and The Institute of Irish Studies, Queens University of

The combined comparative and transnational approach followed in this book is therefore significant in offering a new way of looking at migration. In doing so, it engages with Nancy Green's formulation of comparative history, which posits three approaches: linear, divergent, and convergent. The linear model is clearly important in ascertaining comparisons between country of origin and country of settlement. This study not only undertakes that contrast but also compares it with a convergent model in which the experiences of different groups in one place are examined. Such an approach, however, posits that contrasts will be the result of the groups rather than the destination. Yet this is clearly contentious in studies of migration and must be analysed in concert with Green's divergent model which attributes differences to places of arrival, rather than origin.[16] Yet all models are static unless more than one migrant group is compared.

This book therefore adopts suggestions for comparison by scholars like Kenny and Green but compares not one, but two, migrant groups in different destinations. In undertaking a comparative study it is impossible to compare the totality of the Irish and Scottish migrant experience. Rather, specific questions and problems to be compared must be identified from the sources deployed. As such, this book undertakes systematic analysis of a number of central issues pertinent to the migrant experience, including motives for leaving, the voyage, initial settlement, the development and articulation of cultural identities, and return. In evaluating the Irish and Scottish migrant experience such comparisons are not reliant on secondary sources, but in both cases utilise primary material, thus facilitating systematic rather than impressionistic assessments.

The comparison of the United States with the British World destinations of Australia, Canada, and New Zealand is also a worthwhile venture. First,

---

Belfast, 1996); and Donald M. MacRaild, 'Crossing migrant frontiers: comparative reflections on Irish migrants in Britain and the United States during the nineteenth century', *Immigrants and Minorities*, 18:2&3 (1999), pp. 40–70. For Scottish migration see T. M. Devine, *Scotland's Empire, 1600–1815* (London: Allen Lane, 2003) and Marjory Harper's *Emigration from Scotland Between the Wars: Opportunity or Exile?* (Manchester: Manchester University Press, 1998) and *Adventurers and Exiles: The Great Scottish Exodus* (London: Profile Books, 2003).

16 See Nancy L. Green, 'The comparative method and poststructural structuralism: new perspectives for migration studies', in Jan Lucassen and Leo Lucassen (eds), *Migration, Migration History, History: Old Paradigms and New Perspectives* (Bern: Peter Lang, 1997), especially pp. 67–71. See also Nancy L. Green, 'The modern Jewish diaspora: eastern European Jews in New York, London, and Paris', in Dirk Hoerder and Leslie Page Moch (eds), *European Migrants: Global and Local Perspectives* (Boston: Northeastern University Press, 1996), pp. 263–81. For other perspectives on comparison see Samuel L. Baily, 'Cross-cultural comparison and the writing of migration history: some thoughts on how to study Italians in the New World', in Virginia Yans-McLaughlin (ed.), *Immigration Reconsidered: History, Sociology, and Politics* (New York and Oxford: Oxford University Press, 1990), pp. 241–53.

settlement in the United States is of a longer duration than Canada, Australia, and New Zealand. Second, while Australasia and Canada were part of the British Commonwealth, the United States was independent. The United States also had significant non-British migrant populations, whereas Australia and New Zealand preferred British stock, despite the growing presence of migrants from other European countries throughout the century. Canada, on the other hand, with its strong French settlement, can be viewed as a hybrid between Australasia and the United States.

What, though, is the rationale for comparing the migration of the Irish and the Scots? First, Scotland and Ireland share a long history of emigration into the British Empire and Commonwealth, a stark contrast with other migrant groups in Europe. Second, in numerical terms emigration from both Irish states in the period under discussion replicated that of Scotland, with around 2 million people leaving. Third, both groups were predominantly English-speaking, a feature which clearly demarcates them from other European migrant groups. Fourth, the destinations to which they predominantly moved were also English-speaking and close in cultural terms. Such cultural proximity raises issues relating to adjustment, a phenomenon understood best by personal memory rather than statistics. Furthermore, not only has their geographical proximity facilitated sustained linkages over the centuries, but also the small size of both countries enables comparison to be feasible.[17] Irish and Scottish migrants also provided major contributions to their recipient societies. Some interesting differences also exist in relation to the socio-economic profile of the broader migrant groups. The outflow from Ireland was predominantly composed of the rural young, single, and unskilled, with the gender profile relatively balanced.[18] By contrast, Scots were more likely to be skilled migrants from urban industrial areas.[19]

17 T. M. Devine, 'Making the Caledonian connection: the development of Irish and Scottish Studies', in Liam McIlvanney and Ray Ryan (eds), *Ireland and Scotland: Culture and Society, 1700–2000* (Dublin: Four Courts Press, 2005), pp. 248–57; T. M. Devine, 'Irish and Scottish development revisited', in David Dickson and Cormac Ó Gráda (eds), *Refiguring Ireland: Essays in Honour of L. M. Cullen* (Dublin: Lilliput Press, 2003), pp. 37–51. See also the outputs from a number of symposia: L. M. Cullen and T. C. Smout (eds), *Comparative Aspects of Irish and Scottish Economic and Social History, 1600–1900* (Edinburgh: John Donald, 1977); T. M. Devine and David Dickson (eds), *Ireland and Scotland, 1600–1850: Parallels and Contrasts in Economic and Social Development* (Edinburgh: John Donald, 1983); Rosalind Mitchison and Peter Roebuck (eds), *Economy and Society in Scotland and Ireland, 1500–1939* (Edinburgh: John Donald, 1988); S. J. Connolly, Rab Houston, and R. J. Morris (eds), *Conflict, Identity and Economic Development: Ireland and Scotland, 1600–1939* (Preston: Carnegie Publishing, 1995).
18 Enda Delaney, *Irish Emigration Since 1921* (Dublin: The Economic and Social History Society of Ireland, 2002), pp. 12–14.
19 Michael Flinn (ed.), *Scottish Population History from the 17th Century to the 1930s* (Cambridge: Cambridge University Press, 1977), pp. 452–4.

Personal testimony: collections and methodology

A further comparative element of this book is its use of personal testimony, drawing as it does on such diverse sources as letters, diaries, shipboard journals, and interviews. The predominant primary source, however, is oral interviews. All told, the book utilises 102 oral interviews (ten of which are transcripts) with Irish and Scottish migrants worldwide. The majority of these interviews (72) were undertaken for the Ellis Island Museum project, which was largely concerned with the processes of migration and settlement. Similarly, the interviews with Scots who went to Canada were taken from collections focused on migrants from Lewis who voyaged on the *Metagama* in 1923, though some later migrants with connections to those who went on the same vessel are also included. By contrast, the material from Australia was sourced from the New South Wales Bicentennial Oral History Project, a collection of 200 interviews with individuals born before 1907 who resided in New South Wales between 1900 and 1930. Though movement to New South Wales was a clear theme, these interviews also had larger issues to address, particularly in relation to local history. This is also the case with other interviews drawn from New Zealand which were typically local or institutional oral history projects. This presents an interesting methodological issue in that themes relating to migration and identity were naturally raised during the course of interviews with a broader focus. That such issues arose is significant, for this establishes the importance of migration in the life trajectories of those interviewed and reduces the possibility of bias emerging from one collection.

Additionally, the book draws upon 47 written questionnaires with Irish and Scots who moved to New Zealand after the Second World War as assisted migrants. Again, these written questionnaires were part of a major migration project in which responses were received from 282 individuals. Among other written personal testimony utilised is an extensive collection of 143 letters composed between 1925 and 1938 by Ernest Younger, a Scottish migrant in Canada. A further voluminous collection of 158 letters written by Scotswoman Lorna Carter between 1951 and 1954 is also incorporated. Two shipboard diaries composed by Scottish women who voyaged to the Antipodes in 1929 and 1938 are likewise exploited, along with an extended letter outlining the voyage and early settlement in New Zealand in 1924 of Irishwoman Brigid Dawson. While journals, like letters, were generated contemporaneously, they could contain reflective statements. Journals also tend to be a more private form of communication, yet as with the letters used in this study, these shipboard diaries were composed and then sent home.

All told, then, this book is based on source materials produced by 154 migrants (87 Scots and 67 Irish; 79 male and 75 female). Their age at migration ranged from 2 to 38 years of age. The bulk of these migrants, 91, left during the inter-war period while 63 individuals went after the Second World War. Moreover, the majority of migrants moved to either the United States or New Zealand (72 and 64 respectively). The bias in favouring analysis of migration to these destinations is warranted, because where studies of Irish and Scottish migration in the twentieth century have been undertaken Canada and Australia have received greater attention.[20]

In analysing the major Ellis Island sources, some interesting contrasts are evident. First, the Ellis Island testimony reveals that while Mayo, Galway, and Belfast supplied large numbers of migrants, most Irish counties were represented in the outflow. Scottish migrants, by contrast, emerged predominantly from Glasgow. The age of the migrants also varied. Whereas Irish migrants were primarily in their teens and twenties, more than half the Scottish migrants left as children under ten years of age. A third difference relates to the migrant's age at the time of the interview. Scottish migrants were principally in their seventies and eighties, whereas Irish migrants were in their eighties and nineties. There are, however, several similarities. First, the date of emigration for both groups took place overwhelmingly in the inter-war period, with 40 Irish and 22 Scots leaving at this time. Second, most of the interviews were conducted with these migrants in the 1990s. Third, both Irish and Scottish migrants were predominantly interviewed more than 60 years after their initial emigration.

The use of personal testimonies for studies of migration is well established, though few studies adopt a comparative approach. So too have the benefits and drawbacks of this material been eloquently debated. Crucially, deploying oral testimony enables exploration of aspects of the experience of migration that would otherwise be lost to scholars, for they facilitate penetrating analysis of themes that are best explored through individual stories. Furthermore, the longitudinal nature of oral testimony gives it 'a crucial competitive edge', as Eric Richards has argued, over the contemporary document.[21] By mapping individual accounts over time the consequences of past events can be examined. Yet complications include debates surrounding the validity, reliability, and interpretation of memory and the construction of collective memory, issues discussed further below. Migrants may, for instance, rationalise their motivations in different ways at a later date; they might also

20 In particular, see A. James Hammerton and Alistair Thomson, *Ten Pound Poms: Australia's Invisible Migrants. A Life History of Postwar British Emigration to Australia* (Manchester: Manchester University Press, 2005). Hammerton is also conducting an ongoing project looking at post-war British migration to Canada.

21 Eric Richards, 'Hearing voices: an introduction', in A. James Hammerton and Eric Richards (eds), *Speaking to Immigrants: Oral Testimony and the History of Australian Migration. Visible Immigrants: Six* (Canberra: History Program and Centre for Immigration and Multicultural Studies, 2002), p. 10.

incorporate narratives gleaned from popular history into their own personal stories or omit discussion of key events. Yet these issues and processes of self-interpretation are themselves forms of evidence. Moreover, they can be counteracted by recourse to documentary evidence or comparison with other interviews on the same topic. Interviews are also mediated by the intervention of an interviewer who typically sets the agenda for discussion, edits the interview, evaluates it, and either stores it for posterity or discards it. The level of comfort a respondent feels with questions directed towards them also shapes the interview process. Whether or not the interviewee has a personal agenda in articulating a specific version of events also needs to be considered.[22] We should also bear in mind the strong tradition within both Ireland and Scotland and abroad of printed oral histories and reminiscences.[23] Furthermore the Scots made an easy transition from oral to written, as demonstrated in the extensive use of the Scots language in popular newspapers in Victorian Scotland.[24]

Scholarly concerns about the use of personal letters, meanwhile, relate to the reliability of information contained in personal correspondence and issues of representativeness. Letters, for instance, are composed by the literate and those who wish to communicate. Yet the random and haphazard survival and acquisition of letters means that those that have survived are exceptional and therefore unlikely to be representative of either migrants or letter-writers. Methodological concerns surrounding the authenticity, editing, and presentation of transcripts are also important. Despite such apprehension, the major benefit of emigrant correspondence is in illuminating quite vividly and emotionally the varied migration experiences of individuals. Indeed, the benefits of personal letters in studies of migration are immeasurable. They often provide a two-way perspective, even though many preserved sequences contain correspondence sent in just one direction. Indeed, being an intimate, conversational means of communication, correspondents actively sought responses

---

22 There is a large literature on the theory, method and use of oral history. A useful collection of essays can be found in Robert Perks and Alistair Thomson (eds), *The Oral History Reader* (London and New York: Routledge, 1998). See also Virginia Yans-McLaughlin, 'Metaphors of self in history: subjectivity, oral narrative, and immigration studies', in Yans-McLaughlin (ed.), *Immigration Reconsidered*, pp. 254–92. For useful summaries of the applications of migrant interviews see Richards, 'Hearing voices', pp. 1–19, and Alistair Thomson's 'Moving stories: oral history and migration studies', *Oral History*, 27:1 (1999), pp. 24–37, and '"I live on my memories": British return migrants and the possession of the past', *Oral History*, 31:2 (2003), pp. 55–65.

23 See, for example, David Thomson, *Nairn in Darkness and Light* (London: Hutchinson, 1987) and John Kenneth Galbraith, *Made To Last* (London: Hamish Hamilton, 1964).

24 William Donaldson, *Popular Literature in Victorian Scotland: Language, Fiction, and the Press* (Aberdeen: Aberdeen University Press, 1986).

from recipients. Depending on the recipient, however, tone and content could vary. In addition, letter-writers decided what information they would disclose, and despite their private nature, letters could be read aloud.[25]

Quite apart from their notable differences, letters and oral testimony have similarities. Both, for instance, depend on the selective memory of the correspondent and interviewee, who shape their stories for their specific audiences. Letters and interviews also contain silences and evasions. While the correspondent might well choose to avoid penning seemingly unsuitable or sensitive topics for discussion, a deft interviewee can also elect to evade an uncomfortable issue, or shirk supplying relevant, but delicate, data.

In adopting a primary focus on personal testimony, however, it is not suggested that other sources be ignored. Instead, this book makes use of a range of statistical and documentary evidence drawn from census, immigration, and maritime files. Such sources are used to complement the personal testimonies, either to qualify or confirm statements, or to discuss critical aspects not covered in depth in the testimony, such as the operation of official schemes to assist migrants travelling to the British World. Yet it is important to examine private testimony in its own right, not merely use it to supplement other sources or 'provide color and drama in historical narratives'.[26] As David Fitzpatrick has argued, personal testimonies are vital in illuminating the 'life-long trajectories of personal migration (forwards, backwards, sideways)'.[27]

Private testimonies are therefore deployed in this book to capture the personal experiences of migration and settlement. They can also 'aid the reconstruction of nearly forgotten social institutions, demonstrate continuities and changes in memory and identity over time, and reveal individual and collective reactions to historical events'.[28] By enabling the self-expression and self-consciousness of migrants to be examined, the experience of migration can be viewed from their perspective. Such an approach is necessary because many explanations tend to ignore the self-representations of participants, preferring instead to focus on formal and group-oriented expressions of

25 For valuable discussions of the merits and drawbacks of personal letters see David Fitzpatrick, *Oceans of Consolation: Personal Accounts of Irish Migration to Australia* (Cork: Cork University Press, 1995), especially pp. 18–36; David A. Gerber, 'The immigrant letter between positivism and populism: the uses of immigrant personal correspondence in twentieth-century American scholarship', *Journal of American Ethnic History*, 16:4 (1997), pp. 3–34; Dirk Hoerder, *Creating Societies: Immigrant Lives in Canada* (Montreal and Kingston: McGill-Queen's University Press, 1999), especially pp. 16–21.

26 Gerber, 'The immigrant letter between positivism and populism', p. 4.

27 Fitzpatrick, *Oceans of Consolation*, p. 4.

28 Maria G. Cattell and Jacob J. Climo, 'Meaning in social memory and history: anthropological perspectives', in Jacob J. Climo and Maria G. Cattell (eds), *Social Memory and History: Anthropological Perspectives* (Walnut Creek: Altamira Press, 2002), p. 22.

migration. These and other themes are also blurred in analyses focused on quantitative evidence.

History and memory

By incorporating interviews with migrants conducted many years after their migration, this book is explicitly concerned with issues relating to history and memory. Indeed, the international, interdisciplinary field of memory studies is a particularly vibrant and debated one. In its links to the field of history it is especially concerned with issues of how and why particular versions of the past are represented, received, and rejected. As such it is not concerned simply with the representation of the past but its meaning.[29] Typically, such approaches have focused on competing and multiple versions of collective memory, and the way conflicting versions of the past have been appropriated and shaped by nation states to propagate particular interpretations of the past. In doing so common symbolic identifiers are typically sought to conceal fundamental differences.[30] In this way memory is usually manipulated by political and intellectual elites, who either incorporate personal narratives into general interpretations, or ignore them altogether.[31] Yet so too do individual memories incorporate or reshape formulaic narratives into private recollections. As Penny Summerfield explains, 'Theorists of cultural or popular memory and the life story argue that the discourses of, especially, popular culture inform personal and locally told life stories, in that narrators draw on generalized, public versions of the aspects of the lives that they are talking about to construct their own particular, personal accounts.'[32]

One aim of this book is, therefore, to reclaim individual memory from within the broad field of collective memory to obtain 'glimpses into the lived interior of the migration processes'.[33] This is because the importance of individual memories lies in what they can reveal about past events from the point of self. According to Alastair Thomson this provides entry into a world of knowledge, feelings, fantasies, hopes, and dreams.[34] We can tentatively, as Joanna

---

29 Alon Confino, 'Collective memory and cultural history: problems of method', *American Historical Review*, 105:5 (1997), p. 1395.

30 *Ibid.*, pp. 1399–400.

31 Wulf Kansteiner, 'Finding meaning in memory: a methodological critique of collective memory studies', *History and Theory*, 41 (2002), p. 185.

32 Penny Summerfield, 'Culture and composure: creating narratives of the gendered self in oral history interviews', *Cultural and Social History*, 1:1 (2004), p. 68.

33 Rina Benmayor and Andor Skotnes, 'Some reflections on migration and identity', in Rina Benmayor and Andor Skotnes (eds), *International Yearbook of Oral History and Life Stories*, Vol. 3: *Migration and Identity* (Oxford: Oxford University Press), p. 14.

34 Thomson, 'Moving stories', p. 29.

Bourke indicates, 'recapture a sense of awe about individuals in the past'.[35] Yet the book does not simply replicate individual stories in isolation; instead it analyses them in relation to one another and in connection with formulaic narratives of migration such as adventure or exile. Such an approach is undertaken in the light of Alon Confino's warning that memory is only useful when linked to historical questions and problems.[36] Reclaiming the individual is also warranted, as collective histories can displace experiences which may be better explored through analytical categories such as gender, class, and religion. Moreover, by analysing migration through individual stories we can, as anthropologist Caroline Brettell stresses, ascertain what aspects of the process of migration are general and what elements are particular. This can then be extended comparatively with the experiences of other migrant groups.[37] It is undertaken, however, with the knowledge 'that few actual individual lives fully conform to the master narratives'.[38]

In essence, this book considers how individual memories can become collective memories that fit, modify, or challenge dominant national narratives. It also considers the reverse of this process: the way in which the nation state endeavours to establish a dominant narrative and how the testimony of individuals and groups reinforces this. It puts the individual at the centre of the analysis, examining not only how their experiences merged with dominant narratives and how this was meaningful to individuals, but also how and why their memories deviated from standard scripts.[39] This is particularly the case with the propaganda relating to emigration emanating from both Ireland and Scotland, explored in Chapter 1, which posited emigration as draining the life-blood of these societies. But the book is also alert to the creation of collective experiences from a range of diverse stories, particularly in relation to the shared experiences of organising the passage, undertaking the voyage out, and arriving at Ellis Island (Chapters 3, 4, and 5). The book is therefore centrally concerned with the 'interpenetration of collective histories and individual life stories'.[40] As Bourke put it, individual memories not only contribute to the weaving of collective memory, but they also borrow from it.[41] Exploring the

---

35 Joanna Bourke, 'Introduction: "remembering" war', *Journal of Contemporary History*, 39:4 (2004), p. 485.
36 Confino, 'Collective memory', p. 1388.
37 Caroline Brettell, *Anthropology and Migration: Essays on Transnationalism, Ethnicity, and Identity* (Walnut Creek: Altamira Press, 2003), p. 24.
38 Benmayor and Skotnes, 'Some reflections on migration and identity', p. 15.
39 Thomson, 'Moving stories', p. 34; Anna Green, 'Individual remembering and "collective memory": theoretical presuppositions and contemporary debates', *Oral History*, 32:2 (2004), p. 42.
40 Thomson, 'Moving stories', p. 34.
41 Bourke, 'Introduction', p. 484.

complex intersection between collective histories and individual memories therefore represents the most significant contribution of the book to broader debates about the relationship between history and memory.

Connected to the creation and dispersal of collective memory are 'sites of memory' in which various elements spark acts of recollection and preserve memory.[42] These include physical sites such as monuments and museums in which certain interpretations of the past are extolled in such a way that they prove meaningful for the present and future. This does not necessitate, however, that such interpretations are static; rather, they are constantly changing under fluid political, economic, social, and cultural conditions. Such official commemoration is largely memory formation from above. In essence, the depiction at the Ellis Island Museum is a positive one, emphasising the fortitude of migrants. Similarly, disturbing recollections of their time on Ellis Island echo this portrayal, an aspect shaping Chapter 5. Aware that past recollections are often shaped by contemporary concerns, these memories are also analysed within the broader context in which remembering takes place. Chapter 5 also addresses the first impressions migrants held of New York city, while Chapter 6 examines migrant encounters with new realities in New Zealand, Australia, and Canada.

A further major element of history and memory is the issue of identity. Chapter 7 examines the deep attachments of migrants to specific places in Ireland and Scotland. It considers the ways in which personal networks based on these close kin and regional ties operated once migrants arrived at their new destinations, and then analyses group networks through societies. At a public level, ethnic and national identities are created through literacy and language, political symbols, and the role of intellectuals.[43] The formal nature of ethnic and national identities for Irish and Scottish migrants, as exhibited by language, customs, and stereotypes, is explored in Chapter 8. The relationship between memory and identity is fundamental, with questions such as who we are and where we have come from permeating discussion.[44] Current identities also affect how stories are structured and remembered.[45] This has particular implications for the memories emerging from projects focused explicitly on migration. That migrants are recollecting events as part of a forum giving particular emphasis to their ethnicity means that much of their recollection is shaped around this aspect.

---

42 See Pierre Nora, 'Between memory and history', in Pierre Nora (ed.), *Realms of Memory: Rethinking the French Past*, Vol. 1: *Conflicts and Divisions* (New York: Columbia University Press, 1996), pp. 1–20.

43 Jonathan Hearn, 'Narrative, agency, and mood: on the social construction of national history in Scotland', *Comparative Study of Society and History*, 44:4 (2002), p. 747.

44 Thomson, 'Moving stories', p. 35.

45 *Ibid.*, p. 35.

Yet collective memory can also be a shared identity linking smaller groups such as the family.[46] As Wulf Kansteiner has proposed, a project may pursue the collective memory of the family whose members forge a unified interpretation of the family's origin and identity.[47] Indeed, the family played a crucial role in shaping cultural identities as discussed in Chapter 8. Memory is clearly generational and the book reveals that families played a significant role in the shaping of migration stories. Not only did motives for migration occasionally take on a sensational character, but so too were identities shaped by generational exchanges. The novelty of alleged Irish and Scottish characteristics emphasised in accounts presumably goes some way to explaining the continued interest among the children of migrants. Yet the ways in which these memories were disseminated among the extended descent group awaits another study. The thrust of this book, however, is to argue that individual migrations and memories were fundamentally shaped by networks of family and friends. These ongoing transnational connections also proved vital when migrants considered returning home, as outlined in Chapter 9.

Before proceeding with these themes, the broader context of Irish and Scottish migration needs to be established. Chapter 1 sets the scene by providing a statistical overview of the outflows and considering the broader historiographical issues shaping this book. How extensive was Irish and Scottish migration and how was it perceived? What role did assisted passages and agents play in the process? Where did Irish and Scottish migrants settle and what aspects relating to their identities appear in the wider discourse?

46 Confino, 'Collective memory', p. 1390.
47 Kansteiner, 'Finding meaning in memory', p. 189.

Historiography and context

Background and historiography

In historical and contemporary terms, Ireland and Scotland have extensive pedigrees in relation to migration. The major outflows, however, occurred from the nineteenth century onwards. Between 1801 and 1921 8 million Irish sought new lives on distant shores, while the remainder of the twentieth century saw approximately 2 million people depart the island of Ireland, with at least one quarter of those leaving Northern Ireland.[1] Such was the insatiable impetus of the outflow in the later nineteenth century that Ireland lost almost half its population and ranked first among European countries exporting migrants.[2] The outward surge of approximately 2 million from Scotland in both the nineteenth and twentieth centuries ensured that it was also consistently placed in the top four countries supplying migrants between 1851 and 1930.[3] Indeed, during the inter-war period, the exodus from Scotland was proportionately greater than from other European countries, supplying as it did two-thirds of Britain's net emigration during the 1920s.[4]

How do these two flows compare internationally? First, the statistics are slippery, particularly as no accounts were kept of cross-border flows in to and out of Scotland and Ireland. Yet as earlier, Irish and Scottish migration in the twentieth century was part of a broader exodus, with approximately 60 million

1 David Fitzpatrick, *Irish Emigration, 1801–1921* (Dublin: The Economic and Social History Society of Ireland, 1984), p. 3; Enda Delaney, *Irish Emigration Since 1921* (Dublin: The Economic and Social History Society of Ireland, 2002), p. 1.
2 David Fitzpatrick, 'Irish emigration in the later nineteenth century', *Irish Historical Studies*, 22:86 (1980), p. 126; Dudley Baines, *Emigration from Europe, 1815–1930* (Basingstoke: Macmillan Education, 1991), table 3, p. 10.
3 Baines, *Emigration from Europe*, table 3, p. 10. For figures on Scottish migration see Marjory Harper, *Adventurers and Exiles: The Great Scottish Exodus* (London: Profile Books, 2003), p. 1; Michael Flinn (ed.), *Scottish Population History from the 17th Century to the 1930s* (Cambridge: Cambridge University Press, 1977), table 6.1.1, p. 441; and M. Anderson, 'Population and family life', in T. Dickson and J. H. Treble (eds), *People and Society in Scotland*, Vol. 3: *1914–1990* (Edinburgh: John Donald Publishers, 1992), p. 14.
4 Baines, *Emigration from Europe*, table 3, p. 10; Eric Richards, *Britannia's Children: Emigration from England, Scotland, Wales, and Ireland Since 1600* (London and New York: Hambledon and London, 2004), p. 236.

people leaving Europe for overseas shores in the period 1815–1930.[5] Britain and Ireland, among the four principal suppliers of migrant groups in Europe, provided 11.4 and 7.2 million migrants respectively.[6] Their overall flight was therefore proportionately greater than from other European countries for the period 1851–1930.

Compared with the nineteenth century, the historiography of twentieth-century migration from Ireland and Scotland is somewhat thin, a surprising feature given the numbers involved. Nevertheless, the significance of such unprecedented movement is at least recognised and incorporated in the most recent broad surveys of Ireland and Scotland in the twentieth century.[7] Despite the considerable chasm in knowledge, the extant works specifically concerned with migration provide important insight. Inter-war migration from Scotland, when at least half a million Scots departed for destinations beyond Europe, is examined in Marjory Harper's major study, *Emigration from Scotland Between the Wars: Opportunity or Exile?*[8] This significant work focuses primarily on official sources and is weighted towards Scottish migration to Canada. It also makes use of private testimony, mainly from those who settled in North America. Jim Wilkie also drew on interviews with those who left Scotland on the *Metagama* while Isobel Lindsay utilised surveys conducted with graduate migrants.[9] Scottish migrants are also incorporated, usually without comment, along with their Northern Irish counterparts, in much of the literature on British migration during the twentieth century.[10] Two welcome exceptions distinguishing between the various British groups are Jim Hammerton and

5 Baines, *Emigration from Europe*, p. 7.
6 *Ibid.*, table 2, p. 9.
7 See Diarmaid Ferriter, *The Transformation of Ireland, 1900–2000* (London: Profile Books, 2004); Richard J. Finlay, *Modern Scotland, 1914–2000* (London: Profile Books, 2004).
8 Harper, *Emigration from Scotland Between the Wars*.
9 Jim Wilkie, *Metagama: A Journey from Lewis to the New World* (Edinburgh: Birlinn, 1987 and 2001); Isabel Lindsay, 'Migration and motivation: a twentieth-century perspective', in T. M. Devine (ed.), *Scottish Emigration and Scottish Society* (Edinburgh: John Donald Publishers, 1992), pp. 154–74. Also see Angela McCarthy, '"For spirit and adventure": personal accounts of Scottish migration to New Zealand, 1921–1961', in Tom Brooking and Jennie Coleman (eds), *The Heather and the Fern: Scottish Migration and New Zealand Settlement* (Dunedin: Otago University Press, 2003), pp. 117–32.
10 Australia has dominated the field in this regard. See Michael Roe, *Australia, Britain, and Migration, 1915–1940: A Study of Desperate Hopes* (Cambridge and New York: Cambridge University Press, 1995); R. T. Appleyard, *British Emigration to Australia* (London and Canberra: Australian National University, 1964); Reg Appleyard with Alison Ray and Allan Segal, *The Ten Pound Immigrants* (London: Boxtree, 1988). For New Zealand see Megan Hutching, *Long Journey for Sevenpence: Assisted Immigration to New Zealand from the United Kingdom, 1947–1975* (Wellington: Victoria University Press, 1999).

Alistair Thomson's recent analysis of the personal testimonies of assisted British migrants to Australia, and Eric Richards's synthesis of British and Irish migration since 1600.[11] A number of contributions covering migration from Ireland in the twentieth century also exist, including accounts of the Irish in Britain and New York.[12] Several works have deployed personal testimonies but these predominantly concentrate on the Irish flow to Britain or focus on small-scale qualitative studies of contemporary migrant women, or both.[13]

A number of these works encapsulate the broader historiographies of Ireland and Scotland in the twentieth century, which are predominantly suffused with grim interpretations of the economic incentive to leave home. In Ireland emigration was perceived as a national malaise in which the 'over-arching explanation for the scale of the exodus was the failure of the Irish economy to generate sufficient employment in industry, manufacturing or services'.[14] Historians likewise point to the decline of heavy industry and the rise of mass unemployment pervading Scotland in the twentieth century.[15] As one scholar puts it, '[T]he continuation of heavy out-migration in the 1920s and 1930s, when it was falling off elsewhere in the UK, can be explained by Scotland's characteristic mix of heavy, export-orientated industries which were peculiarly vulnerable for much of the inter-war period.'[16] Similar broad explanations are proffered for the period after the Second World War. Richard Finlay, in his overview of twentieth-century Scotland, observes bleakly,

11 A. James Hammerton and Alistair Thomson, *Ten Pound Poms: Australia's Invisible Migrants. A Life History of Postwar British Emigration to Australia* (Manchester: Manchester University Press, 2005); Richards, *Britannia's Children*.

12 See Enda Delaney, *Demography, State and Society: Irish Migration to Britain, 1921–1971* (Liverpool: Liverpool University Press, 2000); Linda Dowling Almeida, *Irish Immigrants in New York City, 1945–1995* (Bloomington and Indianapolis: Indiana University Press, 2001).

13 Breda Gray, *Women and the Irish Diaspora* (London and New York: Routledge, 2003); Bronwen Walter, *Outsiders Inside: Whiteness, Place, and Irish Women* (London and New York: Routledge, 2001); Sharon Lambert, *Irish Women in Lancashire, 1922–1960: Their Story* (Lancaster: Centre for North-West Regional Studies, 2001); Louise Ryan, 'Moving spaces and changing places: Irish women's memories of emigration to Britain in the 1930s', *Journal of Ethnic and Migration Studies*, 29:1 (2003), pp. 67–82.

14 Delaney, *Irish Emigration Since 1921*, p. 32.

15 See, for instance, Christopher Harvie, *No Gods and Precious Few Heroes: Twentieth-Century Scotland* (Edinburgh: Edinburgh University Press, 2000, 3rd edn) and a number of articles in T. M. Devine and R. J. Finlay (eds), *Scotland in the Twentieth Century* (Edinburgh: Edinburgh University Press, 1996): Peter L. Payne, 'The economy', pp. 13–45; Richard J. Finlay, 'Continuity and change: Scottish politics, 1900–45', pp. 64–84; Ewen A. Cameron, 'The Scottish highlands: from congested district to objective one', pp. 153–69.

16 T. M. Devine, *The Scottish Nation, 1700–2000* (London: Penguin, 1999), p. 485. This replicates comments made in T. M. Devine, 'The paradox of Scottish emigration', in Devine (ed.), *Scottish Emigration and Scottish Society*, pp. 12–13.

'economic factors lay at the heart of the post-war Scottish diaspora.'[17] In such conceptualisations, migration from Ireland and Scotland was fundamentally the result of ominous 'push' factors, rather than an energetic response to captivating attractions abroad, or the important operation of personal networks of family and friends, discussed in Chapters 3 and 4.

These synthesising interpretations of Irish and Scottish migration during the twentieth century differ from the prevailing stereotypes for the nineteenth century, which portray emigration from Ireland and Scotland in both positive and negative terms. On the one hand, the anguish associated with the Highland Clearances and the great Irish famine spawned depictions of emigration as exile, forced movements over which individuals had no control. On the other hand, migration was seen as a safety valve, relieving overpopulated regions and counteracting unemployment. Additionally, the splendid achievements of some emigrants abroad resulted in the generation of hagiographical typecasts such as 'Scots on the make', while the Irish were recognised for their significant role as foot soldiers of Empire, not to mention their successful infiltration of the Labour Party around the world.

In the light of these competing stereotypes for the nineteenth century, why has Irish and Scottish emigration in the twentieth century been represented in overwhelmingly sinister terms? Why have alternative images of emigration as a safety-valve, liberation, or celebrations of accomplishment abroad been largely eschewed? Several reasons can be suggested. First, both Irish states and Scotland experienced significant readjustment in the twentieth century. Ireland, after 1921, was partitioned, while during the inter-war decades Scotland experienced vast industrial reorientation. Connected to these upheavals were claims that the economic policies of respective political parties in Ireland and Scotland failed to counteract the emigrant tide, which led to national debate. The newfound independence of southern Ireland, for instance, was criticised for being unable to stem the outflow, while in Scotland the reverse argument ensued: nationalists felt that a lack of self-government caused emigration.[18] A third factor is that neither Scotland nor both Irish states experienced the strains associated with overpopulation. Independent Ireland, for instance, suffered population decline from just below 3 million people in the early 1920s to 2.8 million in the early 1960s.[19] Although Northern Ireland had continued population growth and Scotland's population grew by 5 per cent between 1921 and 1961, such increases were minimal compared with England's 30 per cent

---

17 Finlay, *Modern Scotland*, p. 302.
18 Delaney, *Irish Emigration Since 1921*, p. 35; Harper, *Emigration from Scotland Between the Wars*, p. 12.
19 Delaney, *Irish Emigration Since 1921*, p. 37.

surge.[20] Emigration was therefore viewed as a conundrum. Fourth, the inflow of other migrant groups created profound tension, for if newcomers could secure employment, why were natives still leaving? This was most evident in Scotland in that while, like Ireland, it experienced minimal immigration from non-European countries, a significant inflow of English and Irish migrants occurred.[21] According to the Scottish Nationalist Party in 1956, 'there is an incredible and dangerous influx of English people into Scotland. This we can only regard as a threat to the survival of our country.'[22] Similar alarm accompanied the inflow, or 'peaceful penetration', of Irish migrants entering Scotland when vast numbers of Scots were emigrating. Allegedly, the Irish were 'poor, improvident, and intemperate, with very little desire to raise themselves in the social scale. They never hesitate to seek relief and to exploit our charities.'[23] Social, moral, and spiritual disruption was supposedly imminent, with headlines sensationally proclaiming, 'Irish immigration Scotland's "grave peril"'.[24]

A fifth explanation for the negative depiction of emigration is that both Ireland and Scotland sought to attribute emigration to external forces. One such tactic involved levelling blame at England. In the early 1920s, for instance, allegations circulated that British authorities were enticing Irish people to emigrate. Consequently, the government of independent Ireland endeavoured to restrict the movement of its people until the 1950s.[25] At times it appears that emigration was a political football in Scotland, as captured in communication from the Nationalist Party of Scotland to New Zealand's Prime Minister Holland in 1956: 'It is our considered opinion that the English government is actively and deliberately fostering a large-scale clearance of our people although, as a nation, we are considerably under-populated.'[26] Given that the Nationalist Party of Scotland's agenda was to obtain self-government, such comments must be viewed sceptically. Indeed, the circulation of such charges was designed to keep the myth of the English threat alive and justify Scotland and Ireland's poor economic performances. Official narratives of migration were therefore fashioned to establish a particular viewpoint justifying activities for self-government.

20 Finlay, *Modern Scotland*, p. 305.
21 *Ibid.*, p. 305.
22 National Secretary of the Nationalist Party of Scotland to Prime Minister Holland, 18 December 1956, in NAW, Suggestions and Criticisms, Part 2, L1/22/1/28.
23 'Irish Roman Catholics "supplanting the Scottish nation."', *Scotsman*, 13 May 1924, p. 9, on line at http://archive.scotsman.com (accessed February 2006).
24 'Irish immigration Scotland's "grave peril"', *Scotsman*, 17 May 1927, p. 6, on line at http://archive.scotsman.com (accessed February 2006). Also see Finlay, *Modern Scotland*, pp. 94–101.
25 Delaney, *Irish Emigration Since 1921*, p. 34.
26 National Secretary of the Nationalist Party of Scotland to Prime Minister Holland, 18 December 1956, in NAW, Suggestions and Criticisms, Part 2, L1/22/1/28.

Agents and assistance

As well as blaming the English government for the declining Scottish population, the Nationalist Party of Scotland also vigorously urged New Zealand's Prime Minister to 'issue the appropriate instructions to your officials to cease forthwith their emigration activities in Scotland and concentrate on our grossly over-populated neighbour, England'.[27] Assessment of agent activity is a key element in the historiography of Scottish migration, but is less extensively covered for the Irish moving abroad.[28] Ministry of Labour offices throughout the UK were equipped with immigration forms, information leaflets, and occupational booklets.[29] A report from 1949 focusing on agent activity at Berwick-upon-Tweed, Galashiels, and Hawick, indicates the type of action that was universally pursued throughout the UK in endeavouring to attract newcomers to New Zealand. Agents undertook to place advertisements in daily and weekly newspapers, prepare short articles on the attractions of New Zealand, show films and lectures, and distribute posters and pamphlets. In Scotland, however, this activity was predominantly confined to the Lowlands, while similar pursuits in Ireland were limited to the north.[30]

Other reports emphasise the particular strategies applied in Scotland and Ireland. In 1948 the chief selection officer, W. G. Simpson, documented his trip to Glasgow, in which just over one thousand individuals interested in migrating to New Zealand were interviewed. Simpson stressed the validity of this approach: 'Selecting one area and confining all our activities – advertising, personal calls, film etc., has a snowball effect in that area which must give better results on the whole'.[31] Gender was also important: 'The success of our advertising campaign in Glasgow and Manchester is now reflected in the increased number of applications. A similar campaign is now being conducted in Northern Ireland, where we are placing the emphasis on our need for young women.'[32] Competition from Australia also provoked complaints from New Zealand authorities: 'A publicity campaign has just finished in Perth and

27 *Ibid.*
28 See, for example, Marjory Harper, 'Enticing the emigrant: Canadian agents in Ireland and Scotland, c.1870–c.1920', *Scottish Historical Review*, 83:1 (2004), pp. 41–58. See also Harper, *Emigration From Scotland Between the Wars*, ch. 2.
29 Report of Chief Selection Officer on Immigration – Activities in Britain, September 1946 to August 1948, p. 1, in NAW, Newsletter and New Settler magazine, L1/22/1/49.
30 Report, in NAW, Suggestions and Criticisms, 1947–51, L1/22/1/28.
31 Report of W. G. Simpson, Chief Selection Officer, on Publicity Campaign in Glasgow and West of Scotland from 12th to 22nd November 1948, p. 1, in NAW, Reports from High Commissioner, London, L1/22/1/37.
32 Report as at 31 January 1949, in NAW, Reports from High Commissioner, London, L1/22/1/37.

I   Emigration display at New Zealand House, London, c.1951–52

Inverness and this unfortunately was not very successful. The response generally was poor and it seems that these districts have recently been thoroughly
gleaned by the Australians.'[33]

Apart from generally promoting the benefits of emigration, agents alerted
intending migrants to the availability of assisted passages, varying throughout
the century according to time and place, offered by the British and dominion
governments. Sporadic nomination, together with schemes such as the Empire
Settlement Act, enabled Scottish and Irish migrants from the north to avail
themselves of subsidised fares.[34] Ex-service personnel, meanwhile, could travel
to Australasia free of charge. Indeed, between 1923 and 1929 one third of
British emigrants to Canada and two-thirds to Australia received assistance.[35]

One of the most popular schemes operated between 1947 and 1975,
allowing British migrants to travel to Australasia for £10. Regulations stipulated that migrants had to be single, under 35 years of age, and accept employment in certain occupations for two years after arrival.[36] The schemes for New

33 Monthly Report, 28 February 1950, in NAW, Reports from High Commissioner, Part
    2, L1/22/1/37/2.
34 For examination of a number of assisted migration schemes in the British Empire see
    the articles in Stephen Constantine (ed.), *Emigrants and Empire: British Settlement in
    the Dominions Between the Wars* (Manchester: Manchester University Press, 1990).
35 Richards, *Britannia's Children*, p. 245.
36 For details of the scheme see Hutching, *Long Journey for Sevenpence.*

Zealand and Australia were similar but Australia's differed in that Britain contributed equally to the costs incurred and married migrants could apply.[37] Further alleged contrasts between Australia and New Zealand included Australia possessing an immigration policy and a target figure of 70,000 migrants a year; New Zealand, on the other hand, apparently had a policy hard to define and no target.[38] It was furthermore believed that 'Australia offers such exceptional facilities for transport and every help on arrival, that New Zealand will lose a large number of splendid settlers unless prompt action is taken in announcing a clear and cordial national welcome.'[39] In addition, 'My association is distressed at the feeble effort which New Zealand is making in connection with transport. We understand that only one ship is completely engaged in bringing migrants to New Zealand, whereas Australia has no less than twentyone vessels engaged in this important traffic.'[40] Both countries, though, shared difficulties such as shipping and housing shortages, public apathy, and opposition to immigration.[41] The dominions were alert to these differences and at an Australian Citizenship Convention in 1954 it was claimed that Australia's advantage over Canada was its better weather during winter and continuous prospects of employment. New Zealand was allegedly less favourable due to a smaller population, poorer industrial range, and weaker industrial development.[42] Australia's rate of intake in relation to existing populations was higher than Canada's by mid-century. Moreover, from the period after the Second World War Australia increasingly accepted migrants from other European countries while New Zealand only partially did so. British migration to the United States, meanwhile, continued to decline in appeal.[43]

As time passed emigration schemes altered according to the type of worker desired. In 1951, for example, New Zealand sought qualified tradesmen between the ages of 20 and 45, particularly in building and engineering trades,

37 *Ibid.*, p. 50. Department of Labour and Employment to Department of Labour and National Service, Sydney, 3 September 1948, in NAW, Australia – Policy, pt 2, L1/22/1/8.

38 *Auckland Star*, 2 January 1948, in NAW, Australia – Policy, pt 1 (pts 2–4), L1/22/1/8.

39 DSPA to Fraser, 20 August 1948, in NAW, Dominion Settlement Association, Wellington, L1/22/1/4.

40 DSPA to Fraser, 23 June 1948, in NAW, Dominion Settlement Association, Wellington, L1/22/1/4.

41 *Auckland Star*, 2 January 1948, in NAW, Australia – Policy, pt 1 (pts 2–4), L1/22/1/8.

42 'Faith in our future', Australian Citizenship Convention 1954, pp. 17–18, in NAW, Australian Commonwealth Policy, pt 4: 1.1.52–31.7.58, L1/22/1/8.

43 Richards, *Britannia's Children*, pp. 258, 264.

and women who were nurses, domestics, and clerics.[44] As part of this reorientation, the relevant authorities responded to enquiries from those seeking employment in New Zealand, by stressing the contrasts between working conditions in the two countries. For instance, the Director of Employment answered a query about hotel industry employment in 1948 by pointing out that 'Licensing laws at present operating in New Zealand differ considerably from those to which he would be accustomed, and general conditions in the trade would be rather foreign to him'.[45] Other trades such as surveyors also differed. In New Zealand surveyors specialised in land surveys, rather than buildings.[46] The problems posed by such restrictions meant that migrants would sometimes have to learn other trades.

Despite the considerable importance of assisted passages, an extensive number of migrants travelled abroad independent of government subsidies. For the period 1921–35, for instance, two-fifths of British migrants migrating to New Zealand paid their own way.[47] A higher proportion – three-fifths – choosing Australia between 1922 and 1931 were also self-financing.[48] For full-fare passengers, booklets such as Cook's set out the full spectrum of charges for fares around the world that were levied by various shipping agencies. By 1928, for instance, P&O were publicising one-class only trips to Australia via the Cape on nine vessels. For between £37 and £53 passengers had access to all services, and those with assisted or nominated passages travelled even cheaper.[49] While refusing to bow to enquirer demands and recommend certain countries, Cook's did set out details of assisted passages available for various destinations.[50] For those travelling to the United States, no schemes of assistance were in operation. Instead, migrants largely had to depend on remittances gleaned from their family and friends or fund their own passage.

Irish migrants wishing to travel to Australasia were also heavily dependent on their own resources or funding by friends, for official assistance was only available for residents of Northern Ireland and those Irish who had served with the British forces. Unlike Britain, independent Ireland was unwilling to enter into an agreement with the Australian government to jointly contribute

---

44 'New Zealand Immigration Scheme' 18 May 1951, in NAW, Reports from High Commissioner, London, L1/22/1/37/2.

45 Director of Employment response, 3 March 1948, in NAW, Post-war Migration to New Zealand, part 1, March 1941–March 1948, L1/22/1/5.

46 Department of Labour and Employment, 29 May 1947, in NAW, Post-war Migration to New Zealand, part 1, March 1941–March 1948, L1/22/1/5.

47 See table 1 in McCarthy, '"For spirit and adventure"', p. 119.

48 Richards, *Britannia's Children*, p. 246.

49 P&O One Class Only brochure, 1928, in NMM, P&O Ephemera.

50 *Cook's Ocean Sailing List with Hints to Intending Travellers by Sea*, May 1928, pp. 12–13, in NMM.

towards assisted passages for Irish citizens. In 1948, however, the Australian government offered to pay up to £35 for individual passages to Australia, the full costs of which at the time ranged from £60 to £100.[51]

Indeed, the assistance provided by family and friends was a key similarity for Irish migrants travelling to Australasia and all migrants moving to the United States. A further resemblance to the United States was the quota systems implemented by the dominions, though admittedly there were differences.[52] While the United States quota was overwhelmingly restricted according to ethnic origins, New Zealand's immigration scheme was dependent on occupations, though priority was accorded to British settlers.[53] The major difference between Australasia and the United States for Scottish and Northern Irish migrants, meanwhile, was the provision of an assisted passage. Whereas those destined for the United States had to pay their own way as well as face restrictions concerning quotas, migrants travelling to parts of the British Empire could avail themselves of assisted passages or, if self-financing, were not subject to quota restrictions. There is, however, debate over the quota restrictions. Whereas Michael Roe has indicated that British migrants never filled the quotas they came close to it for as Kenneth Lines has shown between 1925 and 1931 no less than 95 per cent of British quotas were filled annually.[54] By 1933 Britain only took up about 17 per cent of the American quota.[55]

For many migrants, then, perceived cultural similarities between home and parts of the British Empire were influential in determining their choice of destination. By contrast, 'the United States took in the widest and most evenly balanced assortment of ethnic groups'.[56] Despite this scenario, Scottish and Irish migrants continued to travel there. In part, this was due to the nature of American immigration legislation. Although restricted entry to the United States, particularly following the implementation in 1924 of the Johnson-Reed

51 'Irish Eligible for Assistance', in Tomorrow Australians Magazine, 11 October 1948, p. 4, in NAW, L1/22/1/8 pt 2.
52 In the late 1920s, for instance, New Zealand raised its quota from 10,000 to 13,500 due to shipping strikes. See *AJHR*, 1927, D-9, p. 1.
53 In 1946 timber and metal workers together with coalminers, hospital and factory workers, and domestics were sought, while in 1953 those with building, agricultural, and engineering skills were desirable. See Evidence from New Zealand Federation of Labour, 3 May 1946, p. 4, in NAW, Population and Migration: Figures and Trends, L1/22/1/10, and Director of Employment to Mr James E. Bagwell, 8 June 1953, in NAW, Population and Migration: Figures and Trends, L1/22/1/10.
54 Roe, *Australia, Britain, and Migration*, p. 191; Kenneth Lines, *British and Canadian Immigration to the United States Since 1920* (San Francisco: R&E Research Associates, 1978), p. 110.
55 Richards, *Britannia's Children*, p. 259.
56 Thomas J. Archdeacon, *Becoming American: An Ethnic History* (New York: Free Press, 1983), p. 116.

Immigration Act, the quota allocated to Irish and Scots was not as limiting as that assigned to later migrant groups.[57] That the quota system favoured older migrant groups in the United States, rather than newer inflows from southern and eastern Europe, is evident from 76 per cent of visas being allocated to British, Irish, German, and Scandinavian settlers.[58] Such restrictive policies towards new migrants clearly mirrored the hostility American society directed towards these newcomers, who were perceived as not assimilating, in part because they were less skilled, predominantly Catholic, and more illiterate than the host population.[59] As well as these factors, migrants from eastern and southern Europe generally 'lacked the cultural toeholds' of earlier migrant streams such as the British, Irish, and Germans.[60] This made them susceptible to the discrimination, nativism, and racism endemic in 1920s America. Indeed, one commentator has labelled the 1924 quota system 'the greatest triumph of nativism'.[61] Measures were made, however, to facilitate family reunification, which meant that personal contacts were vital. Indeed, the entry of relatives of United States citizens and those with skills in high demand was facilitated under the 1952 Immigration and Nationality Act. While the migration of Filipinos, Mexicans, and displaced persons shaped policies at certain periods, the quota system continued until 1965.[62]

Child migration schemes

The variety of assisted passage schemes also encompassed efforts to relocate children abroad. Typically, they catered to youngsters such as the Robertson family of Weets, near Kennethmont, Aberdeenshire. In June 1917, Robert Robertson and four of his siblings were admitted to the Orphan Homes of Scotland. Their father John had married twice, producing a staggering ten children with his first wife Susan and a further ten with his second wife Margaret. In 1915 Margaret died and soon afterwards John, a crofter, suffered a stroke. It was determined that 'with loss of memory [he] is quite unfit to maintain the family'. On the recommendation of a merchant from Insch five

---

57 For a brief summary of both the 1921 and 1924 Acts, see *ibid.*, pp. 171–2. In 1923 the Irish were incorporated in the British quota of 77,342. By 1924 independent Ireland had a separate quota of 28,567 while the United Kingdom's quota was 34,000. See R. S. Walshaw, *Migration to and from the British Isles: Problems and Policies* (London: Jonathan Cape, 1941), pp. 70, 45.
58 Archdeacon, *Becoming American*, p. 175.
59 *Ibid.*, pp. 152–3.
60 *Ibid.*, p. 137.
61 Roger Daniels, *Guarding the Golden Door: American Immigration Policy and Immigration Since 1882* (New York: Hill and Wang, 2004), p. 49.
62 *Ibid.*, pp. 118, 58, 115.

of the children were sent to the Homes at Bridge of Weir. They were admitted on 28 June 1917 and maintained by the proceeds of the croft's sale. With the exception of one of the sisters, four of the Robertson siblings who had been admitted to the orphan homes went to Canada, the first (George) in 1922, and the last (Robert) in 1930, the year of his father's death.[63]

The Robertson children were among approximately 150,000 British children who settled in British Empire destinations between 1618 and 1967.[64] Most were sent from a range of children's voluntary societies and charities, and most were orphans aged three to fourteen. The majority – close on 100,000 – went to Canada and were termed 'Home Children'.[65] Contemporary philanthropic explanations surrounding the migration of British children alleged they were leaving dysfunctional and desolate physical surroundings for healthy environments. They would provide cheap labour and benefit 'physically, morally and even spiritually' from this relocation. Yet despite such agendas, they came to be despised and disparaged, with allegations circulating in Canada that they were 'filthy', morally corrupt, and thieves.[66] As Stephen Constantine succinctly put it, 'They carried the double jeopardy of apparent *ejection* from Britain and *rejection* in Canada.'[67]

In recent times, the historiography of these child migrants has been reconstructed. The emerging picture of orphan migration is predominantly one in which these alleged victims triumphed over adversity.[68] Such a reworked positive interpretation is the result of several factors: the testimonies of the children; the achievements they obtained despite oppression; and the reconstruction of child migrant experiences by their descendants after years of silence. The involvement of organisations designed to enable descendants to locate their roots in Britain has also aided this representation. In Australia, meanwhile, the history of child migration is perceived as 'Britain's secret betrayal of a generation', resulting in formal apologies from implicated parties, including government and religious and charitable institutions.[69]

While child migration to Canada came to an almost complete halt in the 1920s, efforts were still undertaken elsewhere in the Empire. In New Zealand,

---

63 Information about the Robertson family was kindly provided by Melanie King.

64 Stephen Constantine, 'The British government, child welfare, and child migration to Australia after 1945', *Journal of Imperial and Commonwealth History*, 30:1 (2002), p. 99. Also see Gillian Wagner, *Children of the Empire* (London: Weidenfeld and Nicolson, 1982).

65 Stephen Constantine, 'Children as ancestors: child migrants and identity in Canada', *British Journal of Canadian Studies*, 16:1 (2003), p. 150.

66 These points are made in *ibid.*, pp. 150–1.

67 *Ibid.*, p. 151. Italics are Constantine's.

68 *Ibid.*, p. 156.

69 Constantine, 'The British government', p. 99.

for instance, four schemes were operating in 1927: the English Public and Secondary School Boys' Scheme, the Flock House Scheme, the Salvation Army Boys' Scheme, and the Church of England Boys' Scheme, all of which were designed to give youths farming experience. The rationale was clear: 'if placed upon the land they have not nearly so great an inclination to drift back to the towns as have older immigrants.'[70] The Big Brother Movement, on the other hand, brought almost 2,000 young men to Australia in the late 1920s.[71] In the 1930s 2,500 children were sent to Australia, while after the Second World War 3,000 went to institutional care in Australia. Child migration predominantly focused on those aged under 14. By the late 1940s it was indicated that the Australian government wished to maintain child migration but keep it limited to organisations such as the aforementioned scheme, Dr Barnado's Homes, the Fairbridge Farm Schools, YMCA, and churches.[72]

Unlike Canada, where children were dispersed to become labourers, in Australia the intention was to raise children in farm schools, such as the Fairbridge Society. Schemes such as the latter were financially supported by the British government in order to sustain links with the dominions. Australia, on the other hand, was more preoccupied with issues of underpopulation, rather than the welfare of the children involved.[73] The founder of the farm schools, Kingsley Fairbridge, had also visited New Zealand but the result of his visit was unrecorded. In 1947 a report considered the viability of his scheme in New Zealand. It concluded that it would not appear the scheme 'could offer a really suitable contribution to our population plan'. Among criticisms were the scheme's limited education – children were only given primary education – and it was felt they 'would not be in a position to compete for jobs with native born New Zealanders'. As the Australian experience revealed, the difficulties of suitable vacant accommodation and obtaining a cottage mother also hindered the scheme.[74] By way of contrast, in 1937 the New Zealand government took over the Flock House Scheme, which provided training in agriculture for young men.[75]

Other schemes were also discussed, though New Zealand officials were

70 *AJHR*, 1927, D-9, p. 2.
71 Geoffrey Sherington, '"A better class of boy": the Big Brother Movement, youth migration and citizenship of Empire', *Australian Historical Studies*, 33:120 (2002), pp. 267–85.
72 T. H. E. Heyes, Commonwealth of Australia, to H. L. Bockett, Director of Employment, Wellington, 18 November 1947, in NAW, Child Migration, 1945–1948, pt 1, L1/22/1/9.
73 Constantine, 'The British government', p. 102.
74 Minister of Immigration, NZ, to Prime Minister, NZ, 14 October 1955, in NAW, Fairbridge Farm Schools, L1/22/1/42.
75 M. J. Savage, PM, to W. Nash, Minister of Finance, 10 July 1938, in NAW, L1/22/1/3.

keenly aware that child migration needed to be kept within reasonable limits for several reasons: attitudes of the UK government to child migration, shipping, costs, and the demand in the UK for child adoption.[76] In 1948 a scheme was implemented to provide free passages to British children aged 5 to 17 years 'whose parents or guardians undertake to release them for permanent residence in New Zealand to the custody of persons desiring to receive them'.[77] The parents or guardians in the UK were to sign an agreement not to interfere in their upbringing or future. Publicity in the first instance was limited to New Zealand, where family members could nominate children to join them. Between 1948 and 1952 more than 500 children went to New Zealand under the Child Migration Scheme. By 1952 the scheme was discontinued, for which several reasons were posited, including high expectations of foster parents, difficult behavioural problems of many children, interference by natural parents, and unsuitable foster parents.[78]

Such a focus, however, excludes the dominant flow of child migrants in the twentieth century: those who voyaged with or to their parents. The reason for such family migration was generally highlighted in propaganda as the desire to provide children with better opportunities. A cleverly crafted example of this was the selection of the 100,000th migrant to Australia: six-year-old Isabelle Saxelby from Possilpark, Glasgow. With her family wearing kilts for the occasion, Isabelle received a koala bear and doll. Her mother allegedly stated, 'We fully believe we are giving the kiddies their best chance in life by bringing them to the sunshine of Australia.'[79] Official accounts reinforced propaganda typecasts: 'Of all the forms of migration that of family migration was probably the most attractive and yielded the best results. Many parents wanted better opportunity for their children and would make great sacrifices to obtain it.'[80] It is the experiences of these children that this book incorporates, by considering the role the family played in shaping the migration and settlement narratives, negative and positive myths.

76 NAW, L1/22/1/9 pt 1.
77 Memorandum for District Child Welfare Officers, Government Immigration Scheme – Child Migration, 20 May 1948, in NAW, Child Migration, 1945–48, L1/22/1/9.
78 Minister of Immigration, NZ, to Prime Minister, NZ, 14 October 1955, in NAW, Fairbridge Farm Schools, L1/22/1/42.
79 Statement by the Minister for Immigration, 23 August 1949, in NAW, Australia – Policy, pt 3, L1/22/1/8.
80 Deputation to PM and Minister of Immigration, 18 February 1938, in NAW, Dominion Settlement Association – Immigration and Settlement in New Zealand (1936–55), L1/22/1/4.

Settlement patterns

The assistance provided to child and adult migrants ensured that the composition of overseas-born settlers throughout the British World remained predominantly British for much of the period covered in this book. What broad findings can be construed in relation to their settlement patterns? In his synthesis of migration out of the British Isles, Eric Richards has indicated that two-thirds of Irish migrants moved to the United States, while two-thirds of British migrants settled in Empire destinations.[81] By 1952, however, the Irish flow significantly altered towards settlement in Britain, with four-fifths of migrants from independent Ireland moving there.[82] There are a number of reasons for this changing destination of choice, including unrestricted access to Britain, the high demand there for labour, and cheap and frequent transport which eased return home.[83] Migrants from southern Europe during the century were also more inclined to engage in short distance migration within Europe.[84] Though England was also a popular destination for Scottish migrants, they continued to migrate further afield, settling predominantly in the United States and Canada, with Australia and New Zealand also proving attractive destinations. Increasing numbers, however, moved to other parts of Britain from the 1920s onwards, until by the 1950s and 1960s a balance was struck between those settling elsewhere in Britain and overseas.[85] One explanation for this contrast is the ability of Scottish migrants to secure assisted passages to parts of the British Empire.

According to the available statistics (see Appendix 1) the Irish venturing overseas between 1921 and 1938 favoured the United States. In part this was due to the shipping system, with vessels voyaging direct from Ireland going to the United States, whereas ships bound for the dominions left British ports. More Scots than Irish, on the other hand, settled in Canada, although the United States was a closely followed favourite. Indeed, Scots were nine times more likely to settle there than their English counterparts.[86] In addition, many Scots moved on to the United States from Canada, thereby presumably surpassing Canada's overall appeal. The emigration of Scots to the United States during the early 1920s was part of a substantial outflow. Yet the peak year, 1923, predominated due to at least three factors. First, there was a

81 Richards, *Britannia's Children*, p. 236.
82 Delaney, *Irish Emigration Since 1921*, p. 8.
83 *Ibid.*, p. 10.
84 Cited in Enda Delaney, 'Placing postwar Irish migration to Britain in a comparative European perspective, 1945–1981', in Andy Bielenberg (ed.), *The Irish Diaspora* (London: Longman, 2000), p. 335.
85 See Flinn (ed.), *Scottish Population History*, p. 442; Anderson, 'Population and family life', p. 14.
86 Finlay, *Modern Scotland*, p. 105.

downturn in Scotland's economy, which hit the shipbuilding industry particularly hard and prompted the exodus of many skilled workers. Second, a large number of Scottish migrants responded favourably to the heavy promotional activities and financial assistance offered by governments in Canada, Australia, and New Zealand. Indeed, Appendix 1 shows that more Scots than Irish were attracted to Australasia. Third, the large outflow in 1923 to the United States may have reflected the forewarning of the implementation in 1924 of the Johnson-Reed Immigration Act, which would restrict the entry of migrants to the United States according to a quota system.[87] Certainly, the available statistics, which starkly reveal the dramatic exodus of Scots to the United States in 1923 compared with earlier years and the equally spectacular dropping off in 1924, seem to support the suggestion that the United States quota system led to a downturn in the influx of Scottish migrants. One possibility, then, is that migrants perceived the quota restrictions as detrimental and increasingly turned their thoughts from the United States without further consideration or further investigation. This, however, excludes those migrants who entered the United States from Canada. The most sensible explanation would be to regard 1923 and 1924 as anomalies, for in subsequent years the direct flow to the United States once again resembled the pattern of earlier years.

Further insight into the Irish and Scottish profile abroad is gleaned through census data. As Appendix 2 demonstrates, Irish migrants were always present in the United States in greater numbers than Scots, and, unlike the Scots, formed a more dominant component of the foreign-born population. The reverse applied in Canada (see Appendix 3). Meanwhile, although the numbers of Irish and Scots were considerably less in Australia and New Zealand, they supplied a greater share of the foreign-born populations (Appendices 4 and 5). There are, however, discrepancies between both countries. While fewer Scots settled in New Zealand compared with Australia, their contribution to the non-New Zealand born population was considerable and relatively stable. In Australia, on the other hand, despite a noticeable increase between 1961 and 1971, the Scottish proportion of the foreign-born population continued to fall, a situation mirrored by migrants from both Irish states settling in Australia, despite actual numbers increasing (Appendix 6). Meanwhile, the Irish population in New Zealand, as contained in census returns, fell dramatically between 1936 and 1945, though it remained relatively stable thereafter (Appendix 7).

The composition of overseas-born settlers in Australia remained predominantly British, with England and Scotland providing the majority of overseas-born migrants recorded in the Australian census between 1921 and 1954 (see

---

87 For a brief summary of both the 1921 and 1924 Acts, see Archdeacon, *Becoming American*, pp. 171–2.

Appendices 8 and 9). These statistics also show that the top ranking countries of origin among Australia's foreign-born population was relatively similar from 1921 until 1947. Thereafter, migrants from the Netherlands, Yugoslavia, Poland, and Malta became increasingly significant, while Italians and Greeks continued to expand from 1933 onwards. Of these groups, migrants from southern Europe were less likely to receive financial assistance from the Australian government.[88] Instead, they relied upon sponsorship from the Italian government and from friends and family already residing in Australia.[89] Such flows led to Australia becoming noted for its ethnic diversity leading to comparisons that it increasingly resembled Canada.[90] While New Zealand also preferred British stock, migrants from Northern and Western Europe were regarded more favourably than their Southern and Eastern European counterparts.[91]

Identities

The presence of various ethnic groups in diverse global destinations raises questions relating to identity. Individuals can hold a range of complementary identities such as religious identities, gender identities, and work identities.[92] As Linda Colley perceptively noted, 'Identities are not like hats. Human beings can and do put on several at a time.'[93] While identities have multiple and fluid meanings, as a concept it is not only a sense of what is intrinsically felt, but is shaped and determined by the wider environment. Migrants could also hold a range of multiple identities, though the testimonies utilised in this book emphasise their local, regional, national, and ethnic ties rather than other identities. Ethnicity, in the formulation of Kathleen Conzen and colleagues, is 'a process of construction or invention which incorporates, adapts, and amplifies preexisting communal solidarities, cultural attributes, and historical memories'.[94] A common ancestry, shared historical past, and

---

88 Geoffrey Sherington, *Australia's Immigrants, 1788–1978* (Sydney: Allen and Unwin, 1980), p. 147.
89 *Ibid.*, p. 115.
90 *Ibid.*, p. 134.
91 James Belich, *Paradise Reforged: A History of the New Zealanders from the 1880s to the year 2000* (Auckland: Penguin, 2001), p. 224.
92 The concept of complementary identities is articulated in Jon Gjerde, *The Minds of the West: Ethnocultural Evolution in the Rural Middle West, 1830–1917* (Chapel Hill and London: University of North Carolina Press, 1997).
93 Linda Colley, *Britons: Forging the Nation, 1707–1837* (London: Vintage, 1996; 1st edn 1992), p. 6.
94 Kathleen Neils Conzen, David A. Gerber, Ewa Morawska, George E. Pozzetta and Rudolph J. Vecoli, 'The invention of ethnicity: a perspective from the U.S.A.', *Journal of American Ethnic History*, 12:1 (1992), pp. 4–5.

cultural symbolism are all considered ingredients in formulating an ethnic identity. In achieving ethnic cohesion out of a multitude of differences 'a constellation of symbols, rituals, and rhetoric' was drawn upon.[95] In this case culture is identity, with symbols the cultural markers of identification.[96] It is, however, the fashioning of an intimate, cultural identity, discernible in their language, societies, customs, and interaction with other expatriates, that is focused on in this book.

Historians of nineteenth-century Scots and Irish abroad have stressed the importance of schools, churches, and societies in maintaining a national identity.[97] Such emphases reflect the domestic historiographies which stress the significance of religious, legal, and educational systems in propagating national identities.[98] Within a Scottish context, the focus has generally been on Highland Gaelic migrants. This has presumably arisen due to the myths generated by enforced Highland migration, the concentrated and isolated nature of much of their settlement, together with the continuing use of the Gaelic language, which makes it easier for historians to trace their presence.[99] Canada has also been a focal point due to little research conducted elsewhere, and its longer history of settlement. Studies of Irish identities, while less insular, have also tended to focus on broad political and Catholic conceptions of Irish migrants.

In exhibiting institutional, as well as emotional, mental, and social versions of their ethnic heritages, this book shows that both Irish and Scottish migrants articulated many aspects of their cultural identities. In the Scottish case this is intriguing given Tom Devine's erroneous suggestion that, at least for the Scottish migrant experience in the United States, 'They may have paid lip service to their identity ... but they no longer required it, and haven't needed it since.' Devine reaches this conclusion by comparing the Scots with the Irish; he suggests that part of the reason for Scottish invisibility overseas

95 *Ibid.*, p. 28.
96 Anthony P. Cohen, 'Culture as identity: an anthropologist's view', *New Literary History*, 24 (1993), pp. 195–209.
97 There is a robust international literature surrounding issues of national and ethnic identities. See, for instance, Steven Vertovec, 'Transnationalism and identity', *Journal of Ethnic and Migration Studies*, 27:4 (2001), pp. 573–82; Conzen et al., 'The invention of ethnicity', pp. 3–41; David McCrone, 'Who do you say you are? Making sense of national identities in modern Britain', *Ethnicities*, 2:3 (2002), pp. 301–20.
98 See, for instance, Dauvit Broun, Richard J. Finlay and Michael Lynch (eds), *Image and Identity: The Making and Re-making of Scotland Through the Ages* (Edinburgh: John Donald Publishers, 1998); Tom Devine and Paddy Logue (eds), *Being Scottish: Personal Reflections on Scottish Identity Today* (Edinburgh: Polygon, 2002), p. xi.
99 Harper, *Adventurers and Exiles*, pp. 331–3. See, too, E. J. Cowan, 'From the Southern Uplands to Southern Ontario', in Devine (ed.), *Scottish Emigration and Scottish Society*, pp. 61–83.

was due to the contrasting nature of Irish and Scottish migration. Whereas the Scots in the United States were apparently voluntary migrants 'on the make' and therefore had no need to resort to exile narratives or voice their ethnic identity for defensive purposes, the Irish did so.[100] Yet this interpretation of identity, focusing largely on its external and practical political applications, is an oversimplified, distorted, and partial reading. Just because Scots do not fit a defensive diaspora Irish model of identity does not imply that Scottishness was redundant among the Scots abroad. For Irish migrants, their cultural institutions served a dual purpose, not only allowing their identity to be proclaimed, but also to actively pursue political objectives. Unlike the political agenda of many Irish cultural organisations, Scots had no campaigns abroad for an independent Scotland. So although Scottish identity was, like Irish identity, visible, it was a positive rather than defensive posture.

Devine, however, is not alone in his view that Scottishness declined in the twentieth century, allegedly continuing an erosion that had begun the century before. Again, this notion is largely derived from consideration of the Scots in Canada, and the Canadian context may well have shaped scholarly opinions. Ted Cowan, for example, has indicated that Scottish letter-writers in Canada referred to themselves as Canadian rather than Scots.[101] His findings are reiterated by J. M. Bumsted, who reckons the Scottish experience in Canada during the nineteenth century 'becomes less visibly distinct and identifiable as the century goes on', in part due to intermarriage and the appropriation of Scottish symbols by Canadians.[102] Marjory Harper has also pointed to the 'decline of many of the symbols of ethnicity in the early twentieth century'.[103] Thereafter, as one study of the American South argues, Scottish identities were revitalised due to the involvement of later generations.[104] The evidence throughout this book suggests that Scots paid more than lip service to their ethnic identities and that group gatherings played a major social role in Scottish adjustment abroad. The cultural, social, and institutional forms of Scottishness evident in these testimonies, however, need to be set against political objectives at the local and national level, an area of investigation

---

100 T. M. Devine, 'Scotland's exiles can follow Irish lead', *The Scotsman*, 27 October 2001.
101 Edward J. Cowan, 'The myth of Scotch Canada', in Marjory Harper and Michael E. Vance (eds), *Myth, Migration and the Making of Memory: Scotia and Nova Scotia, c.1700–1990* (Halifax and Edinburgh: Fernwood Publishing and John Donald Publishers, 1999), p. 64.
102 J. M. Bumsted, 'Scottishness and Britishness in Canada, 1790–1914', in *ibid.*, pp. 98, 101.
103 Harper, *Adventurers and Exiles*, p. 372.
104 Celeste Ray, *Highland Heritage: Scottish Americans in the American South* (Chapel Hill and London: University of North Carolina Press, 2001), p. 2.

missing from a focus on personal testimonies alone. For the purposes of this book, however, it is largely the individual social and cultural manifestations of these identities that are explored.

From this broad overview, the book now turns to consider the experiences of the individuals involved in the processes of migration and settlement. Each chapter begins with an extract from a particular form of personal testimony before moving to consider the themes generated by these snapshots. In the first instance, what critiques of their homelands did Irish and Scottish migrants pinpoint as being influential factors in their decisions to move abroad?

2

'I'll go and find some sunshine': considering going

Ena Hughes was a Protestant migrant born in 1907 at Augher, County Tyrone. Her family were farmers and moved to Sydney, Australia, in 1923–24 on the ship *Ormus*. Ena was sixteen years at the time of the move. Her recollections were recorded in 1987.[1]

Bronwyn Hughes: Now you obviously were very settled in Ireland and was the business, the farm, was it reasonably prosperous in making a good living?

Ena Hughes: Yes, it was quite prosperous and then an uncle in days before my time, an uncle had got ill. TB was very prevalent and a young aunt died from it. I don't remember that happening. And this uncle seemed to be getting a weakness in the lungs and the doctor recommended he go to a hotter climate and to not go alone. The other uncle went with him. Two brothers went together. As a matter of fact one other brother went to Canada and he did die from TB there.

Bronwyn Hughes: So your first inkling of or your first recollection of anyone around you going overseas were the two uncles?

Ena Hughes: No, I don't even remember them going, I think. They were gone. Well then one uncle came back. The one that was sick got better and he came back and he'd had a very brilliant education … so he got the job of you'd call it town clerk here, in charge of the council, and he did that job. Well then the other brother was still in Australia doing very well in business, making money, you know.

Bronwyn Hughes: So you would hear stories about how well he was doing?

Ena Hughes: Hear stories about how well he was doing and buying this and buying property here and there so finally he came home for a trip and my eldest brother didn't like farming, hated it. Wanted to be a businessman. All his life he wanted to be a businessman because we had two uncles that were not, they were only uncles-in-law, aunts' husbands, that had big shops in our village, you see … So then when this uncle came home for the holiday and was going back, this eldest brother was very keen to go back with him.

Bronwyn Hughes: Now how old would he have been at this stage?

Ena Hughes: He was eighteen then and father said, 'No. If one goes, the whole family goes. There will not be a split in the family.' Particularly as he didn't like the uncle's lifestyle.

---

1 Interview with Ena Hughes by Bronwyn Hughes, recorded 1987, in OHC NLA, NSW Bicentennial Oral History Project, Oral TRC 2279/8.

Bronwyn Hughes: Because your elder brother would have gone to live with this uncle?

Ena Hughes: Well, it would have to have been to disappear with him, you see, to Australia. So we packed up. I can remember an auction, selling all the stuff in the house and father didn't get the price he wanted for the farm so he left it behind, let, let it, and off we came to Australia.

Bronwyn Hughes: Now that must have been obviously an enormous decision to do that. Did they plan, did they plan to go forever or did they plan just to go for a while?

Ena Hughes: No, they planned to go forever because they were just, they never thought they would come back to it again, I think. Because in those days it was a big job. We were five weeks and three days on the water in a ship called the *Ormus* taken over from the Germans after World War One.

...

Bronwyn Hughes: Now were you unusual as a family moving in that your reasons were not primarily economic but family ones or were most people emigrating for economic reasons?

Ena Hughes: I think single people emigrating were quite different to a family. I think when a family did it, it was just sort of they wanted to do it and they moved as a family just a single person and I tell you what. Not many single people came to Australia. It was far away. America was the whole thing and I can always remember these people that perhaps had less property and all that, that lived up the mountains. We used to call the mountains the poor places [*laughing*]. Not like Australia. And one person would go from the family to America and they would send back the fares for the next person to go and they'd send back the fares for the next person to go until whole families would go to America. It always amused us because they always came home with, well the first place was gold fillings in their teeth and fancy hats and dresses and things like that and my mother used to laugh and say, 'Yes, but they've usually worked as maids in the house and some of the mistresses give them some of her clothes to come home' [*laughing*].

Bronwyn Hughes: Now was there that sort of expectation about going to Australia to, that it was the land of promise and wealth?

Ena Hughes: We thought it was the land, but the uncles had done very well in it you see so we thought it was a land of promise but I think we were too young to sort of think of that sort of thing very much. It was just we were going to work, we were going to get on alright. It was just the feeling you had kind of.

Testimonies such as that supplied by Ena Hughes contradict stereotypically gloomy economic explanations for Irish migration in the twentieth century. She reveals, for instance, that the family farm in County Tyrone was moderately prosperous. Rather than a fierce impulse to leave home, Ena emphasises that the decision to move to Australia arose from a deep desire to keep the family together. Yet combined with this rationale was the presence in Australia of close family connections and upbeat images touting it as 'a land of promise'. A number of factors were therefore intricately involved in the process of resolving to migrate. The narrative of Ena Hughes exposes the complex layering of memory and highlights the myriad reasons that migrants later seek to identify as spurring their mobility. Case studies such as hers establish that we must search beyond the overarching explanations for mobility that are frequently proffered, and develop more nuanced rationalisations for migration incorporating a number of factors.

How, though, do other migrant testimonies compare with overarching national narratives of an economic impulse pushing unwilling migrants on to distant shores? Or, as indicated in the narrative of Ena Hughes, do other life stories similarly reveal a range of complexities implicated in the decision to migrate? In exploring these issues, the chapter looks firstly at the extent to which circumstances at home, rather than attractions abroad, influenced migration decisions. It then moves to explore the images of potential destinations that circulated in the homelands.

Family obligations

For some migrants, family and household obligations were fundamental in the memories they held of the reasons for migration, and these frequently coexisted with economic uncertainty. Demographic pressure in Hugh Roberton's Glaswegian home following his father's remarriage, for instance, was allegedly the spur for his migration to Australia in 1921: 'We were all growing up very rapidly to be women and men. I should perhaps say here that we were all very large men; none of us were under six feet tall. And so when my brother came back, I decided that I ought to make room for the other members of the family and I came to Australia.'[2] While his coming of age apparently spurred Hugh's migration, the reason for his choice of Australia is unrecorded. The selection of New Zealand for George Gunn and his widowed mother is also unknown. Nevertheless, George frankly conveyed his reasoning for leaving Dundee on the eve of Second World War: 'She was all I had ... She was the purse strings as well. I had no money. So I said I would come with you, with her.'[3] Such accounts are of interest for the memory of migration rather than in pinpointing an exact reason. The migration of the widow Gunn and her son is unusual; the more likely pattern was for the father to initially settle abroad before sending for the remainder of the family, an aspect discussed in the following chapter.

2 Interview with Hugh S. Roberton by Mel Pratt, recorded 8 July 1974, in OHC NLA, Mel Pratt Collection, Oral History Section, Oral TRC 121/53.
3 Interview with George Gunn by Julian McCarthy, recorded 4 December 1996, in ATL OHC, Conscientious Objectors of World War II, OHC-0426.

Family obligations could also relate to health issues. While economic conditions spurred the Crutchleys from Belfast, they were specifically drawn to New Zealand for a range of reasons, including the health concerns of both Ann and her son Robert. As Ann elucidated, 'Well, I'd read a lot about New Zealand and felt it would suit me health-wise. I had nasal problems and so on and I thought the clear air and I'd read about Nelson and it seemed the ideal place to come to.' Furthermore, 'our eldest son Robert had the same kind of health problems that I had. It would have turned to asthma the doctor said and he said he advised us to come. He said the only cure for him really was to get him to New Zealand.'[4] Indeed, the desire for a better future and life-style for their children or themselves was the primary reason cited by 40 per cent of migrants assisted to New Zealand who were interviewed.[5] Publicity by countries like Australia and New Zealand about the benefits to health offered by a conducive climate reinforced such beliefs. The reality will be discussed in Chapter 6.

The climate was a significant spur for the migration of some Irish and Scots in the twentieth century, including almost 20 per cent of a sample of assisted migrants to New Zealand.[6] For Lorna Carter, a 27-year-old living at Oban, the Scottish climate played a significant part in sparking her migration to New Zealand in 1951: 'the weather in Oban the winter before was just dreadful so I thought I'll go and find some sunshine.' When quizzed as to whether this rationale was the real reason for her relocation, Lorna remained adamant: 'It was a bad winter the winter before, just months before, and I thought I've had enough of this.'[7] The climate may have been Lorna's initial spur to leave Scotland, but it fails to explain her choice of destination, which was determined by a number of factors. First, New Zealand was in the British World and therefore not an exotic or foreign-speaking destination, as was continental Europe. Aspects of cultural continuity were therefore more likely. Second, having served during the war, she could avail herself of a free fare. Third, as her letters highlight, Lorna had relatives in New Zealand. That the climate rather than economic conditions in Scotland sparked Lorna's decision is also suggested by the relatively benign Scottish economy in the 1950s, together with widespread work opportunities available for women during the

---

4 Interview with Annie and Bob Crutchley by Megan Hutching, recorded 27 February 1998, in ATL OHC, 1998 New Zealand Citizenship Oral History Project, OHC-0421.
5 BAIQ 007, 042, 075, 107, 115, 135, 157, 160, 165, 172, 173, 177, 178, 179, 208, 212, 230, 264, 276.
6 BAIQ 066, 172, 179, 194, 208, 230, 240, 263, 276.
7 Interview with Lorna Ross by Angela McCarthy, recorded 24 February 2003.

decade.[8] A poor climate at home, a 'cliché of complaint', also motivated many Britons to move to Australia, though for these migrants it was often the 'last straw' in a number of other coexisting factors.[9]

Economic reasons for emigration

Accounts of poor economic conditions at home permeate the testimony of Irish and Scottish migrants. Economic insecurity on the family farm, for instance, allegedly spurred the migration of the Catholic McAleese family from Loughgiel, County Antrim, in 1925. Just four years of age at the time, Annie McAleese, later to become Sister Laboure, suggested, 'I gather from what I've been told that the farm just broke even and it wasn't economic and that really enticed them to apply for assisted emigration to New Zealand.'[10] Sister Laboure's recollection shows the powerful image of economic dislocation among generational memory. That same year, Joseph Brady of Claddy, near Markethill, County Armagh, left for the United States, having acutely assessed that his chances were better abroad than at home: 'I thought that I never could make much money in Ireland, that I would, it was always a hand to mouth existence I felt, and I felt that if I came to America I could do better. I could make some money and be independent, I thought.'[11] In similar vein, fellow Catholic Ann Conway of Esker, County Tyrone, testified bleakly that 'Life was very hard for you couldn't make nothing. You couldn't get no jobs or nothing, don't you know. And there was nothing to be made on the land.'[12] In 1929, with ongoing recession 22-year-old Ann, the youngest in her family, followed her sisters to the United States. Later decades saw a continuation of these economic explanations. The Protestant Crutchleys, a married couple who left Belfast in 1961 with their children, highlighted mediocre economic conditions in Northern Ireland as the prime factor in their departure. Ann

8   Tony Dickson and Jim Treble, 'Scotland, 1914–1990', in Tony Dickson and James H. Treble (eds), *People and Society in Scotland*, Vol. 3: *1914–1990* (Edinburgh: John Donald, 1992), pp. 4–5.

9   A. James Hammerton and Alistair Thomson, *Ten Pound Poms: Australia's Invisible Migrants. A Life History of Postwar British Emigration to Australia* (Manchester: Manchester University Press, 2005), p. 69.

10 Interview with Sister Mary Catherine Laboure McAleese by Jacqueline Gallagher, recorded 19–26 October 1993, in ATL OHC, Reading, Writing and Rosaries: Life Stories of Seven Dominican Nuns, OHC-0554. Permission to publish was kindly provided by Jacqui Foley, Sister Mary McAleese Laboure, and Sister Madeline McAleese.

11 Interview with Joseph Brady by Paul Sigrist, recorded 25 September 1995, EIOHP, EI Series 673.

12 Interview with Ann Conway by Janet Levine, recorded 11 March 1998, EIOHP, EI Series 981.

Crutchley stressed: 'I think finance, the financial situation was the main thing. Bob's wages over there weren't all that big and I wasn't working.'[13]

These standard economic explanations identified by migrants from Northern Ireland were replicated by their southern counterparts. According to Michael Jordan, son of a jarvey driver in Limerick city, who emigrated to the United States in 1924 at 22 years of age, he and his brothers left because 'there was a better opportunity for work here.'[14] Similar views were expressed by County Kilkenny migrant Patrick Shea, who departed in 1925 aged 28. He claimed a lot of Irish were emigrating as the times were not good and there was nothing much for the young people.[15] A more extensive explanation encompassing the broad economic and political context was energetically proffered by orphan Manny Steen, a Dublin-born Jew:

There was no money. There was nothing to do. Ireland was going through a terrible phase, the revolution. What had happened was after 1916 the Irish government was dissolved, I mean the rebels. By 1921 Civil War broke out and it was awful. There was street ambushes and killings and murders, like what's happening in the North, almost as bad as that. And finally in 1922 England signed a treaty with Ireland, they had a hands full. They said that's enough. 1922 Ireland became not a republic, a Free State. England signed a treaty. In the meantime I had applied in 1921. My uncle said the economy does nothing. I mean the country is shot to hell. You see unemployment was rife and what you gonna do?[16]

The issue of Ireland's political context is discussed later in this section. Meantime, personal testimonies echo the widespread disenchantment with economic opportunities in Ireland wrought by the decline of the shipbuilding and linen industries, reduced employment resulting from the introduction of technology into the agricultural sector, and few alternative employment options.[17] Circumstances in Scotland were hardly better: heavy industry declined; foreign tariffs were imposed; unemployment was rife and wages low; there was little diversification of industry; and international markets collapsed.[18]

---

13 Interview with the Crutchleys.
14 Interview with Michael Jordan by Paul Sigrist, recorded 19 October 1993, EIOHP, EI Series 397.
15 Interview with Patrick Shea by Harvey Dixon, recorded 7 May 1980, EIOHP, NPS Series 120.
16 Interview with Manny Steen by Paul Sigrist, recorded 22 March 1991, EIOHP, EI Series 33.
17 See Enda Delaney, *Irish Emigration Since 1921* (Dublin: The Economic and Social History Society of Ireland, 2002), ch. 2; Dermot Keogh, Finbarr O'Shea, and Carmel Quinlan (eds), *The Lost Decade: Ireland in the 1950s* (Cork: Mercier Press, 2004).
18 See especially R. J. Finlay, *Modern Scotland, 1914–2000* (London: Profile Books, 2004), chs 2 and 3, and Christopher Harvie, *No Gods and Precious Few Heroes: Twentieth-Century Scotland* (Edinburgh: Edinburgh University Press), ch. 2. Also

Indeed, economic factors in both Scotland and Ireland were blamed by 23 per cent of assisted migrants moving to New Zealand after the Second World War, with many stressing the impermanency of labour and the competition for jobs posed by the return of ex-servicemen.[19] As with their assisted counterparts moving to Australia, complications and frustration with work conditions at home, rather than outright unemployment, drove many to emigrate.[20]

Earlier migrants also blamed economic conditions for their exodus. John Will, one of five children of Alexander and Jane Will from Cupar in Fife, attributed his father's decision to take the family to the United States in 1924 to 'lousy economic conditions' in Scotland and the availability of more opportunities, including education, for John and his siblings abroad.[21] The combination of poor prospects at home together with perceived opportunities overseas clearly propelled many Scots to seek settlement on distant shores. It was an explanation cited by Sydney Samuels, who left Glasgow in 1933 at 23 years of age: 'I left in Scotland in the Depression and my parents thought that there wasn't much future in the UK in those days and they thought I might have an opportunity going out to Australia.'[22] Economic factors also played a part in the Hunter family's decision to migrate. Jock Hunter, who left Glasgow at 17 years of age, ascribed his family's assisted departure to New Zealand in 1926 to avoidance of his father's creditors.[23] In such cases, economic motives were starkly linked to collective family aspirations.

The most damning of testimonies recounting the lack of economic opportunity in certain parts of Scotland in particular time periods are the recollections provided by inhabitants of Lewis who voyaged to Canada on the *Metagama* in April 1923. This group of migrants were predominantly single male agricultural workers. A number of forlorn statements point to a collective critique of Scottish society's failure to provide economic sustenance to its people: 'There were too many young men there for the opportunities that

---

see David Newlands, 'The regional economics of Scotland', in T. M. Devine, C. H. Lee, and G. C. Peden (eds), *The Transformation of Scotland: The Economy Since 1700* (Edinburgh: Edinburgh University Press, 2005), pp. 159–83 for regional discrepancies. Unemployment, for instance, was localised in particular industries such as fishing and granite in Aberdeen and jute in Dundee.

19 BAIQ 041, 042, 060, 066, 115, 191, 194, 227, 240, 264, 275.
20 Hammerton and Thomson, *Ten Pound Poms*, p. 40.
21 Interview with John Will by Elysa Matsen, recorded 16 September 1994, EIOHP, EI Series 547.
22 Interview with Sydney Samuels by Sarah Dalton, recorded 13 February 1990, in ACL, Special Collections, Glen Innes Oral History Project, 90-OH-012/1–2.
23 Interview with Jock Hunter by Cath Kelly, recorded 27 September 1988, in ATL OHC, Trade Union Oral History Project, OHC-0112. Permission to publish was kindly provided by the Trade Union History Project.

were present'; 'Ordinarily, to get a paypacket you had to leave the island'; 'I left as there was nothing else to do – there was no [work] there. That's why we all left. You had to go somewhere for a livelihood'; and 'There were too many of them and too little employment'.[24] This was hardly surprising given that the economy had quickly declined from a post-war boom, characterised in part by a surge in shipbuilding, into deep economic malaise.[25] Margaret Kirk, who left Glasgow in 1923 at 22 years of age, likewise emphasised the harmful impact of economic recessions and lack of work in Scotland as the overarching reason for migration from Scotland:

There was depression in the country and everybody wanted to come to America. Everybody was putting in for them to get to America, to go to Canada, anywhere, so that that was when everybody came to America. 1918 men came over to America first and then they brought their families over you see, so that it was, that's why so many people came from Scotland because of the depression. There was nothing. There was no work. So they were gasping for a job.[26]

In these accounts, emigration was a powerful individual and collective reaction to the economic insecurities and pressures pervading Ireland and Scotland. How did the political situation compare?

Political reasons for emigration

Just as some Irish and Scottish migrants similarly attributed their departure, predominantly taking place in the inter-war period, to economic factors, their testimonies are likewise complementary in respect of political activities in the homelands. Sectarianism in Ireland and Scotland reared its repugnant head, and again was largely confined to the testimonies of those leaving during the inter-war period. Where the Irish and Scottish experience differed in this regard related to accounts of political violence. Irish migrants, unlike their Scottish counterparts, stressed the anxiety, uncertainty, and fear arising out of the violent landscape of revolutionary Ireland which was composed of numerous phases of militant activity, including the 1916 Easter Rising, the 1919–21 'Tan' War, and the Irish Civil War of 1922–23. It is likely, though, as each version is explored further, that broader collective stories fed into these later individual recollections.

24 See transcript of interviews with Donald 'Tulag' MacLeod and Murdo M. MacLean, transcribed in Jim Wilkie, *Metagama: A Journey from Lewis to the New World* (Edinburgh: Birlinn, 1987 and 2001), pp. 99, 152, and transcripts of oral interviews with Seonaidh Shiurra and Dòmhnall Chrut, in CEN, Emigration folder.
25 Harvie, *No Gods and Precious Few Heroes*, p. 39.
26 Interview with Margaret Kirk by Paul Sigrist, recorded 25 February 1994, EIOHP, EI Series 440.

In January 1930 James Joseph Walls, a 12-year-old Catholic, left Belfast for the United States. When asked why he left at that time he answered, 'I felt that if I come to America I would do better because I'd be free from all that religious prejudice, you know, and I felt there was more opportunity. Of course, I didn't realise I was coming to America I was coming to the big depression, you know, but still in all it worked out.' Elaborating further on this prejudice, Walls attributed it to Catholics being given the most 'menial' of jobs. He explained:

Two-thirds of the people in Northern Ireland are Protestant and one-third is Catholic and the Catholics were persecuted, you know. You had no opportunity for work even if you had an education, you know. The common rule of thumb was when you applied for work and if you qualified but before you were accepted, you know, they'd say, 'Well which school did you go to?', you know. Well I went to Earl Street. Well that could be a little bit misleading. But they were smart too. They'd say, 'Well which school on Earl Street?' See there was one Protestant school and Catholic school.

Such comments reveal that the oppression thesis was still important to migrants in the United States. As well as apparent endemic discrimination, Walls also scathingly discussed the Black and Tans, British veterans of the Great War recruited to the Royal Irish Constabulary. They were, he asserted gravely, 'creating an awful lot of trouble for the Catholics in and around Belfast, as a matter of fact all over Ireland. The Black and Tans were English criminals, mostly people let out of jail to come over and harass the Irish Catholics.' As with other statements by child migrants, however, Walls had little first-hand experience of such deeds. Nevertheless, the experiences of other family members infiltrated his memories, including intimidating tactics such as the burning down of the family house.[27] Although attributing his departure to sectarian animosities, it is interesting that, overall, northern Catholics were less inclined to emigrate than Protestants in independent Ireland, a somewhat surprising feature given that 'northern Catholics were far worse off than their southern Protestant counterparts.'[28]

While not a native of Belfast, fellow Catholic Joseph Brady moved there for a short period of time from Claddy, County Armagh, before emigrating to the United States. He was not quite as young as Walls (Brady was 18 when he left in 1925), but he too summarised both the discrimination encountered by Catholics in the shipbuilding trade and the activities of the Black and Tans: 'They [Catholics] lost their jobs and then they, of course, they started to get

27 Interview with James Joseph Walls by Janet Levine, recorded 20 July 1996, EIOHP, EI Series 771.
28 Peter Hart, *The I.R.A. at War, 1916–1923* (Oxford: Oxford University Press, 2003), p. 242.

guns and try to shoot at these people they figured were discriminating against them. And then, of course, the English soldiers come in, English soldiers, and they were there to try and keep peace.' Asked to recollect his own experiences, Joseph related:

Well, I remember where I was staying, I remember the two, I think four English soldiers came up and they put a machine gun on the ground and just sprayed the streets. There was nobody on the street but I guess to frighten people they sprayed the street with gunfire, that's about the thing I remember about it. Never anything bothered me, you know.[29]

Explosive sectarian tensions in Belfast were likewise replicated south of the border.[30] Many of the existent testimonies are intriguing in that they emerge from those who were mere youngsters during such a menacing period. Among them was James Gleeson, who lived at Monkstown, County Cork, and who emigrated to New York in 1927 at 12 years of age. He described an incident in which self-preservation was vital:

There was one instance. I recall my oldest brother and I were going to go to Confession in Monkstown which is the nearest church and we crossed on, it was dark on Saturday night, and we crossed on to those railroad tracks and we didn't get very far when there was shots fired over our heads and one, the man who was shot at and killed was a soldier from the Free State Army who was patrolling that area. Course we ducked back into the house as fast as we could.

Even more fascinating is the testimony of Edward James Stack, born in 1920 in Listowel, County Kerry. Son of a shopkeeper, Edward Stack emigrated with his parents in 1924. Stack maintained, 'Because of the troubles and amount of hostility my mother felt that it would probably be best if we left the country.' He also claimed to remember the conduct of the Black and Tans, even though he could not have been old enough to recollect the activities he recounts. Nevertheless, his depiction of the recruitment of the Black and Tans is accurate:

I remember the Black and Tans which was demobilised British soldiers that were pressed into service as kind of paramilitary police. They used to drive through the town half drunk and shoot up the square and we lived on the square and my mother used to put mattresses on the window to stop the bullets and I remember crying out to her, 'Shots, mama, shots'. The subsequent incursions of the Black and Tans and the Irish rebels broke into our place once looking for a gun. The British Black and Tans found a revolver which my mother used as a horse pistol. My father, grandfather on my mother's side, was a horse trainer. Anyway, it got

29 Interview with Joseph Brady.
30 For discussion of the experiences of Catholics in Northern Ireland and Protestants in the Republic see Hart, *The I.R.A. at War*, chs 9 and 10.

very serious because at that time holding a gun was almost a death penalty but my mother put the bullets in the mattress where I was sleeping so they only found the unloaded revolver and that ended that. Anyway, it convinced my mother it was time to get out of the country.[31]

John Waters of Ballymote, County Sligo, also attributed his departure in 1929 to activities in Ireland in the early 1920s:

My biggest reason for leaving I says that we come out of a civil war. It's brother against brother I says. You had in Dublin in the Four Courts where the father and the son was inside and two sons outside fighting one another. That's what the civil war was, that's right. So there was terrible enmity amongst the peoples accusing each other of being spies for the other side and all that stuff.[32]

Waters's testimony is intriguing in that, when interviewed in 1974, after the explosive tensions in Belfast during the late 1960s and early 1970s, he failed to refer to sectarian friction or economic recession in Northern Ireland in the late 1920s, but described instead a period of revolution characterised by its intimacy. As Peter Hart's evocative study of revolutionary County Cork reveals, and as Waters emphasises, the war 'was played out within homes and neighbourhoods'.[33] As well as the Civil War, Waters chillingly recounted the activities of the Black and Tan recruits. He narrated the ambush and assassination of a policeman in November 1920 with the Black and Tans, 'rapists and murderers', seeking retribution by shooting everything in sight, and burning down six houses and a creamery. Waters also mentioned animatedly the execution of guerrillas in the Ox Mountains in County Sligo and specified that farmers took doors off their hinges and used them to carry corpses down from the mountain.[34] What is puzzling with Waters's testimony is that he did not emigrate until 1929 at the age of 20, several years after the cessation of the Civil War and these tit-for-tat reprisals.[35] It seems likely, then, that he has integrated personal and collective memories of violence in Ireland to explain his departure in vivid political, rather than drab economic, terms. While this may be possible, the extent to which discussion of the Black and Tans suffused other accounts from Irish migrants indicates that this period of Irish history had a stark influence on their later recollections. It was what Hart

31 Interview with Edward Stack by Paul Sigrist, recorded 23 July 1993, EIOHP, EI Series 356.

32 Interview with John Waters by Margo Nash, recorded 15 February 1974, EIOHP, NPS Series 49.

33 Peter Hart, *The I.R.A. and its Enemies: Violence and Community in Cork, 1916–1923* (Oxford: Oxford University Press, 1998), p. 18; Interview with John Waters.

34 For an account of the civil war in Sligo see Michael Farry, *The Aftermath of Revolution: Sligo, 1921–23* (Dublin: University College Dublin Press, 2000).

35 Interview with John Waters.

has disturbingly detailed as a 'vast everyday traffic in terror and destruction. Beatings, raids, kidnappings, torture, arson, robbery, and vandalism.'[36] Such episodes became deeply ingrained into the minds of Irish migrants, whether they had personally witnessed them or not.

Other testimonies emerged from those who were adults during this period of revolution. While such memories need to be analysed just as cautiously, there seems no obvious reason to discredit these accounts, given the age and background of the migrants. At times, however, such reports appear as standard narratives of Irish republican history. Stephen Concannon, raised on a small farm near Spiddal, County Galway, cited broader incidents of revenge and reprisals in which ten IRA militants were killed for every murdered Black and Tan: 'And I mean it was indiscriminate because lots of time there was some of the innocent got killed, you know. They didn't have nothing to do with the Uprising, you know.' Concannon also claimed to have personally experienced hearing an ambush in 1919 while he dug for potatoes. He concluded pensively, 'The objective was good, to get Ireland free but the method was poor, that's the thing.' Unlike the young emigrants Waters and Stack, Concannon was resolute in stipulating that violence did not influence his resolve to leave Ireland, even though he departed in 1921 at 20 years of age, during a period of intense activity. While a disturbed political situation in Ireland may have provided the backdrop to his departure, Concannon's testimony stressed his own agency in deciding to leave home.[37] Other migrants, while not deliberating on whether such atrocities stimulated their decision to emigrate, did recount personal experiences of these violent commotions throughout Ireland.

One of the most vivid testimonies emerges from Michael Jordan, raised in Limerick until his departure at 22 years of age in 1924, after the cessation of civil war. His reminiscences weaved together broad narratives of revolutionary pursuits with his own personal experiences of violence:

In 1916 I was 14 years of age. We had the IRA, Sinn Fein we used to call them, under the name of Sinn Fein, and on the other side was the Irish Free State. They were willing to accept the British terms which they did in 1922. They guarded in trucks and lorries and the men with the IRA was at that side of the street and the Free State soldiers which were backed by the British, they got guns from the British, they used to pass each other in the streets in Limerick city when I was a boy. So it came to such a bad end that the IRA men attacked the barracks where the British soldiers, the Irish Free State soldiers were. They attacked the barracks and it turned into a guerrilla war and that went on into 1922.

36 Hart, *The I.R.A. and its Enemies*, p. 51.
37 Interview with Stephen Concannon by Janet Levine, recorded 16 September 1992, EIOHP, EI Series 212.

Jordan, however, also claimed to have joined the Army and discussed at length an effort to capture Republicans on a hill in County Cork where he was stationed. Intelligence had revealed that a Republican brigade meeting was taking place on top of a hill. With his group's arrival, Michael Jordan found himself exposed in the middle of the shooting:

I could see nothing, only hear the shots firing and the leaves on the trees flying beside me so I ran like blazes this way back and got behind a hedge and I got, when I got behind the hedge I got one of the soldiers. He was bleeding, shot near the heart. We picked him up, three other guys, and we picked him up and took him in a farm house and he's bleeding and these fellas followed me in there and they had machine guns, they were called Thompson guns. They were not long range, they were only about a hundred, a hundred yards [*word unintelligible*] so they followed us to the farm house and they started shooting at the house where we were. But in the meantime reinforcements came up behind us and these guys they took off then. That's my only experience.[38]

Michael Jordan's account illuminates the fear and horror that many individuals residing in Ireland's most violent county endured.[39] As with many migrant testimonies and narratives of trauma, these memories are intimately linked with geographical locations. It is not yet possible, though, in the absence of other migrant testimony from specific locales, to establish the effect of such assaults on local narratives of shared memory.

Female migrants likewise recalled accounts of sectarian violence in Ireland, but their testimonies were less extensive than their male counterparts. In some ways, then, the Irish revolution was remembered along gendered as well as religious lines. Kathleen Lamberti, originally from Brackney, County Down, and latterly of Belfast, left in 1921 at 22 years of age. The Catholic daughter of a teacher, she joined the British Army and remembered uneasy times in Belfast, including armoured cars chasing citizens down the road at night and British soldiers firing on Protestants who would attempt to prevent Catholics from attending church. Her recollections were made in the knowledge of what was to follow: 'It was a sad time in Belfast and we had come out here then and it got worse after we came here.'[40] Meanwhile, Julia Joyce Carmody, who was 18 when she emigrated in 1921 from Toormakeady, County Mayo, portrayed the Black and Tans as 'sons of guns'. She declared that British recruits would arrive unannounced, and revealed an incident in which they searched for guns in the milk held in her cousin's house.[41]

38 Interview with Michael Jordan.
39 Hart, *The I.R.A. and its Enemies*, p. 50.
40 Interview with Kathleen Lamberti by Paul Sigrist, recorded 25 February 1994, EIOHP, EI Series 439.
41 Interview with Julia Carmody by Paul Sigrist, recorded 18 July 1996, EIOHP, EI Series 767.

Intriguingly, most reports of Irish revolutionary violence emerged from those individuals who settled in the United States. Only one Irish migrant in Australasia attributed her departure to the uncertainty permeating Ireland in the early 1920s. Trudie Lloyd, the daughter of wealthy Catholic landholders in County Westmeath, recalled how the family's property was burned down by Republicans 'because Dad and mother both had brothers in the British Army'. Despite being in the throes of moving to Killiney in Dublin during the attack, the family's money was fast disappearing, which prompted Trudie's father to remark, 'when you haven't any money the place to come is New Zealand'.[42] Trudie's father allegedly based this statement on his previous experience of New Zealand as a boy.

While it remains difficult to establish the veracity of existing accounts, what is striking is the persistent reference to this period of Irish revolutionary activity in migrant testimonies. Interviews show that while recitation of various phases of revolution may have been influenced by recent historical interpretations and contemporary events, these coexisted with personal experiences. In such ways, then, a collective memory of revolution developed and was merged into migrant life stories, perhaps to set up the contrast between Ireland as a land where freedom was eagerly sought, and the United States, where liberty was supposedly awaiting. The critical episodes and themes in the Irish revolution of 1916–23 are therefore replete in migrant recollections. Such stories give special texture to what Hart has unequivocally, vigorously, and evocatively portrayed as a 'nightmare world of anonymous killers and victims, of disappearances, massacres, midnight executions, bullets in the back of the head, bodies dumped in fields or ditches'.[43]

Why, though, were accounts of the revolutionary period so pertinent to those Irish Catholics who settled in the United States? One explanation is that the republican tradition in the United States has always been stronger than in other areas of the Irish diaspora. Comparing the reactions of Irish migrants to war and revolution in Ireland, Malcolm Campbell states, 'the Irish-Australian response to developments in Ireland was throughout the period always more constrained and timid than that found among Irish immigrant communities in the United States.'[44] More plausibly for this study is that fewer interviews

---

42 Interview with Trudie Lloyd by Judith Fyfe, recorded 20 April 1990, in ATL OHC, Women's Division Federated Farmers of NZ (Inc) Oral History Project, OHC-0115. Permission to publish was kindly provided by Trudie Lloyd and the Women's Division of Federated Farmers.

43 Hart, *The I.R.A. and its Enemies*, p. 50.

44 Malcolm Campbell, 'Emigrant responses to war and revolution, 1914–21: Irish opinion in the United States and Australia', *Irish Historical Studies*, 32:125 (2000), p. 76. See also his 'Irish nationalism and immigrant assimilation: comparing the United States and Australia', *Australasian Journal of American Studies*, 16:2 (1996), pp. 24–43.

have been sourced from those Irish who left during the inter-war period for countries other than the United States.[45] Few testimonies have likewise been discovered from the period after the Second World War. Only one oral interview conducted with Irish migrants in New Zealand points to this sectarian friction. Jack Brotherston, a Protestant raised in Belfast, argued candidly that mixed marriages in Ireland could not be prevented: 'I would say that 90 per cent of the mixed marriages have to move out of Ireland or did in those days to live comfortably, to go to England, America or Canada. They couldn't live in the country north or south.'[46] Such unions therefore posed severe challenges to family solidarity.

Of those questionnaires completed by assisted Irish migrants moving to New Zealand after the Second World War, only three out of eleven cited sectarian issues as spurring their departure. Among them was Sylvia Nicholson, the daughter of a policeman at Killyleagh, County Down. She attributed her departure in 1952 to 'Sectarian trouble just beginning, could see it was going to continue for a long, long time.'[47] Her husband George echoed this: 'Could see sectarian trouble brewing and economy declining.'[48] Mixed marriages were particularly potent in this atmosphere and Joan Dunn, also a policeman's daughter, left Belfast in 1949 in order 'To get married, which was impossible having different religions. To stay would have caused friction between the families.'[49] Others emphasised a desire for change, an uncertain future, a better lifestyle, and employment difficulties as reasons for leaving.[50]

We must be careful, however, not to assume that an overarching collective memory of sectarian tension pervades all migrant testimonies. Several migrants, for instance, recalled Irish life in more positive terms. In County Cork, James Gleeson, while exposing some friction between Catholics and Protestants in the 1920s, also remembered 'a family named Johnston. They were not Catholics; they were Protestants. They were from a little town close to the school and I remember I used to, they were let out to play during the

45 One exception is a series of interviews with Northern Irish migrants who moved to New Zealand in the 1970s held at the Alexander Turnbull Library. Regrettably, during research for this book the interviewer placed an embargo on access to those interviews.
46 Interview with John Bell Brotherston by Judith Fyfe, recorded 1 June 1989, in ATL OHC, New Zealand Society for the Intellectually Handicapped (Inc) Oral History Project, OHC-0080. Permission to publish was kindly provided by the New Zealand Society for the Intellectually Handicapped.
47 Sylvia Nicholson, BAIQ 192.
48 George Nicholson, BAIQ 191.
49 Joan Dunn, BAIQ 065.
50 BAIQ 28, 140, 66, 75, 107, 191, 227, 240.

catechism quiz and I wished I was a Protestant then [*laughs*].'[51] Despite that memory of childhood innocence, Gleeson would presumably have been thankful he was Catholic during a period when Protestants in the south were vigorously targeted.[52] Joseph Brady also accentuated 'very cordial' relations between Protestants and Catholics at Claddy, County Armagh, in the early 1900s:

> if one of the Catholic people died and they brought the remains to the church always some of our Protestant neighbours would come and come to the ceremony, come to the church, and, and if anything, if anything happened among the, any misfortune happened among the, one of the Catholics, Protestants were there to help out and same with the Catholics with any of the Protestants they went to. We knew they were Protestants but there was no big, no big distinction.[53]

At Gortnamoyah, County Derry, Rose Loughlin was also reared a Catholic and acknowledged being surrounded by Protestants in the early 1900s, but not knowing any difference between the two faiths. She indicated that her school had a Catholic schoolmaster while the teacher was a female Protestant. Rose would even stay over weekends with the schoolteacher's daughter.[54]

Even by mid-century, Catholics depicted amicable relations with Protestants. Upon describing her experiences before her departure in 1950, Elizabeth Griffin from Ballyshannon, County Donegal, observed that there were no problems. Nevertheless, she admitted, 'there was definitely a division. I mean, you knew who was Protestant. It's like the Protestants and the Catholics lived different types of lives in a way but it was kind of taken for granted and you didn't think anything of it, you know.' When asked what contrasts existed between Catholics and Protestants, Elizabeth felt that distinct schools and different churches distinguished the two faiths. She also recognised approvingly that 'the Protestants had names that we envied like Daisy, Pansy, really, names after the flowers and totally different from Kathleen and Bridget and Mary and all the Catholic Irish names we were so used to. There was no problem about friends. You were friends with anybody. I mean children all mixed and played together.'[55] Irish Catholic migrants, then, appear to have clearly distinguished between personal relationships with Protestants in their local areas, and confrontations conducted in a public arena. Their recollections

51 Interview with James Gleeson by Janet Levine, recorded 15 April 1993, EIOHP, EI Series 277.
52 See, for instance, Hart's chapter 'Taking it out on the Protestants' in Hart, *The I.R.A. and its Enemies.*
53 Interview with Joseph Brady.
54 Interview with Rose Loughlin by Janet Levine, recorded 30 April 1995, EIOHP, EI Series 607.
55 Interview with Elizabeth Griffin by Andrew Phillips, recorded 26 May 1989, EIOHP, DP Series 38.

also suggest that hostilities were generally confined to particular areas, especially Belfast and Lisburn.[56]

Violence and victimisation likewise existed in Scottish society, but by and large the extant evidence suggests that it was Scots of Irish descent who were subject to such discrimination. Testimony from John Patrick Daly of Dumbarton, for instance, alleges that his father moved from Ireland to Scotland as he was sought by the IRA.[57] The Comerford family also had origins in Ireland. In 1921 Jim Comerford voyaged from Glasgow to Australia before being joined by his family the following year. Attempting to explain his father's move, in what seems like family lore, Jim Comerford Junior pointed to the 1921 British coal lockout and the apparent persecution his father experienced:

He was a member of the Independent Labour Party and during the lockout he was in the local pub selling the Independent Labour Party's paper, *The Glasgow Forward*. The mine manager was there and the old man bursted up to him. He had a premise. He said 'Would you like to buy the *Forward*, Dave?' And as he told it to me the manager spun round and said, 'You bastard, you'll never work here again.' And he didn't. That's what he was victimised for. And so we came out here. I'm glad he was victimised.

Despite attributing his father's relocation to the incident, when quizzed further Jim acknowledged that the move probably would have occurred without the affair, given his father's previous migration to the United States and Nova Scotia and his mother's fascination with Queensland. While this reveals the problems historians can face in using oral evidence uncritically, it also shows the value of interviews, in that respondents can reflect further and deeper on their initial explanations. Moreover, later in the interview, Jim disclosed that 'my father came from a very strong Catholic background. Might be one of the reasons he came out here.' The son of Catholic migrants from County Waterford in Ireland, Comerford Senior may well have experienced the rife sectarianism rampantly infiltrating the west of Scotland in the early twentieth century. As Jim evoked of his own experience: 'The Catholic school was opposite our public school in Scotland and very often by mutual consent we'd meet in the road and get stuck into each other and that was so bloody stupid. You see the Irish troubles were on while I lived over there and that split Scotland right down the middle.'[58]

56 Hart, *The I.R.A. at War*, p. 247.
57 Interview with John Patrick Daly by Elysa Matsen, recorded 16 September 1994, EIOHP, EI Series 558.
58 Interview with Jim Comerford by Marjorie Biggins, recorded 15 May 1987, in OHC NLA, NSW Bicentennial Oral History Project, Oral TRC 2301/54. For further examples of victimisation experienced during the 1921 lock-out see Ian MacDougall (ed.), *Militant Miners: Recollections of John McArthur, Buckhaven; and Letters, 1924–26, of David Proudfoot, Methil, to G. Allen Hutt* (Edinburgh, 1981), especially 49–59, and

Other migrants likewise referred to sectarian tensions in the west of Scotland. According to Anne Quinn from Paisley, her family was considered Irish because of their name, which she maintained made it difficult to obtain work in Harrison in the United States: 'And we were Catholic, Roman Catholic, which was another blot against us in Scotland because Scotland is a very Protestant country. They're more narrow and biased than England.'[59] Fellow Catholic Agnes Schilling also testified:

[T]his particular town, Motherwell, was like a town in, it was like Belfast, Ireland. There was such fighting with the Catholic and Protestant and I used to feel sorry for the priest coming around on his cycle, on his bicycle and his bicycle being disrupted and things done to it and my religion was strong that I think that's why I wasn't so in love with Scotland and also when we had a May procession my mother would dress us up in pretty white dress and a veil and these people would stop and pull our veils off and molest us on the way.

Agnes Schilling also chronicled events on the Twelfth of July when Orangemen 'always wanted to pass the Catholic church and play, you know, terrible things about the Pope'. She was, however, quick to qualify her remarks by comparing such individuals with contemporary populations in the United States: 'I don't want you to get that impression and Scottish people are very nice, they're very kind, very hospitable, but it was like a certain element like you would get in New York or Brooklyn, you know, some and usually the scum, not real nice people that caused these problems.'[60]

These accounts are important on several fronts. First, the recollections suggest a merging of individual and collective memory. Many Irish migrants drew upon personal events which they allegedly witnessed, though it is just as likely that stories of revolutionary activities not personally observed infiltrated their testimonies. Second, the brutality of such actions ensured that their legacy would coexist with accounts of migration during that decade. While sectarian issues also affected Scotland during the inter-war period, Scots did not have an outside force to which they could attribute such cruelty; where they experienced victimisation it was by their own countrymen. They were generally, however, descendants of Irish migrants in Scotland. Third, some of these accounts are provided by migrants who were either very young at the time of revolutionary activities or who left Ireland and Scotland as children in

---

footnotes 10 (ch. 5) and 3 (ch. 8). For sectarianism see T. M. Devine (ed.), *Scotland's Shame: Bigotry and Sectarianism in Modern Scotland* (Edinburgh and London: Mainstream Publishing, 2000).

59 Interview with Anne Quinn by Dennis Cloutier and Peter Kaplan, recorded 8 December 1983, EIOHP, NPS Series 146.

60 Interview with Agnes Schilling by Janet Levine, recorded 16 June 1992, EIOHP, EI Series 172.

family groups. A more sensational story accounting for their family's relocation may therefore have been passed down through the generations to enter-
tain as well as explain. In a sense, then, incorporating memories of Ireland
during this period was almost obligatory in these accounts, and irrespective
of whether they were 'true' or 'spun', the nature of the country's accepted,
familiar history meant they had to be made. Yet despite stressing dramatic
incidents as spurring migration, the reality may well be that medium- to long-
term forces were more important.

The search for adventure

As many theorists of migration acknowledge, the decision to emigrate is a
combination of several reasons, including economic, social, demographic,
political, and cultural factors.[61] This is evident in testimonies including that
of Isabella Peat, who left Lanarkshire with her family in 1926. Although
supposing that the 1926 Miners' Strike sparked the family's relocation, the
family also considered that a better life was attainable abroad. As daughter
Isabella, twelve years old at the time of the family's migration, later imparted:
'It was great excitement for Jim and I. We thought this was a wonderful adventure. But my mother was very diffident about it. She wanted to come because
she thought it would be, you know, they would be making a better life for
themselves but she hated coming away from the rest of the family.'[62] Isabella's testimony not only shows the complex feelings involved in the process of
relocation, but also raises the issue of female agency.

Adult migrants also testified to migration being an adventure. Although
Margaret Kirk supplied an economic explanation for the mass movement of
Scots during the inter-war period, her personal reasons differed considerably:
'I was adventurous and my, oh my father. I said I would like, I would like to see
what America is like. I would have gone to India. I would have gone anywhere.
I was going to travel so I said I'd like to go and see.' Moreover, as Margaret
Kirk further elucidated, there was no downbeat economic impulse for her to
leave Glasgow: 'I had no reason because I had a nice home. I was in an apartment house, a nice home, and my father was nicely fixed. We went away, every
year we went away on a vacation and that's what a lot of people in Scotland, in

---

61 For a summary of various disciplinary approaches to emigration see Caroline B.
    Brettell and James F. Hollifield (eds), *Migration Theory: Talking Across Disciplines*
    (New York: Routledge, 2000).
62 Interview with Walter and Isabella Solly by Rosie Little, recorded 16–20 August 1985,
    ATL OHC, Nelson and Golden Bay Oral History Project, OHC-0053. Permission
    to publish was kindly provided by Bev and Walter Solly, Rosie Little, and the Nelson
    Provincial Museum.

Glasgow, can't say'.[63] As with Margaret Kirk, the testimony of those migrants from Lewis who departed on the *Metagama* in 1923 likewise endeavoured to place a positive perspective on the migration process, empowering themselves as decision makers within the broader context of poor employment opportunities. They did this by retrospectively reinventing their motives along stereotypical lines in which adventure and tradition were articulated at the expense of broader structural features of the economy. Donald 'Tulag' MacLeod, for instance, reckoned that 'emigration was in the blood of the Lewismen going way, way back to the Hudson Bay Company'.[64] Likewise, Murdo M. MacLean mused: 'I think the wanderlust is always there, though. I think it is a Celtic trait.' As for himself, 'I wanted to see everything and experience everything.'[65]

While many accounts emanating from Scottish migrants who left in the inter-war period emphasise the economic downturn in Scotland, sometimes in combination with a sense of adventure, later Scottish migrants were more inclined to convey the idea that their movement was an exciting escapade, without reference to economic factors. While this may reflect the context of their departure with rising wage levels, greater employment opportunities, and increased immigration into Britain, Scots continued to supply a disproportionate number of migrants.[66] For 21-year-old Andrew Rae of West Calder, new challenges and opportunities were at the forefront of his migration in 1948. He posited thoughtfully, 'Coming from a race of people that have been exploratory over many, many years you think not to emulate them but at least put yourself into the same race.'[67] Clearly, then, Rae was attuned to the historical nature of Scottish mobility.[68] Fellow Scotsman, Robert Paton, a 25-year-old from Ferryden near Montrose, left in 1954. According to him, 'I came to New Zealand for spirit and adventure'.[69] In common with Robert Paton, the lust for exploration, wish for change, curiosity, and desire to travel was cited by 21 per

---

63 Interview with Margaret Kirk.

64 Transcript of interview with Donald 'Tulag' MacLeod in Wilkie, *Metagama*, p. 99.

65 Transcript of interview with Murdo M. MacLean in *ibid.*, p. 152.

66 Eric Richards, *Britannia's Children: Emigration from England, Scotland, Wales and Ireland Since 1600* (London and New York: Hambledon and London, 2004), p. 260.

67 Interview with Andrew Rae by Robert Paton, recorded 9 December 1991, in ATL OHC, Labour Movement Oral History Project, OHC-0056. Permission to publish was kindly provided by Joyce Paton.

68 For overviews of Scottish migration see T. M. Devine, *Scotland's Empire, 1600–1815* (London: Allen Lane, 2003); Michael Fry, *The Scottish Empire* (East Linton: Tuckwell Press, 2001); Marjory Harper, *Adventurers and Exiles: The Great Scottish Exodus* (London: Profile Books, 2003).

69 Interview with Robert Paton by Joyce Paton, recorded 1982–84, in ATL OHC, Hawkes Bay Oral History Project, OHC-0438.

cent of migrants assisted to New Zealand mid-century.[70] Possibly they were de-emphasising an inability to do well at home, and recasting emigration as voluntary and empowering. Or they may have chosen to reshape their personal experiences in order to mirror the extant stereotypes of the mobile Scot and Scots on the make. Some Irish migrants did likewise. County Kilkenny native Ted Dowling had spent time in Coventry, England, and in 1956, after six years there, he left for New Zealand. Aged 33 at the time of his migration, he volunteered a number of explanations for his move. Not only was he disillusioned with Coventry and the English winter, but 'I thought, well, there must be more to life.'[71] County Mayo-born John Gallagher, a decade younger, also left England that same year, after five years there. He explained, 'Ever since I was young I always wanted to go somewhere, you know.'[72] So too did Dannie Madden, originally from County Galway, confess, 'I had the wanderlust ... I wanted to go some place.'[73]

While such accounts suggest that these migrants were from a middle-class background which facilitated their desire for exploration, whereas working-class migrants needed a job, they might also reflect the ongoing quest for exhilarating experiences that these men had encountered in their previous mobility. Most, for instance, had spent a period of time in England before electing to relocate elsewhere. Indeed, available statistics show that Scottish migrants during the 1950s and 1960s were just as inclined to settle in England as overseas, a pattern that resembled their mobility in certain periods of the nineteenth century.[74] Interestingly, accounts from female migrants during this period rarely indicate that a quest for adventure drove them abroad. This contrasts substantially with assisted British migrants to Australia in which young single women emphasised travel and adventure.[75] This divergence may well reflect the portrayal of Australia as an exotic travel destination, compared with New Zealand and the United States.

70 BAIQ 015, 028, 063, 099, 100, 126, 140, 206, 271, 278.
71 Interview with Ted Dowling by Ian Robertson, recorded 4 August and 27 September 1995, in ATL OHC, Wellington City Transport European Immigrants Oral History Project, OHC-0012. Permission to publish was kindly provided by Ian and Elayne Robertson.
72 Interview with John Gallagher by Robert Paton, recorded 1 September 1993, in ATL OHC, Labour Movement Oral History Project – Part II, OHC-0059. Permission to publish was kindly provided by Joyce Paton.
73 Interview with Dannie Madden by Janet Levine, recorded 25 October 1993, EIOHP, EI Series 402.
74 M. Anderson, 'Population and family life', in Dickson and Treble (eds.), *People and Society in Scotland*, p. 14; T. M. Devine, 'The paradox of Scottish emigration', in T. M. Devine (ed.), *Scottish Emigration and Scottish Society* (Edinburgh: John Donald Publishers), pp. 11–12.
75 Hammerton and Thomson, *Ten Pound Poms*, p. 66.

Although the above discussion has drawn upon only a few brief accounts, it is pertinent to ask, how do these versions reflect the remaining testimony? First, most migrants emphasising economic and political factors as impinging on their decisions left Ireland and Scotland during the inter-war period. In later accounts there is a growing propensity to view migration as an adventure, without reference to economic factors. Overall, however, scrutiny of the available evidence reveals that migrants attributed a number of reasons in which the decision to leave was made. Indeed, while the grim economic climate in Ireland and Scotland was a critical motive for many migrants, it was nearly always supplemented by other considerations or explanations in their retrospective accounts. Yet migration was not simply the result of a number of interconnecting circumstances at home. Knowledge of conditions abroad was also crucial in the final decision to migrate. But whether perceived prosperity elsewhere was more important than recession in Ireland and Scotland in generating movement has yet to be determined. Meantime, as the following section indicates, many representations about potential destinations permeated the minds of Irish and Scottish mirants.

Images and the influence of return migrants

The compelling images that migrants held of potential destinations were a particularly significant feature in the process of migration.[76] Apart from propaganda, such images circulated in two ways: by the correspondence of their family and friends already settled overseas, and through their close kin who had returned home after a period abroad. Indeed, returned migrants were a crucial source of information in directing Irish and Scots abroad and highlight the significance of prior experience of mobility shaping further migration flows. Such riveting descriptions could either seduce or repel. According to Allan Gunn, who left Glasgow in 1925 at nine years of age, two competing destinations preoccupied his family: 'My uncle kept writing he would like us to come to Australia and my father was leaning to going to Australia. The other neighbour came to America. He used to write and tell us how nice it was here.' Eventually the family settled upon the United States due in part to the neighbour's writing to say, 'How nice the climate was for one thing. The winters were so nice compared to our winters which were very dreary and mostly very damp. We don't get much snow. And he said kids seem to have so

---

76 These factors were also crucial in directing the flow of nineteenth-century migrants from Europe. See, for example, articles in Dirk Hoerder and Leslie Page Moch (eds), *European Migrants: Global and Local Perspectives* (Boston: Northeastern University Press, 1996), and Dirk Hoerder and Horst Rössler (eds), *Distant Magnets: Expectations and Realities in the Immigrant Experience, 1840–1930* (New York: Holmes and Meier, 1993).

much more fun over that way. They seem to have more things and enjoy life.' The United States was also chosen because Allan's mother thought Australia was too distant. 'So evidently she convinced my father to try America first,' Allan deduced.[77] Ongoing links to Scotland were therefore central to the act of leaving, and women also played a pivotal role in the decision-making process.

The most extensive images migrants held prior to migration related to the United States. While their youthful age meant that many interviewees had no knowledge of the United States prior to their departure, others had positive, if somewhat exaggerated, impressions of the country. Anne Quinn, who left at nine years of age in 1928, reported that her mother viewed the country as a land of opportunity, a belief shared by Josephine Materia from Belfast.[78] Eighteen-year-old Mary Dunn, who worked in a milliner's store, left Stirling in 1923 likewise anticipating the United States in these terms, believing there would be gold in the streets and money growing on trees.[79] For Irish-born Jewish migrant Manny Steen of Dublin, his impressions derived from his brother. He figured America was 'Somehow cowboys and Indians and the streets were paved with gold, not actually paved with gold but we knew that you could you could do terrific over here. You only had the good news, you understand'.[80] Sarah McQuinn, daughter of a small farmer at Dromore West, County Sligo, likewise pictured the United States as replete with riches when she decided to leave at 24 years of age in 1924: 'Oh there was nothing but money here [*laughs*]. Nothing but money [*laughs*]. That's all I heard then. But I found out that it's not that easy to get it.'[81] The following year Joseph Brady emigrated at 18 years of age, also focusing on the opportunities to acquire money in the United States, though his impressions were tempered by a degree of reality:

Well, I knew of course that if you were willing to work in America that you could always get a job which wasn't the case in Ireland and that if you did, I always thought that if you did work here and were sober and watched your step that you could make quite a bit of money, that you would be quite comfortable and I knew that the price of certain things, that, you know, in Ireland you would have to work about two weeks to make the price of a suit of clothes and here you could buy a suit of clothes with one week's salary and have some money left for yourself. That's about all I knew about.[82]

77 Interview with Allan Gunn by Paul Sigrist, recorded 20 June 1992, EIOHP, EI Series 179.
78 Interview with Anne Quinn; Interview with Josephine Materia by Janet Levine, recorded 22 June 1994, EIOHP, EI Series 482.
79 Interview with Mary Dunn.
80 Interview with Manny Steen.
81 Interview with Sarah McQuinn by Janet Levine, recorded 12 June 1996, EIOHP, EI Series 755.
82 Interview with Joseph Brady.

The dominant impression, then, was of wealth, and return migrants were crucial in the proliferation of this stereotype. Michael Jordan of Limerick city was similarly conscious of their inspiration:

All I knew was that, that Americans, what we call Yanks, when they came back, we call them Yanks, when they came to Ireland they always had more money than us and were free spenders in them days, you know. They always gave us, you know, if we'd sing and my brother used to sing songs they gave him 10 shillings which was a big sum which would be taken off the kid and he'd get a couple of pennies and my grandmother keep it for the treasury.[83]

Another who fell under the influence of returned migrants was Bridget Jones, the middle of eleven children. The daughter of a small farmer at Castlefrench, County Galway, Bridget became a sales girl after leaving school. She decided to move to the United States in 1923 at 19 years of age, claiming, 'I used to meet people that came from America and they were telling me "oh if you were out in America you'd be making so much money, you'd have it so nice" and I said, "oh well, I'm going".'[84] Decisions were rarely so simple, but return migrants were clearly viewed with astonishment and admiration. Mary Jo Lenney of County Mayo endorsed this collective mentality: 'America was the land of, what shall I say, money grew on trees, that was the impression. My aunts would come home and they seemed to be very comfortable and they had nice clothes and they never spoke about any of the problems in the States. It was always very, very rosy.'[85]

Indeed, the clothing adorned by return migrants was a major visible measure of success that lingered in the minds of potential migrants. Clothing, together with manners and money, continued the proliferation of the stereotype of the returned Yank in the Irish imagination.[86] As Anne O'Connor remarked:

Everybody came home and they had lovely clothes and they had gold tooth as I'd say. We always thought that any Yank always had gold teeth, that's what we thought as children growing up. You weren't a Yank if you didn't have a gold tooth in your head. That I remember. And I remember the women going, coming home was some relation to me maybe distant relations of my mother's that used to tell us stories about this country.[87]

83 Interview with Michael Jordan.
84 Interview with Bridget Jones by Margo Nash, recorded 15 November 1974, EIOHP, NP Series 78.
85 Interview with Mary Jo Lenney recorded by Paul Sigrist, 21 August 1996, EIOHP, EI Series 793.
86 See Arnold Schrier, *Ireland and the American Emigration, 1850–1900* (Chester Springs: Dufour Editions, 1997; 1st edn 1958), ch. 7.
87 Interview with Anne O'Connor by Janet Levine, recorded 26 October 1994, EIOHP, EI Series 559.

While the stereotype of the returned Yank failed to dominate the Scottish discourse of migration to the same degree as in Ireland, the visible appeal of returnees made a similarly arresting impression. Motherwell–born Agnes Schilling, who left at 15 years of age in 1922, was entranced by the seductive glamour of returned migrants: 'I think I was very impressed with visitors coming over from United States and Scotland and I guess I was always sort of style conscious. Their clothing, their manners, everything impressed me that I thought it must be beautiful, it must be a nice country, lovely to be over there, to go there.'[88]

These images, as the testimonies reveal, were predominantly recalled by Irish female migrants. Perhaps Irish women moving to the United States required more encouragement by way of inflated rhetoric and visible signs of success connected with clothing which suggested that they too could make material gains. Such recollections may also reflect the character of the interviews utilised, with most Irish testimonies emanating from those who emigrated as young, single adults, rather than as children, as is the case with the Scottish recollections. Indeed, the only male migrant who recalled in any depth resounding images of the United States prior to his family's move was John Patrick Daly. Just six years of age when his family left Dumbarton, he mused wistfully, 'I remember in Scotland I'd hear people singing a song, "I know a happy land far, far away, where you get ham and eggs ten times a day". So there was apparently this kind of image of this panacea country some place.'[89]

Though such images should be treated with caution, given their historical inaccuracy, in many emigrants' minds the United States promised an elixir of success and satisfaction. The representations of competing destinations in the British World, by way of contrast, differed in content. Whereas images of the United States were dominated by symbolic signs of financial success, the physical environment and its inhabitants preoccupied migrants intending to venture to the British World. As Isabella Solly recalled before her family's departure from Strathaven to New Zealand, her mother 'wrote to my uncle when we were thinking about coming and said, "is there any snakes out there?"'.[90] Other migrants had prior experience abroad and this influenced their subsequent choice of destination. Doreen Wilkinson's father, for instance, had spent time abroad and this was a critical consideration in determining the family's permanent relocation from West Calder to New Zealand in 1946. His experiences clearly took priority over her mother's prior stint in Australia:

88 Interview with Agnes Schilling.
89 Interview with John Patrick Daly.
90 Interview with Walter and Isabella Solly.

Dad had been out here before and he always loved New Zealand so I think mainly it was that and then, of course, just after the war years I suppose they thought well it being quite a good thing to get out of Britain and so they came to New Zealand … they more or less knew what they were coming to although my mother wouldn't come here the first time round because she was scared of earthquakes. That's why she went to Australia.[91]

The parents of other migrants had likewise resided abroad, including Bob Crutchley's father, who had spent time in New Zealand. As Bob mentioned, 'He talked about New Zealand all the time although he had been to Canada for a couple of years. He had spent two years in Sydney in Australia and but New Zealand to him was the only place worth thinking about.'[92]

In some testimonies the images came close to replicating the astonishing appeal of the United States but, again, not in monetary matters. Lewisman Angus MacDonald remembered images of an enticing climate: 'There was a meeting in Bragar and they showed slides. You know, they showed apples and oranges – but no snowdrifts! Canada was "the land of sunshine and opportunity", and in a way it was for me.'[93] In similar vein, Trudie Lloyd recounted how her father, George Kelly, had spent time in New Zealand as a young boy: 'Dad used to tell us about lovely Maoris and the peaches growing on the side of the roads and everything was free and happy and the sun shining all the time.'[94] Not surprisingly, the family ventured there in 1926. Scots migrant Angus MacDonald was able to draw upon the tantalising information about Australia that his father, a master mariner working for the merchant navy, had supplied: 'Oh, I heard about it. I'd heard Dad talking about it because Dad came out here quite a bit with the O'Connell line … Oh, he said it was good, it was an up and coming country. Said it had good prospects what he saw of it. It's going to be a place of the future.'[95] As Hammerton and Thomson have indicated in their recent study of Australia's assisted immigrants, 'sun, surf and wide open spaces' dominated the minds of intending migrants.[96] Meanwhile, in 1939, when George Gunn left from near Dundee for New Zealand a friend told him, 'It is the most militaristic country in the British Empire and you'll find it's even more British than the British.' Pondering his participation as a conscientious objector during the Second World War, George Gunn declared, 'I had been opposed to the monarchy when I was a young man in

91 Interview with Doreen Wilkinson by Sarah Smith, recorded 1995, HCL, OH0253. Permission to publish was kindly provided by Doreen Wilkinson and HCL.
92 Interview with the Crutchleys.
93 Transcript of interview with Angus MacDonald in Wilkie, *Metagama*, p. 131.
94 Interview with Trudie Lloyd.
95 Interview with Angus Macdonald by Paula Hamilton, recorded 1 September 1987, in OHC NLA, NSW Bicentennial Oral History Project, Oral TRC 2301/137.
96 Hammerton and Thomson, *Ten Pound Poms*, p. 40.

Scotland. You can't be born in a mining village in Scotland and believe in the monarchy.'[97]

Intriguingly, Irish and Scottish migrants choosing the Antipodes generally failed to reflect on what was known of the economic situation in the distant shores to which they went. In a sense, their focus on other factors suggests that they attempted to downplay their helplessness in the face of economic imperatives, deciding instead to emphasise their self-will and control. Concentration on the quality of life in Australia and New Zealand rather than jobs and freedom, which characterised the United States, may also reflect the later conceptualisations of each country.

Popular literature also enabled migrants to acquire knowledge about potential destinations. According to Ann Crutchley, her father had wanted to come to New Zealand but 'My mother said definitely no … She didn't know what New Zealand was like. Dad was like me. He had read a lot about it and thought it would be a good place to come but she just wasn't willing'.[98] Ted Dowling of County Kilkenny had likewise eagerly devoured books and rigorously studied maps on Pacific countries. Yet, as with the Crutchleys, multiple explanations account for his choice of settlement in New Zealand. He had diligently followed the progress of New Zealand rugby and cricket teams touring Britain, read advertisements stipulating the need for bus drivers in New Zealand, and his confirmation in the early 1930s was conducted by the Bishop of Dunedin, James Whyte, a native of Kilkenny back home on a sabbatical.[99] Meanwhile, Johanna Flaherty recalled, 'my father had four sisters in this country and about four or five brothers and every once in a while somebody would take a trip home to visit their father and mother. Their father was dead at that time but the mother was still living so I mean all you would hear about America was what they would tell you or what you would read in a newspaper. That's really all I knew about America.'[100]

There is, then, plentiful evidence to emerge from the personal testimony of these migrants concerning the extent to which prior movement influenced intending migrants. This relates not so much to the previous mobility of the migrants who were interviewed, but the prior and substantial movement of their family members, usually of an older generation. Moreover, this movement was not just confined to England or the closer destination of North America, but included prior travel to Australasia, and spanned all the decades for which testimony has been collected. Such first-hand experiences from

97 Interview with George Gunn.
98 Interview with the Crutchleys.
99 Interview with Ted Dowling. James Whyte was Bishop of Dunedin from 1920 until his death in 1957.
100 Interview with Johanna Flaherty by Debra Allee, recorded 29 May 1986, EIOHP, AKRF Series, 182.

close family members clearly had an influential effect on a migrant's choice of destination.

In addition, stories of the settlement abroad of earlier generations may also have been pivotal. These earlier generations were also probably following in the footsteps of predecessors. Unlike ethnic groups such as the Italians, Jews, Slavs, Greeks, and Finns, who were part of a new flow of migrants abroad, Scots and Irish, like the Germans and Scandinavians, could build upon an extensive tradition of global migration.[101] We might therefore ask whether earlier movements are both responsible for and blend into later emigrations. For the twentieth-century migration accounts so far obtained, there is certainly abundant evidence to suggest that movement from Scotland and Ireland before the First World War set the dynamic for mobility during the remainder of the century. While not dismissing attempts to view migration in phases, this finding does suggest that such phases may best be viewed generationally, rather than looking solely for economic and political imperatives.

Conclusion

These testimonies reinforce the futility of endeavouring to attribute migration to one sole factor. As shown, migrants frequently combined a number of explanations for emigration in their testimonies, including economic, political, and demographic factors. These, however, could alter over time, with later migrants more likely to emphasise a sense of adventure for their relocation abroad. Images of potential destinations and the inspiration of return migrants were also considerable factors in the migrant imagination. For both Irish and Scots, recollections of conditions at home were also influenced by family stories across the generations, and the role played by these extensive networks of family and friends is further explored in the following chapter.

There are, however, some striking contrasts not just between the testimonies of Irish and Scottish migrants, but also differences according to the destinations to which they gravitated and the timing of their departures. The most vivid divergence between the two groups is the ample attention Irish migrants gave to the tense political atmosphere in Ireland, particularly sectarian grievances, and the reign of terror conducted by the Black and Tans (though little comment is made on the underhand conduct of the rebels). Clearly this is not surprising in the light of the volatile events that generated a sustained collective awareness among many Irish migrants. By contrast, there is little in the testimony of Scottish migrants to quite match this political unrest. Related to these contrasts, while women voiced their thoughts and feelings, men were prone to comment more substantially upon such matters.

101 Thomas J. Archdeacon, *Becoming American: An Ethnic History* (New York, 1983), pp. 127, 116.

When considering the destinations to which Irish and Scottish migrants moved, two distinctive differences emerge. First, reminiscences of Ireland's political turmoil were more prevalent in the recollections of those Irish Catholics who settled in the United States than throughout the British World. Second, whereas both Irish and Scottish migrants viewed the United States positively according to its supposed promise of monetary gain, other countries of settlement were viewed optimistically but for alternative reasons. A pleasant climate, easygoing lifestyle, and sense of familiarity were considerable enticements. The perpetuation of such impressions arose from both family and wider networks as well as propaganda, and it is to the organisation of migration that we now turn.

3

'A tearful goodbye': organising the move

Paul O'Dwyer, the youngest of schoolteachers Patrick and Bridget's eleven children, was born on 29 June 1907 in the parish of Bohar, County Mayo. Paul emigrated on the *Doric* to the United States at 17 years of age in 1925, four years after his father's death. He was 86 years of age when interviewed in 1993 about his decision to leave Ireland.[1]

Paul O'Dwyer: My brother Frank who was next in line. He's the one who came here with whom I had close association. He sent me the ticket, bought the ticket here and sent it home, or to Ireland for me, but he urged me not to tell anybody about it, just go, and I couldn't do that because we were a very close family. Our relationship to each other was very close and I didn't feel that I could, well, pack up and leave and say, well, bye to my mother and my sisters. My brothers had gone by this time.

…

Paul Sigrist: When your brother Frank sent you the ticket, did you know he was going to do this or did this just sort of come out of the blue?
Paul O'Dwyer: No, I didn't know he was going to do it but it, it didn't, it was no surprise because he's a member of the family quite devoted to the welfare of the kids in the family and so forth so it did not surprise me anyhow.
Paul Sigrist: Did you want to come to America?
Paul O'Dwyer: Yes.
Paul Sigrist: Why?
Paul O'Dwyer: I'd come to a point, I was in, I was getting nowhere, I was in the university, National University of Ireland in Dublin, wasn't doing too well with my studies, didn't know whether or not I would pass my exams or not, so I, in a certain sense it gave me a double reason to escape, and this other reason that Frank gave me I would no longer be a burden upon my sisters was helpful in the sense that I now had a noble reason for going.
Paul Sigrist: And they were really responsible for your welfare, your sisters?
Paul O'Dwyer: Yes they were.
Paul Sigrist: How did your parents react to your decision to go?
Paul O'Dywer: My father was dead.
Paul Sigrist: That's right.
Paul O'Dwyer: My mother reacted badly, although she thought it over and she said that like many, most Irish mothers at that point that if the emigrant ship

1 Interview with Paul O'Dwyer by Paul Sigrist, recorded 17 July 1993, EIOHP, EI Series 362.

was the way to go that was the way. She wasn't going to interfere with it. She could not, she could not permit herself to be in the position later in life if she was dead and gone of having prevented me from going a road that I had determined to go and which was for my own welfare.

Paul Sigrist: What do you suppose she objected to the most about going? Was it simply that you would be not near her or?

Paul O'Dwyer: Well, I think what she objected to was that I was going, period, and that there must be some other way of staying in Ireland. I knew there wasn't.

Paul Sigrist: How long was it from the time that Frank sent you the ticket till you actually left?

Paul O'Dwyer: Few months.

Paul Sigrist: Do you recall any of the details about getting papers and that sort of thing?

Paul O'Dwyer: Oh, yes indeed. You made application to the American authorities in Dublin, filled out an application to migrate, and then you got some people whom they designated to recommend you that you didn't have any criminal record or whatever else was necessary and then you had to travel up to Dublin to the American consul and someone would go over your papers there with you and check them off and talk to you about them and so forth and so on. They were mostly interested in whether or not you'd become a public charge in America. And that wasn't a big problem at the time because immigrants were coming all the time and they were making out one way or another so it wasn't really a big serious problem for the immigration authorities.

Paul Sigrist: Did you have to undergo any physical exams in Ireland during this process?

Paul O'Dwyer: No. Later on because of the fact that I got a second-class ticket rather than a third-class which was the cheaper one that gave me certain privileges crossing and my brother Frank who knew all of that was able to recommend that I have the second-class ticket which would mean that I was relieved of the process of being deloused number one, and that second-class ticket gave you a little bit more privileges at the table, breakfasts, lunch, and dinner.

Paul Sigrist: Did you understand that when you got the second-class ticket and did that mean anything to you?

Paul O'Dwyer: No. I think it did. You know emigrants talk to one another, those that are on their way, those that are going, and they meet at a local church or something like that to discuss when they're going and where they're going and to whom they are going so that it becomes a sort of a subculture and, yes, I knew that these things were helpful.

Paul Sigrist: May I assume that Frank had actually come over third-class and had lived through the bad experience himself?

Paul O'Dywer: Yes, right.

Paul Sigrist: Before you left did you spend time with your mother at the house?

Paul O'Dwyer: No more than usual.

Paul Sigrist: Was there some kind of a send-off dinner or a gathering of some sort to commemorate your leaving?

Paul O'Dwyer: Yes there was. It was called, known as the American wake where somebody like myself, 17 years of age, would be going, probably never coming back, and the people from the neighbourhood would come in, say goodbye, and they'd come in with money, and they'd not really in a position to give any money but they all did. That would be two shillings, a shilling, three shillings, all amounted to thirty shillings I remember, and I took it and was grateful for it. And then the following day, the following morning, a horse was hitched up to the trap and I was left at the railway station to pick up the train to go to Cork.

Paul Sigrist: Did your mother go with you or any family members go with you?

Paul O'Dywer: As far as the local railway station, yes, but nothing further than that.

Paul Sigrist: Do you remember what you were carrying, what kind of luggage, or what you were bringing with you to America?

Paul O'Dwyer: I had a razor. I'd just begun to shave and it was my special introduction to manhood.

Paul Sigrist: Do you remember saying goodbye to your mother?

Paul O'Dwyer: Oh yeah, that was a tearful goodbye.

As Paul O'Dwyer's testimony highlights, a complex range of factors acted as crucial ingredients in the organisation of migration, once the decision to move abroad was made. The most critical factor was cost. Many migrants like Paul O'Dwyer relocated overseas aided by the economic resources of close family and friends. Others who were British, especially those moving within the British World, were subsidised under official schemes of financial assistance. This chapter examines the ways migrants depended on these two sources of finance and looks too at the range of preparations they undertook having elected to migrate. In doing so the chapter relies not solely on migrant testimonies, but on a range of shipping sources to assess claims made in personal accounts. It broadly argues that similar elements operated in the process of organising migration, even though certain specifics differed according to the nationality of migrants and their chosen destination.

The role of personal networks

If conditions at home together with images of potential destinations had a role in the decision to migrate, the presence of personal networks abroad was the most crucial element in the decision to leave and the choice of destination. These networks could encompass both family and friends, and existed across time and space. Numerous studies of migration in the twentieth century have documented the role of these networks in shaping the choice of destination.

Given the longevity of Irish and Scottish migration together with restrictive immigration policies, it is not surprising that individuals from Ireland and Scotland likewise drew heavily upon such connections when opting to relocate overseas.

The father of Lillian Hopkins, for instance, left Glasgow in 1923. Lillian's mother remained in Scotland and worked as a housekeeper while her father 'kept sending money over for her to get our, to save for our fare over which she did and then she sold everything that was in the apartment'.[2] Nine-year-old Lillian accompanied her mother and two siblings to the United States in 1925, thus reuniting the family. The father of Jack Whitecross Carnegie, meanwhile, went to New Jersey in 1918 and was joined by his wife and children in 1921. As Dundee-born Jack informed, 'He wrote and he sent money and then his employer found out that he was saving, saving up his pay to bring his family over and he gave him the money to bring us and then he worked it out'.[3] Some migrants, however, had their passages paid by family members, other than their father. Glaswegian Joseph Delaney's fare, for instance, was paid by his stepfather's brother, while Lewis woman Mary MacIver who went to Canada revealed: 'It was my brother who came out and he sent me my fare.'[4]

For Irish migrants moving to the United States the provision of a passage seems to be constructed along gendered lines, with female migrants being funded by both male and female family members, while male migrants were primarily sponsored by male connections. Aunts, for instance, paid Elizabeth Dalbey's passage from Blackwater, County Meath, in the mid-1920s and Mary Jo Lenney's from Ballina, County Mayo, in 1935.[5] Catherine English, meanwhile, had her journey enabled by sisters, eventually leaving Bellavary, County Mayo, in 1924.[6] Mary Harney, on the other hand, was facilitated in leaving County Roscommon in 1925 by her eldest brother Thomas, while

2 Interview with Lillian Hopkins by Kate Moore, recorded 18 July 1994, EIOHP, KM Series 70.
3 Interview with Jack Whitecross Carnegie by Janet Levine, recorded 15 February 1996, EIOHP, EI Series 729.
4 Interview with Joseph Delaney by Dana Gumb, recorded 5 September 1985, EIOHP, AKRF Series 23; transcript of interview with Mary MacIver in Jim Wilkie, *Metagama: A Journey from Lewis to the New World* (Edinburgh: Birlinn, 1987 and 2000), p. 126. For more detailed discussion of the operation of networks for Scottish migrants in North America see Angela McCarthy, 'Ethnic networks and identities among interwar Scottish migrants in North America', in Angela McCarthy (ed.), *A Global Clan: Scottish Migrant Networks and Identities Since the Eighteenth Century* (London and New York: Tauris Academic Studies, 2006), pp. 203–26.
5 Interview with Elizabeth Dalbey by Paul Sigrist, recorded 29 August 1995, EIOHP, EI Series 662; Interview with Mary Jo Lenney recorded by Paul Sigrist, 21 August 1996, EIOHP, EI Series 793.
6 Interview with Catherine English by Paul Sigrist, recorded 19 September 1991, EIOHP, EI Series 91.

Eileen Lynn farewelled Athlone, County Roscommon, in 1953 thanks to the assistance of her Uncle Patrick.[7] An uncle also funded Stephen Concannon, who left the Spiddal parish in County Galway in 1921.[8] These practices seemingly continued after the Second World War, with Malachy McCourt financially aided by his brother in 1952.[9] That same year John Joe Gallogly elected to leave County Leitrim for the United States, explaining, 'I couldn't see any future staying in Ireland so I decided I'd come out to America and I had uncles here who sent me the paperwork and sponsored me to come out and I came out to America. My father sold some animals and I decided to come out because I had a lot of friends who had left before I did.'[10]

While Irish and Scots both drew upon family contacts, the major contrast between the two groups concerns the way in which this relocation was structured. Testimony for Scottish migrants indicates that the male head of household frequently moved abroad one to three years before the remainder of his family. By contrast, Irish migrants were more inclined to move as young adults and, once established, send for the remaining unmarried members of the family. The purpose of this early movement was to evaluate the United States as a place of settlement, find a job and housing, and remit funds for the remainder of the family to reunite, aspects discussed in Chapter 6. Analysis of the Ellis Island shipping registers would be a fascinating research agenda to confirm whether these initial conclusions can be substantiated among a wider sampling.

For migrants moving from independent Ireland to Australasia, the financial support of family and friends was also vital, given restrictions preventing them from accessing subsidised fares for British migrants. The staggered chain migration of the Killeen brothers from County Galway is especially instructive in this regard. James Killeen, who emigrated at age 23 in 1929, stated overtly: 'My brother left first at the time of the Black and Tans. We were three or four of us were in the IRA and when the Black and Tans left in 1921 we started working again and he borrowed his passage money off our neighbour and the next thing was my oldest brother he sent for my oldest brother

7 Interview with Mary Harney by Paul Sigrist, recorded 11 October 1991, EIOHP, EI Series 107; Interview with Eileen Lynn by Janet Levine, recorded 31 July 1994, EIOHP, EI Series 509.
8 Interview with Stephen Concannon by Janet Levine, recorded 16 September 1992, EIOHP, EI Series 212.
9 Interview with Malachy McCourt by Margo Nash, recorded 20 March 1975, EIOHP, NPS Series 89. Both Malachy and his brother Frank have penned their memoirs. See Frank McCourt, *Angela's Ashes: A Memoir of a Childhood* (London: Flamingo, 1997) and *'Tis* (London: Flamingo, 2000); Malachy McCourt, *A Monk Swimming* (London: Harper Collins, 1999).
10 Interview with John Joe Gallogly by Janet Levine, recorded 6 March 2001, EIOHP, EI Series 1194.

and in another year's time they sent for my third brother. And that's how we came from Ireland now.'[11]

Migrants availing themselves of assisted passages were also guided in their choice of destination by friends and family abroad. This aspect is particularly evident from an analysis of the migration of assisted migrants to New Zealand in the period after the Second World War. Of 47 Irish and Scottish migrants participating in the questionnaire, 38 per cent were nominated by connections already in New Zealand. Of those nominated or not, 30 per cent had relatives in New Zealand.[12] This, though, falls well short of the evidence from the testimony of Irish and Scots moving to the United States, all of whom had family or friends living there and shows the significance of an assisted passage to the Antipodes.

Destination, assisted passages, and agents

While the presence abroad of close connections was the overarching reason why particular destinations were chosen, official propaganda and facilities also played a part. A particularly intriguing point arising from analysis of oral evidence relates to the consideration of other destinations for settlement. According to a study of assisted British migrants to New Zealand from 1947 to 1975, Megan Hutching found that just under half of all assisted migrants who responded to her questionnaire considered other countries for settlement, primarily Canada, Australia, or South Africa.[13] New Zealand was eventually chosen by Hutching's respondents because it was small and comfortable, friends or relatives had settled there, it was considered similar to the UK, and it was cheap to get to.[14]

Among those contemplating several destinations was John Gallagher. A native of County Mayo, Gallagher had considered moving to Canada before selecting New Zealand: 'When I was 17 I almost went to Canada. And I would have gone but I was reading it was cold and snowy and I thought, well, it's no better than Ireland.' Gallagher also flirted with the idea of settlement in Australia; he added:

I knew nothing about New Zealand, actually nothing, because we never learned anything about it at school, but I knew about Australia and I thought I'll go to Australia. And I went down the Strand in London one day to go to Australia

11 Interview with James Killeen by Madeline McGilvray, recorded 13 April 1999, in ATL OHC, Southland Oral History Project, OHC-0464.
12 Analysis of BAIQ.
13 Megan Hutching, *Long Journey for Sevenpence: Assisted Immigration to New Zealand from the United Kingdom, 1947–1975* (Wellington: Victoria University Press, 1999), p. 82.
14 *Ibid.*, pp. 82–5.

House and I saw New Zealand House in Pall Mall and I thought, well, I'll go in there and see what's there. So I went in and had a look around and saw all the photographs of the sheep and lovely countryside and I thought, well, that doesn't look too bad, I'll go there.[15]

Gallagher's recollection shows that migrants frequently chose their final destination by comparing the prevailing conditions in several competing destinations. Yet in some ways his testimony shows a degree of impulsiveness, in that New Zealand was chosen solely on a visit to New Zealand House. On first reading, testimony from other migrants also shows that destinations could be chosen in a seemingly spontaneous manner. Lorna Carter, for instance, had the option of migrating to either New Zealand or Australia: 'I wrote to New Zealand House and Australia House and whichever one was going to answer me first I was going so it was New Zealand and then I just, all the arrangements started from there.'[16] As an ex-servicewoman, Lorna was able to claim a free passage to New Zealand. She accurately described its conditions: 'I was in the Wrens during the war and they had this scheme and I got there for nothing but you had to do two years in a government job and if you left your job or got something better or whatever you had to pay the whole big sum of £60 for your voyage out'.[17] Migrants under the scheme could also be nominated by family or friends and Lorna was able to obtain the support of her mother's cousin in Wellington. Indeed, it was as a result of this latter initiative that Lorna obtained a complimentary passage to New Zealand, one of approximately 77,000 migrants who went to New Zealand under the scheme.[18] Despite her decision to migrate, Lorna Carter's selection of New Zealand was not clear-cut, for as she emphasised, with some exaggeration, she had 'thousands' of relatives in both Australia and New Zealand, which made both countries appealing. Nevertheless, given that both Australia and New Zealand were so far away, the final destination was probably of less importance than the decision to move to Australasia. Such deliberation is not clear from Lorna's contemporary correspondence, but emerges in her interview. The failure to cite in her letters consideration of Australia as a place of sojourn is understandable, as the correspondence was composed after Lorna's choice was made. This example, however, does show the value of interviews, in that migrants can be asked to reflect on such areas of analysis absent in contemporary documentation.

15 Interview with John Gallagher by Robert Paton, recorded 1 September 1993, in ATL OHC, Labour Movement Oral History Project – Part II, OHC-0059.
16 Interview with Lorna Ross by Angela McCarthy, recorded 24 February 2003.
17 *Ibid.*
18 Hutching, *Long Journey for Sevenpence*, p. 74.

Access to an assisted passage was probably the most determining influ-
ence in a migrant's decision where to go, all other factors being equal. The
McAleese family of County Antrim also had two choices: the United States or
New Zealand. As Sister Catherine Laboure divulged:

I have discovered that they had applied for America, the States, or New Zealand,
and I say I don't know whether they were turned down for the States but, you see,
we already had relatives who had gone to the States. I suppose there was that way
of looking at it. But at that time there were quite a number of people coming to
New Zealand under the British government and I don't think my parents ever
regretted it.[19]

Similarly, Scotsman Robert Paton acknowledged that 'the government brought
me here, paid my way'.[20] This assistance was crucial, as we saw in Chapter 1,
and determined Paton's selection of settlement in New Zealand rather than
Rhodesia: 'The reason I chose New Zealand was that the government paid
the whole of the fare whereas I would have to pay £100 or something to get to
Rhodesia.'[21]

As well as the presence of family and friends abroad, emigration agents
were also a vital factor in facilitating knowledge of potential destinations and
providing assisted passages, as several testimonies demonstrate. Mary MacIver
related how the agent on Lewis for the *Metagama* 'was going to different
schools throughout the island and showing pictures of out west; of the farmers
and the wheat and all that they were growing, and this looked so wonderful.
They would come in the evenings and there was a slide show.'[22] Among those
leaving Lewis on the ship in 1923 was Donald 'Tulag' MacLeod, who stated
that the agent 'worked for Canadian Pacific and told us of the opportunities
in Canada'. Donald MacLeod furthermore remarked, 'We all had to take out
a loan from the Canadian Government for our fares, and we had to pay that
back. It was $90 (£16–£18) from Lewis to Toronto.'[23] Angus Macdonald, a
native of North Uist, was likewise facilitated in moving to Australia in 1929
by the influence of an agent and the provision of an assisted passage: 'A local
man came up out to see us, out to the Lochmaddy and he was apparently
from Immigration, Australia House. And I signed up and came out … They
advanced me my fare which was thirty-three pounds. I had to pay back sixteen

19 Interview with Sister Mary Catherine Laboure McAleese by Jacqueline Gallagher,
   recorded 19–26 October 1993, in ATL OHC, Reading, Writing and Rosaries: Life
   Stories of Seven Dominican Nuns, OHC-0554.
20 Interview with Robert Paton by Joyce Paton, recorded 1982–84, in ATL OHC, Hawkes
   Bay Oral History Project, OHC-0438.
21 *Ibid.*
22 Transcript of interview with Mary MacIver in Wilkie, *Metagama*, p. 123.
23 Transcript of interview with Donald 'Tulag' MacLeod in *ibid.*, pp. 100, 104.

pound ten out of it over a two-year period. Plus three pound landing money.'[24] The decisive role of agents, assisted passages, and the presence of family and friends abroad therefore combined with other factors to affirm and facilitate a move from home.

Preparations for leaving

Once the decision to leave home was made, but before their eventual departure, intending migrants had to undertake a range of preparations. Migrant testimonies, together with surviving handbooks for passengers, ephemera from major shipping lines, and guidelines from agencies such as Thomas Cook and Sons, provide clear insight into the elaborate procedures necessary before, during, and after departure. For migrants travelling to the United States a passport bearing a relevant and valid visa was obligatory. Also required for entry was a letter from a firm or individual vouching for the character, health, and financial ability of the traveller, and the purpose of their journey.[25] This was typically sought from a respected member of society. Joseph Brady, who was 18 years of age when he left Claddy, County Armagh, in 1925, willingly documented his exertions to secure a testimonial:

I remember especially going to my parish priest who was new in and he said, 'How do you expect me to give you a reference? I don't know you. I've only been here a short time.' So I was pretty spicy. I said, 'Well, don't mind Father', I said, 'I know Mr Irving, he's known me a long time', and he's also a pastor, that is a Protestant clergyman. I said, 'I'm sure he'll give me, he'll give me a whatever kind of a reference I need.' 'No', he said, 'I'll give it to you' [*chuckles*].[26]

Sponsors were particularly important in the United States especially after 1924 when stringent entry regulations were enacted. Margaret Kirk, who was 22 when she left Glasgow in 1923, remembered waiting two years to get a visa because:

America was very fussy about who they let in to the country ... No woman could come in to America in these days unless she had a sister claiming her or a brother claiming her but he had to show that he was her brother but it was mostly a sister or an aunt claiming you because they were afraid of prostitution or whatever it would be but no girl could come in here without somebody claiming her.[27]

24 Interview with Angus Macdonald by Paula Hamilton, recorded 1 September 1987, in OHC NLA, NSW Bicentennial Oral History Project, Oral TRC 2301/137.
25 *Cook's Ocean Sailing List with Hints to Intending Travellers by Sea*, May 1928, p. 7, in NMM.
26 Interview with Joseph Brady by Paul Sigrist recorded 25 September 1995, EI Series 673.
27 Interview with Margaret Kirk by Paul Sigrist, recorded 25 February 1994, EIOHP, EI Series 440.

An application for permanent residence had to be directed to a local United States consulate, which could be a protracted and vulnerable process. For Irish migrants wishing to secure passports and visas, a trip to Dublin or Belfast was necessary. As Mary Jo Lenney of Ballina, County Mayo, declared, her aunt 'had to show credentials that she was able to take care of me that I wouldn't become a burden to the state. You had to go to the American Consulate in Dublin and you had to go through an examination there, both the mental and physical, and then they decided and it took approximately a year.'[28] Thirteen-year-old Mary Jo eventually voyaged in 1935. The examinations she undertook were designed to circumvent the protracted processes associated with arrival in early periods at Ellis Island. Some migrants also made use of official agencies in arranging their passage. Mary Dunn from Stirling chronicled her arrangements in the 1920s: 'We had to go to Glasgow to go through all this passport stuff and visa and all this kind of stuff and then you had to wait until a number came up for you, for your time to come'. After being notified by the British Council of her eligibility to travel, Mary mentioned, 'We travelled in care of the Travelers' Aid, you know, the Travelers' Aid. They have them when you arrive in the country and they kind of give you advice and tell you what you should say and what you shouldn't say'.[29] For those going direct to Canada during the same period, passports were not required, unless the migrant planned to return to the United Kingdom.[30] Nor was a passport needed for assisted or nominated migrants to New Zealand; instead, they were supplied with Landing Permits in advance of their departure.[31]

Once permission to travel was granted, migrants were either allocated a ship on which to voyage or an application was made to travel on a vessel of their preference.[32] It is unknown whether migrants had much knowledge of the particular ship on which they would journey, although extensive newspaper advertisements, published voyage accounts in the press, media coverage of the launching of new vessels, and detailed information from personal networks presumably alerted intending migrants to the range of shipping companies and vessels plying the migrant routes of North America and Australasia. Travel agencies and their resultant advice and promotional literature were

28 Interview with Mary Jo Lenney.
29 Interview with Mary Dunn by Dana Gumb, recorded 23 January 1986, EIOHP, AKRF Series 127. The Travelers' Aid movement began in 1851 and is the oldest, non-sectarian, social welfare organisation in the United States.
30 *White Star-Dominion Line: Facts About Canada* [c.1924], p. 9, in NMM, Ephemera Collections, White Star.
31 *Shaw Savill and Albion Line to New Zealand Direct via Panama Canal, Official Guide and Handbook* [c. 1928], p. 24, in NMM, Ephemera Collections, Shaw Savill, folder titled 'Shaw Savill Line II'.
32 *Cook's Ocean Sailing List*, p. 6.

2 White Star Line Belfast to Canada advertisement

also significant sources of information. An instructive overview of agents operating in Ireland and Scotland in the mid-twentieth century can be found in a passenger list for 1953. Agents in Scotland were located in Greenock, Aberdeen, Kirkcaldy, Perth, Kilmarnock, Paisley, Kirkwall, Dundee, and Dunfermline. Meanwhile in both Irish states agents were operating in Belfast, Ballymena, Killarney, and Dublin.[33]

These agents acted for a number of shipping companies dominating the worldwide migrant route. For instance, companies commanding the passage to the United States included the Cunard Line, the Anchor Line, the White Star Line, and the United States Line. Among those plying the route to the Antipodes, meanwhile, were Shaw Savill Albion, the New Zealand Shipping Company, and the Union Steam Ship Company of New Zealand. The Orient Line together with the Peninsular and Orient Line (P&O) could be found on the Australian route. In endeavouring to seduce potential migrants and travellers, such companies flagrantly flaunted the facilities of their ships. For Scottish migrants, the Anchor Line proved particularly popular. A Glasgow-based firm, it boasted a number of prominent vessels including the *Columbia*, *Caledonia*, *Cameronia*, and *Transylvania*, the latter three being newly built just after the First World War. Both the destination and choice of ship were therefore important factors in the process of movement abroad.

As established, the most crucial consideration was cost and this determined the class on which migrants could travel. With the advent of the US Immigration restrictions in 1924, however, demand for third-class passages dropped. As a consequence, shipping companies undertook extensive alterations, including the introduction of a new 'tourist' class. Companies providing ships for other destinations also adopted one-class vessels. One of P&O's ships, the *Baradine*, had just undergone a major refit with cabin accommodation servicing 586 one-class passengers.[34] It was claimed: 'A lot of attention had been given to catering, the dining saloons were greatly improved and a late dinner served. For their entertainment, passengers had cinema facilities and gramophone music for dancing on deck. Once the ships were into warmer

---

33 Among those agencies in Scotland were Thomas Black and Son (Greenock), Munro's Tourist Agency (Aberdeen), Mays Ltd (Kirkcaldy), D. L. Edward (Perth), J. Brown and Son (Kilmarnock), A. K. Duncan Ltd (Paisley), A. M. Morgan and Son (Kirkwall), Fleming and Haxton (Dundee), and Mays Shipping and Travel Ltd (Dunfermline). Meanwhile, in Northern Ireland, W. McCalla and Co. (Belfast), Greer's Travel Office (Ballymena), and N. Canning Ltd (Co. Antrim) were cited. In Ireland Counhian's Travel Agency (Killarney) and Thomas Cook and Son in Dublin were listed. See NMM, Shaw Savill Collections, Shaw Savill & Albion Co. Ltd Passenger Office Records: Outward Passage Money Sheets, SSS2/31.

34 Neil McCart, *20th Century Passenger Ships of the P&O* (Wellingborough: Patrick Stephens, 1985), p. 77.

waters large canvas swimming pools were rigged on deck.'[35] By 1932, Shaw Savill had also converted its passenger steamers via the Panama Canal to one-class vessels.[36] Cabin class vessels levied higher fares and offered higher standards of service and accommodation. Tourist class, on the other hand, supplied modern comforts at economical rates, of which the *Arawa* was one steamer.[37] To protect such investment, shipping companies ordered that passengers treat the furniture with care and that cigarette ends not be thrown overboard, as 'Several instances have occurred where lighted cigarette ends have blown into portholes and caused considerable damage.'[38]

Deciding what to take on the voyage was the final fundamental consideration. Again, surviving shipping documentation shows that various recommendations were made. Those intending to undertake agricultural tasks were advised not to bring farming tools from their place of origin due to their unsuitability in Canada.[39] The cost of baggage allowance also varied according to the date and destination of settlement and this restricted migrants in what they could take. For those going to Australasia with Shaw Savill in 1928, third-class migrants were only allocated 15 cubic feet of personal baggage.[40] The passenger's initials and port of destination together with the steamer's name had to be marked clearly. Baggage required during the voyage had to display a label 'Wanted on the Voyage', to which they could have access once a week.[41]

Given the variety of climates that passengers would encounter during the voyage, they were supplied with advice by shipping companies. Generally, migrants to the Antipodes were given more explicit instructions because of the length of their voyage – approximately six weeks. Shaw Savill, for instance, recommended 'some light thin clothing', but overall 'the clothing should be warm and heavy, as sea-breezes are always more or less chilly in every latitude. Passengers should provide sufficient linen to last the voyage, as no regular washing is done on board.'[42] Despite this latter instruction, testimony reveals that migrants often did undertake washing duties on board ship. Brigid Dawson, for instance, disclosed of her journey to New Zealand in 1924, 'I did wash a few times and Ironed them but that could be done before breakfast time'. She further indicated, 'We got free soap a[nd] towels for our own

35 *Ibid.*, p. 78.
36 'The ideal route to England via Panama Canal' booklet, in NMM, Ephemera Collections, Shaw Savill, folder titled 'Shaw Savill Line II'.
37 *Ibid.*
38 Notice to Passengers Issued by New Zealand Immigration Department, in NAW, UK Immigration, L 1/22/6.
39 *White Star-Dominion Line: Facts About Canada*, p. 14.
40 *Shaw Savill Handbook*, p. 24.
41 *Ibid.*, p. 26.
42 *Ibid.*, p. 14.

use but not for washing the clothes. We had [to] buy this and it was a shilling a pound Rinso 6^d starch blue or anything we had to buy was just double what it was at home.'[43] Eighteen-year-old Mary Dunn of Stirling who went to New York in July 1923, commented on the instructions she had received:

We were told to bring warm, warm clothes for the winter time. But when we went on, the three days that we were on the ship we almost went naked because it was ninety degrees up on the deck, you know, in New York. And we had the least amount of clothes we could wear, really. I remember I had, I had a dress and it was made of tussah silk. Remember the tussah silk? It was real silk but we called it tussah silk. I thought I was dressed for [*word indecipherable*]. I did have a coat with a fur collar, I remember that. And we all wore hats at that time.[44]

Apart from clothes, migrants also took a range of items, carefully packed in trunks bound with straps and cords for protection. Some accounts reveal that china was carefully wrapped by the migrant, but cracked due to the inconsiderate handling of trunks. Irish Catholic migrants revealed the importance of various religious icons with statues of the Blessed Mother, prayer books, and rosary beads being taken.[45] Others took gifts for relatives already settled abroad.[46]

Once all preparations and procedures were fulfilled, migrants then had to make their way to the port of departure. For those migrants sailing from Irish ports, their transit was generally made by jaunting car or train.[47] Ann Conway, on the other hand, took a bus to Omagh to connect with a train bound for Derry before taking a tender to her ship, evidence of the technological developments facilitating movement in general.[48] John Joe Gallogly of County Leitrim was able to make good connections in 1952 due to the railroad passing through his townland:

the Narrow Gauge Railroad run through our land and there was a small train station there which was only a quarter of a mile from where we lived. So I took the train from there and there was about 30 people at the train when it was leaving my family and the neighbours and they all gave me presents or little money and good

43 Brigid Dawson (Wanganui) to her sister Ellen Quinn (Armagh), 30 July 1924. This letter was kindly supplied by Joan Leonard.

44 Interview with Mary Dunn.

45 See, for instance, interviews with Anne Craven by Paul Sigrist, recorded 2 October 1991, EIOHP, EI Series 102, and Mary Jo Lenney.

46 Interview with Elizabeth Schmid by Janet Levine, recorded 20 June 1992, EIOHP, EI Series 177.

47 See, for example, interview with Mary Harney; Interview with Julia Carmody by Paul Sigrist, recorded 18 July 1996, EIOHP, EI Series 767; Interview with Desmond Black by Janet Levine, recorded 12 March 1998, EIOHP, EI Series 982.

48 Interview with Ann Conway by Janet Levine, recorded 11 March 1998, EIOHP, EI Series 981.

luck and off I went and that's how I took the train from there from Drumran to Drumich, a town the name of Drumich, that was as far as the Narrow Gauge went, and then I picked up the bigger train and that went to Dublin and from Dublin then I had to change planes [sic] in Dublin and that took me to Cobh down in Cork and that's where the ships went from.[49]

In 1921 Kathleen Lamberti emigrated with her mother and siblings to New York. She discussed the preparations and voyage in 1994 when she was 95 years of age. Hailing from Brackney, County Down, the family had travelled to Liverpool to take the liner *Celtic*. 'It was snowing like mad,' Kathleen described evocatively. 'One of those sloppy snowy nights and yet you weren't allowed on the deck on that little boat going across there to Liverpool and I'll never forget that night. It was dreadful.'[50] The sight and feel of snow inevitably added to the drama of the evening and kept the memory of her departure fresh in Kathleen's mind. Scottish migrants pursued similar strategies to Kathleen's family. Those leaving ports such as Greenock travelled there by train and then took a tender to the ship. Some testimonies, though, indicate that others went to Liverpool and London to voyage from there. Firms such as Shaw Savill laid on a special train from Waterloo in London to Southampton. Return tickets at reduced rates were also available for friends and family wishing to farewell the passenger.[51] As Angus Macdonald acknowledged of his trip to Sydney in 1929, 'The trip was a good trip out. We left Tilbury about half past two in the afternoon. We joined the train at St Pancras at half past ten in the morning, straight down to the ship. The ship was tied up at Tilbury and we left Tilbury wharf about half past two I think it was.'[52] A key difference between Irish and Scottish migrants voyaging to Australasia was that vessels left ports in the UK, so Irish migrants had to make a preliminary voyage across the Irish Sea to make the connection. Some Irish also had to undertake this journey to travel to North America, though ships on this route were often inclined to stop over in Ireland to collect additional passengers.

Prior to a vessel's departure, third-class migrants underwent a medical examination. Again this procedure caused concern as migrants could be rejected if in poor health. For those voyaging to Australasia and Canada the inspection was undertaken by the Board of Trade, and as Shaw Savill warned, individuals 'are liable to be refused permission to embark if they are found to be by reason of any bodily or mental disease unfit to proceed, or likely to

---

49 Interview with John Joe Gallogly.
50 Interview with Kathleen Lamberti by Paul Sigrist, recorded 25 February 1994, EIOHP, EI Series 439.
51 *Shaw Savill Handbook*, p. 23.
52 Interview with Angus Macdonald.

endanger the health and safety of others in the Vessel'.[53] A range of disabilities for which migrants could not travel were then specified, including physical defects, illiteracy, insanity, disease, chronic alcoholism, and criminal convictions.[54] Similarly, a free medical examination by a Canadian Medical Officer at Liverpool, Glasgow, Southampton, Belfast, and Cobh, prior to departure for Canada, was required. Unlike those bound for Ellis Island, a medical examination on arrival was not demanded unless disease developed during the voyage.[55] Prohibited classes in Canada included immoral persons, professional beggars or vagrants, anarchists, and those aged 15 or above unable to read.[56]

For those relocating to the United States, an examination was conducted at the port of departure by consular staff of the United States government. This procedure was in the interests of shipping companies as they were not only fined for transporting inadmissible migrants, but were also liable for the expenditure of taking migrants home if denied entry to the United States on medical grounds.[57] The intensity of the procedure was captured in several accounts. Patrick Shea, for instance, had to pass the inspection of three doctors in Cobh in 1925, while at the same port that year Anne Craven indignantly claimed: 'Me and everybody that was going on that ship, that was coming on the ship, had to spend three days in Queenstown to be examined. We had to go through terrible, when I think of these people coming in illegally today it kind of annoys me, we had to spend three days in Queenstown to be examined by doctors.work. Our clothes were fumigated and there was many sent back.'[58]

Implied in these stories is the sense of fear surrounding the inspection process and relief that they had been deemed suitable for passage. The heightened tension accompanying the process, given the potentially negative consequences, presumably contributed to migrants maintaining vibrant memories of the inspection. Their recollections would also have been influenced by their subsequent traumatic experience of being medically examined on Ellis Island, explored in Chapter 5. Accounts such as Anne Craven's, which compare their experiences with those of contemporary migrants, are also discussed further in Chapter 5.

53 *Shaw Savill Handbook*, p. 19.
54 *Ibid.*, p. 22.
55 'Canadian Pacific sailings to and from Canada short seaway to United States', April 1931, p. 7, in NMM, Ephemera Collections, Canadian Pacific, Entertainments etc.
56 *Ibid.*, p. 7.
57 Pamela S. Nadell, 'United States steerage legislation: the protection of the emigrants en route to America', *Immigrants and Minorities*, 5:1 (1986), p. 65.
58 Interviews with Patrick Shea by Harvey Dixon, recorded 7 May 1980, EIOHP, NPS Series 120, and Anne Craven. Although Queenstown became known as Cobh in 1922, the testimonies reveal that migrants still associated the port with its pre-partition name.

The ache of farewell

At the dock the farewell ceremony was recalled in contradictory terms. Two examples serve to illustrate this. According to Mary Jo Lenney, who left Ireland in 1935, the departure was deliberately scheduled for the evening in order to prevent excessive displays of distress:

I remember getting on this small what we call a tender or a ferry and you got on that in the evening, that was the plan, and they whisked you out to the ocean liner which was I don't know how many miles out on the ocean because it's not deep enough for the big ocean liners to come in. And we got on board ship probably about 7 or 8 o'clock in the evening and then you had a nice meal and the next morning when you were out in mid-ocean you, Ireland was gone and there was a reason for that because people did not want to say goodbye, you know. It was all over by the time they got up in the morning. It was too emotional.[59]

Almost two decades later, however, John Joe Gallogly depicted a somewhat different leavetaking, in which a multitude of well-wishers commandeered the dock for what might have been a last glimpse of their loved one. The spectacle was poignant:

I stayed at the hotel and the next morning I took the tender – there was 164 immigrants on the ship – we took what they called the tender out to the ship because the ship couldn't pull in to port. We took the tender out to the ship and it was like a big monster out in the ocean and the waving of the people – there were hundreds of people on the dock – waving goodbye to all their friends that were leaving and got on the ship and off we went.[60]

These conflicting farewells are less evident in the testimony of migrants before they left their home for port, for the majority of Irish migrants from all regions frequently and with great emotion conveyed deep despair at leaving home. Such impassioned farewells are evident in the broader historiography, particularly for the nineteenth century.[61] The act of separation or the preliminal rite, identified as the first phase in Arnold van Genepp's rites of passage, resulted in poignant goodbyes.[62] These not only fed into the maintenance of national narratives, but knowledge of such chronicles heightened emotions for participants at the time of departure. Sr Rose O'Neill, for instance, recalled

---

59 Interview with Mary Jo Lenney.
60 Interview with John Joe Gallogly.
61 See, for instance, analysis of the 'American wake' in Arnold Schrier, *Ireland and the American Emigration, 1850–1900* (Chester Springs: Dufour Editions, 1997; 1st edn 1958), ch. 5.
62 Arnold van Genepp, *Rites of Passage*, translated by Monika B. Vizedom and Gabrielle L. Caffee, with an introduction by Solon T. Kimball (London: Routledge and Kegan Paul, 1960), p. 21.

3 Clandonald settlers leaving Scotland for Alberta, 1924

a bonfire when leaving and spent every night in tears.[63] Anne Walsh, 77 at the time of her interview, reflected on her departure in 1922 at 14 years of age. She spoke of getting 'on the train, I didn't cry much. Cried more when I got to the ship.'[64] Ann Conway reckoned that everyone was sorry to see her leave and that a convoy of people arrived to farewell her by dancing and playing music.[65] Mary Jo Lenney was thirteen when she emigrated in December 1935. A native of Ballina, County Mayo, she was accompanied by her mother on the voyage. Mary Jo forlornly portrayed the trip to Cobh as 'a long, lonesome trip'.[66] Irish men recounted similar scenes. According to James Killeen, 'My mother and I were great friends. We done a lot of jobs together. She said, "Don't cry in the station, Jim", she said to me. Well I didn't cry in the station but I shed buckets, buckets full after that. I used to write. I tried to write but I had to put it into the wastepaper box and it took me weeks and weeks to get over that.'[67] Meanwhile, John Joe Gallogly meditated on his sorrowful farewell: 'When it was leaving then of course it was very sad, you know, and a lot of tears and my father said

63 Interview with Sr Rose O'Neill by Paul Sigrist, recorded 3 June 1998, EIOHP, EI Series 1003.
64 Interview with Anne Walsh by Nancy Dallett, recorded 26 June 1986, EIOHP, AKRF Series 200.
65 Interview with Ann Conway.
66 Interview with Mary Jo Lenney.
67 Interview with James Killeen.

4 Crowds at dock, Stornaway, Western Isles, Scotland, 1924

to me, he said, "I saw so many leave", like his brothers and sisters, and he said, "I hope you're not that would lose communication with home", so I never did.'[68] Such testimonies indicate that the legendary 'American wake' of the nineteenth century, in which emigration was portrayed as death, continued well into the twentieth.[69]

Indeed, several migrants represented departure from Ireland in that terminology. When Joseph Brady of County Armagh was asked why it was referred to as a wake he responded:

Because in those days they figured once you went to America you were dead. You were never, never came back. Very few, prior to that time, very few people went to America. They stayed here. They never, never came back because they got married here and then had children and I suppose never could get the, enough money for a passage.[70]

Scottish migrants, by contrast, were less likely to recall any grief surrounding their departure, either from home or from port. The exceptions are High-landers and some female migrants. Highlander Angus Macdonald, for instance, acknowledged that at the outset of his journey, 'I was standing at

68 Interview with John Joe Gallogly.
69 See especially Schrier, *Ireland and the American Emigration*, ch. 5.
70 Interview with Joseph Brady.

the stern of the ship when she was going down the Thames. I was a bit lonely then, a bit sad.'[71] Migrants from Lewis bound for Canada also commented bleakly on their departures. Among them was Angus MacDonald from Ness: 'I remember when she was goin' by the Butt o' Lewis, well, they were blowin' the horn all the time, and everybody in Ness was out makin' bonfires. Even my father was cryin'.'[72] Murdo M. MacLean fervently evoked the depressing atmosphere surrounding their exodus:

Most of the population of Lewis were in Stornoway that day, and I remember two things that made the situation worse than it was – if that's possible. The Gaelic psalms – if you're a Gaelic speaker, it gets you right here in your heart – and the band marching up and down. It was really pathetic to see these people embarking on that boat ... and the mothers crying, 'We're never going to see you again.' And, you know, 90 per cent of them were right.[73]

The sense of exile in assessments of departure from Lewis was presumably amplified by the group character of the exodus, leaving direct as they did from Stornoway and Lochboisdale. In addition, the publicity surrounding these departures may also have fed in to the later testimony of migrants. Reports of the Hebridean departure from Lochboisdale to Canada in April 1923, for instance, conveyed such evocative expressions as 'a touch of sorrow', 'the separation is more than ordinarily painful', and 'the pain of parting'.[74] Such emotive terminology, then, not only arose from accounts of individual movers but also fed into individual and collective imaginations.

Accounts such as these convey a sense of exile, which has traditionally been attributed to those Scots leaving in the nineteenth century as a result of clearances. The majority of Scots in the twentieth century, however, failed to depict their leaving in such emotional language. What explains the relative lack of sorrow accompanying Scottish departures? First, many Scottish migrants were from urban industrial areas with strong shipping industries; perhaps such familiarity helped lessen the anxiety accompanying departure. This explanation, however, fails to incorporate the awareness of northern Irish migrants with shipbuilding traditions. A more plausible explanation for the minimal grief imbuing the testimony of Scottish migrants is that the majority of interviewees travelled in family groups, whereas their Highland and Irish counterparts were more prone to relocate as single adults. That Scots had a greater propensity for return migration may also have eased the gloomy atmosphere surrounding their departure.[75]

71 Interview with Angus Macdonald.
72 Interview with Angus MacDonald, transcribed in Wilkie, *Metagama*, p. 112.
73 Interview with Murdo M. MacLean, in *ibid.*, p. 152.
74 'Hebridean emigration: economic pressure', in *The Scotsman*, 16 April 1923, p. 6.
75 One scholar has estimated that for the period 1899–1924 the British return rate was just

Conclusion

With regard to their organisation of the move, the main contrasts between migrants from independent Ireland and Scotland relate to the accessibility of assisted passages, and there is also a clear difference according to the destination they were bound for. The activities of agents, for instance, was discussed among those moving to the dominions, whereas those destined for the United States made greater use of family connections. Yet in the case of the United States, and for those leaving Ireland for all destinations, both groups drew upon the support of friends and relatives already settled abroad. Nor was gender a major factor in the process of organising a passage. A general experience of organisation can therefore be discerned in arranging the assistance, packing, and obtaining the relevant documentation.

Clear differences, however, emerge when both groups are scrutinised in detail. First, there are marked divergences in the demographic structure of the two migrant streams. Whereas Irish migrants were more likely to move as young, single adults joining other family members already abroad, Scots typically went as youngsters in family groups, usually to reunite with their father. This social mix of the migrant streams presumably explains why Irish migrants were more prone to ceremonially and symbolically characterise their departure from home in terms of a 'wake', emphasising the painful emotions associated with leaving friends and family. By contrast, Scottish recollections were mainly from those who emigrated as children, who were seemingly less aware of such powerful feelings. The divergence in this perception may reflect the traditional representation of such departure from Ireland, which was historically portrayed as forced exile, rather than a depiction of 'Scots on the make'. The emphasis given to the preliminal or separation phase for Irish migrants, then, suggests that they saw their emigration in a more sensitive, disturbing light than did many Scots. How did both groups react during the liminal phase of their rites of passage?

under 20 per cent, double that of the Irish. See Mark Wyman, 'Emigrants returning: the evolution of a tradition', in Marjory Harper (ed.), *Emigrant Homecomings: The Return Movement of Emigrants, 1600–2000* (Manchester: Manchester University Press, 2005), pp. 16–17.

4

'Nothing but water': getting there

Mary Gibson was born at Bannockburn on 6 July 1905, the eldest of eight
children of coalminer John Gibson. She had been courted by Neil Macfarlane,
who continued to correspond with her after his departure for New Zealand in
1934. After Neil made a return trip in 1936, Mary followed in his footsteps,
leaving Scotland on 28 April 1938. The couple married in Auckland within
a few days of her arrival on the vessel *Remuera*. During her passage Mary
maintained a shipboard journal and posted it home as soon as she arrived in
Auckland. Selected extracts are cited below.[1]

30th

I woke this morning early & knew by the movement the ship was on its way & we
have left England behind. We didn't get a last look at it seeing they started at 2 in
the morning. Our tea as usual & the clock put back 25 minutes again. Then breakfast at 8.30. Stewed prunes I had, fish then bacon and Egg. I'm able for it alright
& I've never been sick touch wood Eh. The morning passed Lying in a deck chair.
By the way we had instruction how to put on the life belts and where to go and so
forth in case of accidents.

...

After Lunch at 1 oclock we are resting from 2 till 4pm when we go for afternoon
tea. I'm writing this in my bunk now. They don't allow any noise from 2 till 4 as it
is the official rest hours, so I thought I'd do the same, as I shouldn't be so sleepy
at night time but I'll see. After dinner we went for a walk. You go for a walk on the
ship alright back & forward the deck till you feel you've walked a few miles. That's
what we did with Sat night & ended with a blether to the Engineers. There is one
from Glasgow & he acts like Charlie Chaplin, but he is nice looking. What *what*
a comic. I like to meet him as they get a good laugh at him & I speaking Scotch.
Then to bed.

1st May

Sunday morning tea as usual in bed then up for breakfast. No church this morning,
so went for a walk again till [*?oft*] the storm. Boys O boys, what a gale. We ran into
bad weather. Fancy on Sunday. Some say its because they didn't hold a service.
The purser blames the Hockey girls for singing on Sunday morning the hymn
(For those in peril on the sea). He was swearing them & said it was a bad Omen.
It always is wild whenever that is sung on board, & I missed Lunch on Sunday
feeling sick. Went to lie on my back with whiskey & was ready for tea at 4 and never

---

1 Shipboard journal of Mary Gibson, 1938. This was kindly provided by May Tapp.

5 Mary Gibson, 1938

felt bad since. I got up on deck in the fresh air & felt it kept me better. Costume, coat, & rug on. Most of the tables were empty on Sunday night but I was able for Dinner. 6 instead of 12 at table.

Monday 2nd May.
I never slept all night. Not being able to lie in bed for rocking I tried to get fixed but no good. Things getting worse & to crown it all we got our Cabin flooded last night through a ventilator. My shoes were full of water & everything is soaking.

You should see the rugs. Everything went flying. Cups & saucers of the dressing table but I went & had bacon & Egg for breakfast. I was <u>one</u> of <u>three</u> at our table this morning, nine absent, all the men missing & the poor cook. The ships cook got swept off his feet & broke his collar bone & his leg. When the boy came to ring the Gong one of the stewards says to him You are expecting someone to turn up for lunch. Its awful yet Stewardess says Im weathering it well & the steward at table says I'm pluckier than the others. I choose fish, cold ham & salad beetroot etc. They say to stick to those things & you get on better but I feel I must have a good feed so end with biscuits & cheese & the steward laughs when I won't take butter. I was telling him (safety first) no coffee. I'll survive on these things till I gets a bit calmer.

…

This is 3rd May. I got a good sleep last night after I fell over. It was still wild but no water came in on us. Nothing but creaking all the time. It was the knocking about kept me from sleeping the night before. I tried a*t* pillow at my back to keep me from rolling so much & at last I fell asleep & heard no more till morning. Stewardess brings me hot water & lemon these two mornings since the storm. She says this is best in the meantime, but eat. I can eat like a horse. I had stewed pears, haddock & then sausage & bacon & potatoes this morning. So I'm not sick. I wasn't right sea sick on Sunday but went to bed at the beginning & I feel OK. All the smart guys who were yarning about where they have been, have disappeared these 2 days. They aren't so big noises now. I knock about on my own now. I've met lots of folk travelling alone. You get used to this. I just go where I please & never mind the cabin pal. I was speaking to an old man after lunch today. He says he hopes we get (across the pond alright). This is his first trip too. He has a yorkshire terri*o*r with him. One with the hair over its eyes and he had to pay £9 for the dog. It's not the size of Bruce.

…

4th Wed.
Got up fit & went to see land. The Azores are Islands. We could see white patches on them. They say it was villas & we did see a sailing ship also today. We are seeing things today. Its getting warm now. I can go for a walk with jumper & skirt in spite of the breeze. Cabin pal & I walked quite a bit this morning. She is feeling better. I never had sea sickness. Just felt rotten for (3 hours only) but took whiskey and have been OK since. Sat on Deck till lunch time & walked in the afternoon up and down, up and down. If it was in Stirling they would be talking about us. You should see the crowd. Everyone does it. We were present*at*ed with the passenger list at Lunch. I'll send it when we got a decent P. Office.

…

(7th May they say its Sat)
I have an awful job to mind the day and date. After breakfast we didn't walk much. It's getting very hot. We have lovely big deck chairs with cushions like the blue one for the bed chair. You can lie in them but in the sun its awful. Later we went

to the (top deck). There is a lovely deck behind on top. There are more places than you see in the plan of the ship. There's plenty of room for sunbathing, but Im wearing my linen hat well & sun classes over my own. You don't need to screw up your eyes with them on. It makes a difference. Then a game of bowl board & then the ice cream came on the scene, & after I did a bit of washing, I'm doing it often & its easier just to rinse them out. You feel your skin all sticky with the sea air. I've never saw any kind of fish yet, unless on the table. The sailor boys are in their white suits now & they say the table stewards will soon be in white also. Some of the hockey team is nice, & the rest are <u>snobs</u> roaring and laughing and showing off. That's what they do & you should see them in shorts, & no corsets on. Gee. The thin ones arent so bad.

...

Sunday 8th

Everyone is wishing we were at Panama. Although plenty of games they tire of them. I went to Church. I had my white Satin blouse on with my skirt & white shoes, & Linen hat. It was held in the dining room of the first class. The tables were covered with maroon table cloth & curtains on the portholes the same & finished with gold. The chief officer & the captain took the service. The bible was on a cushion covered with the Union Jack. It was an English Service, but I knew all the hymns. Then walking a lot today & evening & they had community singing tonight till bed time. I hear them at it yet.

...

12th May

We see another ship a passenger one on the horizon & some more small Islands in the distance. Its hazy today and we cant make them out well. We arrive at Curaco tonight & the young sailor boys are delighted to get off. They got a lecture not to go with girls and not to go in any of the places. I was telling them thats what mother would have been telling them. They are all nice boys just 18 yrs old & going to N.Z for 3 yrs. So if we go off tonight we will get a glimpse just to give us an idea what the west indies is like. Well we go off but it was moonlight but we could see everything just O.K. Plenty of darkies, & what struck me first of all was how lovely & clean the wharf was. It was as clean as the decks here on board, & they are scrubbed with sand stone every morning. Instead of a sweeping brush its a big sandstone fixed like a brush & push it back & forwards to clean the decks.

...

Sunday 15th

...

We got off at 3 oclock in the afternoon just in time for a 3 hours run around the places by car to see the different places. We were at Old Panama, new Panama & some of the outlying districts, some of Old & New Panama. Had narrow streets like (Baker St) & we just said to each other we would rather drive than walk through these places. All kinds of darkies in this part & the girls & woman with the gaily coloured flocks looked lovely. I saw & spoke to a Panamean woman & her black baby. The baby was 8 or 9 months old but it was a beauty. They are nicer looking than the niggars & the baby had its ears pierced and lovely gold ear[r]ings in. I couldn't believe my eyes when I saw her ear[r]ings & lovely black curls & her face was as black as coal.

…

19th

Warmer this morning. Walked, played games & sewed today & finished sewing off tea cosy cover. In the afternoon the crossing the line service was set agoing which was fine looking on. They were questioned & examined by doctor and if they didn't go straight forward they were all the harder done to. They got pills to swallow & slapped all over hair face & body with paste out of a pale & Distemper brush. Some got the brush slapped across their face & then flung into the tank or bathing pool I should say. Neptune was up on top of them & he said what treatment they were to get. He had his stick [*drawing*] like this & his followers were dressed up like Zulu's, and a director that is travelling to N.Z was head [*word illegible*]. When it came to the sailor boys turn, they took charge & flung all the head [*word illegible*] into the water. They didn't expect that & what a laugh we got. Neptune would say how many times they were to be dipped or how many pills they were to get etc. Others would get a pail of water thrown on them from behind & what a mess the paste made. They would hold them down & plaster mouth eyes & everything with paste but it was a laugh when Neptune & his colleagues got thrown in. I nearly died laughing.

…

24th

This is Empire day so we are told there's to be a party tonight, so we got over the day as usual. Its still warm & not much of a breeze. Thats why we think its warmer here. Always you hear them talk now of how many days till we get there (Auckland). Everybody is getting to know who's who & some we get to know too well & they get the go-bye. I like a talk with Mrs Connell & a Mrs McRae. They come from Glasgow & theres a Miss Murray an elderly lady from Edinburgh. So they all understand me alright. An Australian likes to torment me because he doesn't know what I say in Scotch, so I just give them all the more Scotch. The German Jew couldn't see how I knew English & yet was Scotch. I think he got mixed up because the English don't understand Scotch & yet I understand them in English. He can talk so much English the German Jew & he tells me he can't get his money from Germany. All he'll get is his passage paid for him on the boat to go to N.Z. & the money for landing & drinks (Lemonade) etc from the ship. He doesnt get handling money & only 18/- allowed at Panama & any left over goes back to Germany & they won't give any more. I was telling him NZ will treat him better than that. They are very nice, him & his wife & 2 girls.

The place is decorated with flags all round & a concert seeing its empire day, singing God save the King to start the thing & the same to finish. Some of the first class are glad to mix with us. They are bored stiff as there is very few first class.

If the hockey girls & the sailors hadn't been travelling with us there would have been less here too.

…

25th Wed

…

I was telling them they've never played a Scotch dance yet. I don't think they can play them but we will see if they can do anything like that by the time we go off. Mrs Connell & I were doing patronella, Highland Schottiche etc on our own often to let some of the Ausies & N.Zs see how we dance. I fairly enjoyed the fancy dress. I've enjoyed all the voyage but this is more so and the dancing on our own finished the [*word illegible*]. Then some got happy & started rehearsing the Maori war cry. What a laugh. They were half drunk. What a laugh it was. The Captain had to chase them to bed.

…

June 4th

We had to have the cabin trunks taken away at 9.30 this morning. Everybody is looking after their luggage now & we have just got word we have to arrive at 10 o'clock tomorrow forenoon. Thats sooner than we expected but everyone is delighted at the idea of the journey coming to an end. Its a lovely day today & the sun is shining. The sea is quite calm with us. This is the 4th Sat but its really Sunday 5th in NZ. [*erased: ?*] We miss Sunday & call tomorrow the 6th owing to the time being put back. We have taken 5 weeks and 4 days for the trip. Ive enjoyed it but its too long a journey without seeing anything for so long. If we hadn't called at pitcairn as the other ships do, we would have been 3 weeks without seeing a particle of land the longest spell without seeing land on any journey. Now we have only a few hours to go. I can hardly believe it.

We arrived in Auckland at 9.30 in the morning. What a good impression I got at the very beginning coming in to Auckland. Its lovely to see all the houses with red roofs in all the bays. Everybody is dying to get off. Its been such a long journey. Now Neil & his pal to meet me.

Mary Gibson's travel story encapsulates the uncertainty and dislocation caused by departure from home. Although official accounts together with pertinent information provided by expatriates settled abroad gave migrants a sense of what to expect, personal testimonies show that the process was one of displacement as migrants confronted a vast range of novel contrasts. This is vividly demonstrated by Mary Gibson's encounter with shipboard regulations, her interaction with other ethnicities, and disruption to the ship in foul weather. Voyaging was a liminal experience, with the transition providing the second element in their rite of passage.[2] Being betwixt and between, migrants

2 Arnold van Genepp, *Rites of Passage*, translated by Monika B. Vizedom and Gabrielle L. Caffee, with an introduction by Solon T. Kimball (London: Routledge and Kegan Paul, 1960), p. 21.

were subject to disorienting, unfamiliar surroundings. Change and a decline in hierarchical relations are seen as key elements of this theory, and examination of the voyage both affirms and challenges this assumption.

Deploying official publicity tracts by shipping companies in combination with personal testimonies facilitates exploration of a number of critical themes relating to the voyage out: preparations for the passage, facilities on board ship, and life at sea. The novelty of the journey meant that some migrants penned captivating descriptions of their passage, their daily activities recorded for longevity. Such narratives, though, may have been influenced by the likelihood of an audience at home, for in Mary Gibson's case, her journal was sent to her father. Meanwhile, the confusion encountered during such a life-changing transition ensured that recollections of the voyage continued to be vividly documented decades later. That such stories were also retold and rehearsed to audiences of family and friends over the years also kept such memories fresh, though presumably not without an element of embellishment.

Weaving together individual narratives and broad overviews of the journey, the chapter argues that despite migrants being unprepared for many experiences encountered during their passage, the transition enabled them to anticipate the many contrasts they would eventually confront at their destination. Moreover, the blending of such diverse source materials enables the construction of a 'typical' twentieth-century migrant voyage. Memories of an assisted post-war passage to Australia, on the other hand, resulted in British migrants structuring voyages along conflicting lines: luxury cruise versus nightmare at sea; seasickness versus romance.[3]

Image versus reality

Having experienced the dislocation of separation from family and friends, migrants sought their on-board accommodation. Third-class berths were usually allocated on the day of travel, and occasionally one or two days prior. Those voyaging on quotas to the United States, however, were not entitled to travel in the newly established 'Tourist Third Class'.[4] Their onward journeys via rail, however, could be booked in advance. Angus Macdonald in 1926 travelled on the *Bendigo*, revealing, 'She was a P&O branch line boat and she was also a cargo/passenger ship. She carried passengers to mid-ships, a few,

3 A. James Hammerton and Alistair Thomson, *Ten Pound Poms: Australia's Invisible Migrants. A Life History of Postwar British Emigration to Australia* (Manchester: Manchester University Press, 2005), p. 101.

4 *Cook's Ocean Sailing List with Hints to Intending Travellers by Sea*, May 1928, p. 6, in NMM.

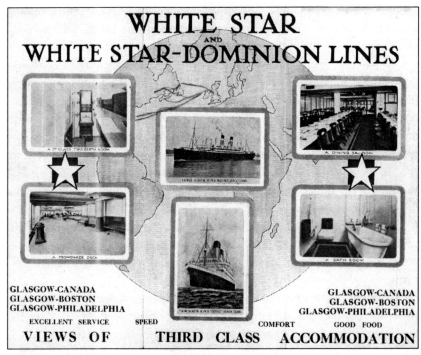

6 White Star Line Views of Third Class Accommodation

homeward bound. But when she was on her way out here all the holds and there was cabins, temporary cabins knocked up for migrants.'[5]

Although most promotional tracts from shipping companies were aimed at first- and second-class passengers, intending settlers were occasionally targeted, including those considering migration to Canada with the White Star Line. Details about the ships bound for Canada, their capacity and facilities also appear. The amenities of the ships included 'Excellently equipped bath rooms', 'an orchestra of skilled musicians', and 'unusually extensive' promenade decks – though deckchairs had to be hired.[6] A specimen bill of fare was also included. Passengers to Canada from Belfast were also targeted by the White Star Line, with a fortnightly direct service to Quebec and Montreal being offered on Belfast-built ships. In an effort to attract third-class passengers it was asserted that sleeping accommodation was 'well ventilated and well lighted … whilst there are numerous bathrooms with hot and cold showers. There are three Dining Saloons in the Third Class quarters extending the full

5 Interview with Angus Macdonald by Paula Hamilton, recorded 1 September 1987, in OHC NLA, NSW Bicentennial Oral History Project, Oral TRC 2301/137.
6 *White Star-Dominion Line: Facts About Canada* [c.1924], p. 15, in NMM, Ephemera Collections, White Star.

width of the ship, besides excellently equipped Smoking and General Rooms.'[7] A promotional tract of Cunard's dating from October 1924 likewise specified the opportunities available in Canada and outlined the spaciousness of the third-class accommodation. In addition, 'Curtains decorate the port-holes in the public rooms, and well-chosen pictures on the walls tend to produce a homely atmosphere.'[8] For those voyaging further afield, fine accommodation was a priority. It is not surprising, therefore, to find the Shaw Savill Line attesting in 1928 that 'The accommodation in third class is excellent ... In this class Passengers are provided with bedding, linen, table requisites, etc., and the food is cooked and served by the Ship's Servants. The quarters are kept clean by the Ship's Stewards.'[9] In a reproduction of a voyage account on one of the company's steamers, *Arawa*, it was observed that the dining saloon was 'furnished with revolving chairs, and there is a smoke-room set apart for their exclusive use. Each cabin has its own wash-stand, mirror, etc., whilst in addition there is a splendidly equipped lavatory, with a tessellated flooring, and an abundance of fresh water.'[10]

How, though, did migrant impressions of their accommodation compare with the publicity generated by shipping companies? The depictions of the shipping facilities already cited stem from companies transporting migrants to parts of the British World. Personal testimonies by migrants moving to Canada, New Zealand, and Australia by and large reveal satisfaction with the facilities they encountered. Among those conveying their contentment with the amenities on offer was Annabella Sinclair from Onziebust on the isle of Wyre, Orkney. Journeying to Australia on the *Baradine* in 1929 she penned: 'Now we get on board our liner and get conducted to our cabins which is a nice four berth place one bunk for each of the boys one for Duncan and one for myself and baby.'[11] Almost a decade later, Mary Gibson, sailing on the *Remuera* to New Zealand, wrote, 'I find there are plenty seats for everybody. We got away from the crowd to a quiet part of the deck by ourselves when it was lovely and quiet.'[12] An intriguing similarity of official versus private accounts is discernible in the testimony of Lorna Carter. Though she provided little comment on

7 'Belfast to Canada direct service by Belfast built steamers – White Star Line' [c.1922], in NMM, Ephemera Collections, White Star.
8 'Cunard to Canada', p. 4, October 1924, in NMM, Ephemera Collections, Cunard, Brochures 1, folder titled 'Brochures: destination Canada'.
9 *Shaw Savill and Albion Line to New Zealand Direct via Panama Canal, Official Guide and Handbook*, p. 12 [c.1928], in NMM, Ephemera Collections, Shaw Savill, folder titled 'Shaw Savill Line II'.
10 *Ibid.*, p. 52.
11 Shipboard journal of Annabella Sinclair, 1929, in OA, D1/118. Extract dated 13 April 1929.
12 Shipboard journal of Mary Gibson, 1938. Extract dated 30 April 1938.

the vessel, she commented favourably on the provision of frequent showers and was grateful for 'plenty of lounge & deck space'.[13] These observations reiterate official publications, which lauded the *Atlantis* for its 'spacious decks, comfortable lounges, a swimming pool, an inside cinema and additional equipment and space so that films can be shown on one side of the ship whilst a dance is being held on the other side. There are plenty of bath rooms and shower rooms, and there is no restriction on the use of fresh water for baths and showers.'[14]

By way of contrast, migrants moving to the United States indicated that their accommodation sometimes failed to live up to the image proffered in glossy publicity tracts. Anne Walsh found it to be 'a dread ship I got on. Oh God, it was terrible. When I went to go to bed at night, something was creeping on the pillow. And there was bugs on the pillow.'[15] According to Della Gleckel who voyaged on the Anchor Line ship *Cynthia* in 1925, 'It was just a little dump away down in the boat. It was steerage or, you know, third-class which was the cheapest. So it was just like a little bunk away down in the boat. But to me, you know, it meant nothing because we weren't accustomed to luxury.'[16] The accommodation on the White Star Line's *Celtic* was also considered inferior by some: 'We were steerage, that was one of the lowest of the low because we had no money,' Kathleen Lamberti explained. 'I can imagine telling you it was very dirty and there were bugs and things that we had never seen.' The cabins, she maintained, 'were dreadful. You wouldn't put a dog in them today.'[17] With the conversion of the *Celtic* to a cabin steamer, however, a glossy publicity tract boasted that its cabins had an 'air of cosiness and privacy, are complete with every modern device to ensure cleanliness'.[18] The disenchantment conveyed by these migrants may well be the result of the contrast between the journey and the subsequent comfort they found in the United States. Those travelling to Empire destinations, on the other hand, frequently noted after arrival that their surroundings were quite primitive. Alternatively, perhaps those moving to the United States had been influenced by stories of the nineteenth-century voyage in which discomfort and unsanitary conditions were commonplace. More likely, however, is that ships bound for Australasia tended to maintain

13 Lorna Carter (*Atlantis*) to her parents (Oban), 19 August 1951, 27 August 1951, in ATL, Carter family letters, MS-Papers-7377.
14 Immigration Newsletter, No. 3, January 1949, p. 2, cited in Megan Hutching, *Long Journey for Sevenpence: Assisted Immigration to New Zealand from the United Kingdom, 1947-1975* (Wellington: Victoria University Press, 1999), pp. 107-8.
15 Interview with Anne Walsh by Nancy Dallett, recorded 26 June 1986, EIOHP, AKRF Series 200.
16 Interview with Della Gleckel by Paul Sigrist, recorded 2 May 1995, EIOHP, EI Series 611.
17 Interview with Kathleen Lamberti by Paul Sigrist, recorded 25 February 1994, EIOHP, EI Series 439.
18 '*Celtic* and *Cedric* Tourist Third Cabin' brochure, in NMM.

high standards of quality and cleanliness on account of the length of the trip and desire to attract migrants through offers of assisted fares, features also reminiscent of nineteenth-century voyages to the Antipodes.

Food

One particularly extensive account of third-class accommodation was provided by Johanna Flaherty, who voyaged on the *Adriatic*, belonging to the White Star Line, in 1923:

The trip wasn't bad, but we were down in steerage. Now, that's the bottom of the boat, absolute bottom. And you could not open your window because the water was, you were like under water. It was splashing up against the porthole the whole time. And we had bunk beds, of course. And the food was good, pretty good, but I was sick most of the ways across. I was seasick. And I really didn't care if I ever saw food. Just a glass of ginger ale, that was all I really wanted. Then I'd go upstairs and lay down on the deck and roll my coat up and put it under my head and I'd sleep there half the day. I was really very sick. But what made us worse was on our way down to our bunks we had to pass the kitchen. And the smell of that cook cooking food, it used to make us nauseous, because we were nauseous anyway [*laughs*].[19]

Food was an especially intriguing aspect of the voyage for migrants. Shipping companies too recognised the importance of provisions, with promotional material acclaiming the liner's benefits in this department. As Shaw Savill claimed in 1928, the Company's cuisine was 'unsurpassed by that of any Line in the world ... Third Class Passengers have a full supply of the best provisions, and a very liberal allowance of fresh meat and fresh bread.'[20] Dining facilities were also advertised by shipping companies. Canadian Pacific declared that its Duchess steamers had capacity for 252 passengers at one sitting, dining at small tables holding between two and six passengers.[21] Moreover, on special occasions such as St Patrick's Day and Burns Day menus featuring Irish and Scottish fare were created. Cunard's *Queen Mary*, for instance, celebrated St Patrick's Day in 1966 by offering a range of dishes from Irish regions on a menu boasting a shamrock and lines from 'The dear little shamrock'.[22] A 'Scottish Landfall Dinner' was also operated by P&O on the *Moldavia* in June 1937. The menu featured a snippet from Burns together with traditional Scottish fare which echoed the Scots language with its 'tatties' and 'a hunk

19 Interview with Johanna Flaherty by Debra Allee, recorded 29 May 1986, EIOHP, AKRF Series 182.
20 *Shaw Savill Handbook*, p. 31.
21 'Canadian Pacific Duchess Steamers', November 1927, in NMM, Ephemera Collections, Canadian Pacific, Brochures (Specific) 2.
22 NMM, Ephemera Collections, Cunard, Menus.

o'cool frae the hielands'.[23] Other migrants indicated that separate dining times were established for adults and children. As Annabella Sinclair divulged in her contemporary shipboard diary on board the *Baradine*, her children ate separately, though in her presence. Her own dining typically consisted of the following: 'soup stewed [*word illegible*] potatoes roast mutton pudding e*ct ect*. For breakfast we get Ham, eggs potatoes, stewed prunes & rice. Afternoon tea at four, dinner at seven. Soup again meats of all sorts pudding & fruit to finish up with.'[24]

For some migrants the food they encountered on board proved to be a novelty, and established many contrasts that would again be encountered at their destinations. Apart from cornflakes and orange juice, for many it was the first time they had eaten corn on the cob. Several migrants, for instance, claimed that corn was fed to cows at home and humans would not consume it. As Mary Dunn of Stirling disbelievingly indicated:

Well, the only thing I remember, the first time I ever saw corn on the cob and I said, 'My God, I wouldn't eat that stuff, we feed that to the cows at home.' Which was true, you know. And I never, I never cared too much for corn on the cob. And we just got, one cob would be cut in about three pieces, you know. Just a little bit. That was one of the things I remember that I didn't like. I wouldn't even eat it.[25]

Similarly, Ena Hughes mentioned eating pumpkin during her voyage to Australia in the mid-1920s on the ship *Ormus*: 'Another thing they used to give us was boiled pumpkin and we said, "How do people eat that awful stuff?" It was Australian you see. We didn't have pumpkins in our place and they used to give us this rather sloppy boiled pumpkin with the meal and we just hated it. We thought it was dreadful.'[26] Other migrants were similarly unimpressed, with Ann Walsh groaning 'the food was perfectly dreadful food. You see, when you grow up on the farm, you have fresh eggs and fresh chickens and all good food.'[27] For many post-war migrants, however, the availability of food on the voyage contrasted strikingly with food rationing in place at home.

As well as encountering new foods, migrants were also confronted by the dilemma of selecting the correct silverware. As John Joe Gallogly admitted coyly, 'I was on the ship for Thanksgiving and I never saw more food or dishes or silverware and we would look at each other. We all sat together and we didn't

23 'P&O Menu', in NMM, Ephemera Collections, P&O.
24 Shipboard journal of Annabella Sinclair, extract dated 7 April 1929.
25 Interview with Mary Dunn by Dana Gumb, recorded 23 January 1986, EIOHP, AKRF Series 127.
26 Interview with Ena Hughes by Bronwyn Hughes, recorded 1987, in OHC NLA, NSW Bicentennial Oral History Project, Oral TRC 2279/8.
27 Interview with Anne Walsh.

know which knife or fork or spoon to pick up.'[28] Presumably the bemusement, curiosity, and awkwardness accompanying these social situations meant that such contrasts remained fixed in migrant memories.

Seasickness, storms and safety

Apart from the difficulties posed by cultural contrasts, migrants also experienced physical disturbance. Seasickness was the greatest culprit in this regard and plagued many for the first few days at sea. Some counteracted this by taking a teaspoon of brandy![29] Others were subjected to cabins being saturated. Yet some migrants saw the humour among the rolling waves. Lorna Carter, for instance, hilariously described one storm encountered during her voyage to New Zealand on the *Atlantis* in 1951:

Well, well, there is a storm today – a real smasher – huge waves and spray all over the place. Sitting in the cabin a wee while ago it just felt as though the ship were going down huge steps, giving great shudders each time. Things are crashing about and we have the edges up round the table to keep the dishes on!! E and I had our games of table tennis as usual. When we weren't sprawled half way over the table we were running for yards down the deck to rescue the ball!! Working under difficulties we were, then we tried walking round the deck!! We soon gave it up and subsided on to a seat amidship where it is fairly steady. The rocking didn't stop the Scottish Country dancing Lass. There they were doing Scottish Reform, which was managed fairly successfully, but when they started the Gay Gordons – laugh I was 'ungry!! especially when they came to the twirly bit.[30]

Indeed, encountering storms was perhaps the most widespread event in which migrant testimonies contradict official publicity tracts. While most shipping companies implied a stable voyage by emphasising a ship's comfort, explicit descriptions can also be found in official publications. Cunard, for instance, attested to the importance of a 'steady sea-going ship',[31] while the size and equipment of the *Berengaria* 'make it ride smoothly over the roughest seas'.[32] In relation to the *Baltic*, *Cedric*, and *Celtic*, the White Star Line similarly proclaimed 'the exceptional steadiness of these steamers at sea'.[33] Official publicity also emphasised that the *Atlantis* 'has exceptional

28 Interview with John Joe Gallogly.
29 Interview with Sr Rose O'Neill by Paul Sigrist, recorded 3 June 1998, EIOHP, EI Series 1003.
30 Lorna Carter (*Atlantis*) to her parents (Oban), 26 September 1951, continuation of letter 1, 22 September 1951, in ATL.
31 *Cunard to Canada* (October 1924), p. 6, in NMM, Ephemera Collections, Cunard, Brochures 1.
32 *Berengaria*, in NMM, Ephemera Collections, Cunard, Brochures 1.
33 *White Star Line Royal and United States Mail Steamers*, p. 9, in NMM, Ephemera Collections, White Star.

stability in rough weather'.[34] Lorna Carter, as we have just seen, thought otherwise. During another gale she wrote, 'One minute we were on our toes waltzing away and the next minute we were talking to the side of the ship as she rolled!'[35] In similar vein, Ernest Younger, bound for Canada in October 1929 on the Anchor-Donaldson Line's *Athenia*, reported, 'During the night the sea didn't behave very well & I didn't sleep so good. The boat was tossing too much.' The following morning he felt 'a little seedy' and two days later a dance was cancelled as the sea was 'too rough & the boat was rolling'.[36] Meanwhile, the *Manhattan* proved unstable for Mary Jo Lenney: 'The cabin was very, very nice except it was rough that you were knocked from one side to the other or if you walked down the corridor you couldn't walk a straight line and I remember one night when we were out in the middle of the ocean all the dishes and the food and everything went flying off the table. It was exciting.'[37] Such encounters caused some ships to be vigorously derided. The *Cameronia*, for instance, 'shook along her whole length rather like a dog shaking water off his coat'.[38]

The responsibility of conveying so many people across sometimes treacherous seas meant that a number of safety elements associated with seaboard life were documented in shipping policy. The Royal Mail Line Ltd regulations in 1950, for instance, stipulated that 'Captains must conduct an Emergency Fire and Boat Stations Drill at a convenient opportunity at least once each week and make an entry in the Official and Deck Log Books that this has been carried out. Officers and Crew must wear their Lifejackets.' In addition, 'Passengers must be invited to attend an Emergency and Boat Station Drill immediately after leaving port, and whenever such drill is being carried out.'[39] Testimonies reveal that lifeboat drills were often held during the voyage. Lorna Carter, journeying in August 1951 on the *Atlantis*, a vessel chartered by The Royal Mail Lines Ltd for four years to carry emigrants from Southampton to Australasia,[40] mentioned such drills in her correspondence. On other occasions, the scenario was not a rehearsal, as Kathleen Lamberti eagerly illustrated: 'we were all given lifebelts and everybody the Irish are all in the corners kneeling

---

34 Immigration Newsletter, No. 3, January 1949, p. 2, cited in Hutching, *Long Journey for Sevenpence*, pp. 107-8.

35 Lorna Carter (*Atlantis*) to her parents (Oban), 19 August 1951, in ATL.

36 Ernest Younger (*Athenia*) to his parents (Tillicoultry), 5 October 1929, in NLS, Acc. 9407/2.

37 Interview with Mary Jo Lenney by Paul Sigrist, recorded 21 August 1996, EIOHP, EI Series 793.

38 R. S. McLellan, *Anchor Line, 1856-1956* (Glasgow: Anchor Line, 1956), p. 86.

39 *Royal Mail Line Ltd Regulations 1950* (London, 1950), in NMM, RMS/67/1.

40 Duncan Haws, *Merchant Fleets: Royal Mail Line, Nelson Line* (Crowborough, Sussex: TCL Publications, 1982), p. 73.

"Holy Mary Mother of God" praying away and the boat's going this way and this way and well they really thought they'd had it'.[41] Scotsman Patrick Peak also remembered a renowned blackspot during the voyage out, though he presumably meant that although the waves may have reached forty feet, the water breaking over the forecastle was significantly less:

There's one spot, they call it the Devil's Hole … It's a very stormy area nine times out of ten. And I remember the waves were coming over the deck about twenty, thirty, forty feet high. And I thought, at the time, the ship was going down, because that captain, at that time, took it on himself to put on a rehearsal for abandoning ship, you know. And I remember we were all up on the deck and they were showing us how to buckle the lifebelts on, and how to get into the lifeboats. And to me that's what I was thinking, this ship is going down, you know. But that's all it was. It was just a rehearsal in case something did happen, you know.[42]

Encountering such events was clearly a staggering contrast with what migrants were accustomed to. Unsurprisingly, the sheer terror experienced in such circumstances left clear impressions in migrant minds. Yet some migrants confessed to being innocent because of their background. Della Gleckel, raised on a hilly farm at Tuam, County Galway, supplied a thoughtful interpretation:

the great part of being naïve was that I had no feeling about anything ever happening like, you know, drowning or anything like that because we only had rivers see. I can't, don't know how to swim because we had no place where you could learn. We had no pools, the ocean was 24 miles away and transportation, we had no transportation except a bicycle and to cycle eight miles was really a big cycling job to go into this other town and come back the same day, that was like 16 miles you cycled one day so I don't know how to swim so naturally I had no fear of the water. But I just looked out and saw nothing but water and it was, even though kind of scary, you thought oh I'd just love to see land or a house or something because I had never seen that mass of water. I had never seen the ocean until I got to Queenstown to sail and that wasn't like being out in the boat.[43]

Faith and frivolity

A further regulation for The Royal Mail Line Ltd in 1950 was for the Captain 'to see that Divine Service is duly and reverently held on board every Sunday at sea and a note must be made in the Deck Log Book to that effect. If Divine Service is not held during any Sunday at sea the reason must be stated in the

41 Interview with Kathleen Lamberti.
42 Interview with Patrick Peak by Nancy Dallett, recorded 15 November 1985, EIOHP, AKRF series 84.
43 Interview with Della Gleckel.

Deck Log Book.'[44] While Lorna Carter's contemporary letters do not mention religious practices on board ship, in an interview she revealed, 'Every nationality had a church service they could go to and, of course, Una had to go to her service and first day first Sunday she said, "oh I haven't got a hat", so my hat, it was a beret, went to church every Sunday with Una.'[45] Faith proved crucial when death occurred at sea. Again, however, makeshift arrangements had to be undertaken. Ann Conway explained the procedure as follows:

Oh there were a few buried at sea when going over. I felt so sorry that they didn't put them into a coffin, you know, they died at sea and then they hadn't money enough to take them off and they just wrapped burned canvas over them and captain told us all to get up on deck so went all up on deck and opened a wee gate after he said some prayers or something and shoved them into the sea. I thought it was so sad.[46]

Uncertainty also surrounded the length of time migrants spent at sea, though the journey to the United States in the twentieth century took approximately six to ten days. Throughout the period, shipping companies competed against each other by claiming that their transit was faster. In June 1924, for instance, Canadian Pacific boasted that its express Empress steamers spent only four days at sea.[47] By contrast, those making their way to the Antipodes were on the seas for six weeks. As Brigid Dawson amusingly quipped of her voyage to New Zealand in 1924, 'No doubt its a long Journey six weeks and a day night and day and had nothing to do only sit about that left the time to seem longer. From to much work to no work abal kilt [*about killed*] me.'[48]

In an effort to counteract the boredom of long days at sea, particularly during voyages to Australasia, shipping lines boasted of extensive entertainment. Among those activities publicised by Shaw Savill in 1932 were 'swimming, deck sports, horseracing, dancing, indoor and outdoor games, and card and social parties'.[49] Novel names were formulated in connection with such events, especially the card and dice game of horseracing. Those with an Irish or Scottish flavour included in the First Pacific Meeting of the *Rangitata* in June 1959 were 'Mr Brady's Partition by Ulster out of Eire', and 'Mr Dunlop's

44 *Royal Mail Line Ltd Regulations 1950.*
45 Interview with Lorna Ross by Angela McCarthy, recorded 24 February 2003.
46 Interview with Ann Conway by Janet Levine, recorded 11 March 1998, EIOHP, EI Series 981.
47 '*Canadian Pacific* to Canada & USA third class steamer accommodation', June 1924, in NMM, Ephemera Collections, Canadian Pacific, Brochures (General) 1.
48 Brigid Dawson (Wanganui) to her sister Ellen Quinn (Armagh), 30 July 1924. This letter was kindly provided by Joan Leonard.
49 'The Ideal Route to England via Panama Canal' (Wellington, March 1938), in NMM, Ephemera Collections, Shaw Savill.

Canadian Pacific Spans the World

Exercise
for the
Energetic

DECK GOLF

A GYMNASIUM

DECK TENNIS

SHUFFLE BOARD

7 Exercise for the Energetic on board Canadian Pacific

Scotland the Brave by Bagpipes out of Scotland'.[50] Dancing was a particular
passion of Scottish migrants making the lengthy voyage. A particularly enthusiastic participant was Lorna Carter: 'I danced Scottish Reform this morning,
but am conserving my energy for tonight when there's to be an all Scottish

50 *Rangitata*, 1 June 1959, in NZMM.

dancing session.'[51] Ships making shorter crossings to North America also boasted of pursuits on board. 'Orchestral music, Cinematograph entertainments, Concerts, Dancing and Deck Sports' were all offered to third-class passengers by Canadian Pacific.[52] Overall, though, the trip to Canada and the United States tended to be poor in the way of entertainment, with passengers making their own festivities such as dancing, singing, playing music, and competing at shuffle board and cards.[53] Ernest Younger related happily during his 1929 trip to Canada, 'I haven't played so many different card games in my life before. I know a lot of new ones.'[54] Many passengers possessed musical instruments such as those who shared John Joe Gallogly's trip to New York on the *Brittanic* in 1952:

quite a few of the immigrants had musical instruments with them. They had melodeons and fiddles and tin flutes and concert flutes and we had a great time. We had such a good time in our department that a lot of the people from first class came down and joined us and it was just great.[55]

The luxury of participating in such convivial and relaxing events for a period of several days or weeks at sea would have impressed many migrants accustomed to gruelling work habits at home. It is therefore not surprising that they fondly recalled these social activities.

For those destined for Australasia, crossing the equator was a novel undertaking, and one that would rarely be forgotten, given the pomp and circumstance surrounding the procedure. Annabella Sinclair reported it like this in 1929:

It is the custom at sea [*erased: ?*] as we cross the line whoever crosses it for the first time is fixed and carried away and held under a tap of water to get a good [*word illegible*] … Its just carried on as a custom same as some of our old customs at home same as diving for apples on hogmanay night and so on.[56]

51 Lorna Carter (*Atlantis*) to her parents (Oban) 20 September 1951, in ATL.
52 '*Canadian Pacific* to Canada & USA third class' brochure, April 1926, p. 2, in NMM, Ephemera Collections, Canadian Pacific, Brochures (General) 1.
53 See, for instance, interviews with Lamberti; interview with Anne Craven by Paul Sigrist, recorded 2 October 1991, EIOHP, EI Series 102; interview with Ann Conway; interview with Frances Hoffman by Janet Levine, recorded 20 February 1997, EIOHP, EI Series 853; interview with Mary Kelly by Paul Sigrist, recorded 10 September 1997, EIOHP, EI Series 936.
54 Ernest Younger (*Athenia*) to his parents (Tillicoultry), 5 October 1929, in NLS, Acc. 9407/2.
55 Interview with John Joe Gallogly.
56 Shipboard journal of Annabella Sinclair, extract dated 3 May 1929.

Port calls and views of 'others'

Despite the choice of vessel, migrants were restricted according to the routes they travelled. For those moving to Australasia, several exotic territories were visited along the way. If travelling via the Suez Canal, ports of call included Colombo, Bombay, Aden, Port Said, and Gibraltar. Shore excursions were a major feature of this journey, a key distinction of their passage from those travelling to North America. The Shaw Savill Line went via the Panama Canal and called at Colon and Panama, cities situated at either end of the Canal.[57] Quite apart from the 'travel thrill' of the transit through the Canal, Shaw Savill also proclaimed this route benefited from 'smoothness of seas and moderate temperatures'.[58] Migrants frequently described the exotic character of these ports of call, expressing immense astonishment at the contrasts with their homelands and fellow passengers. Annabella Sinclair epitomised the mixed feelings accompanying such forays. At Malta traders came on board to sell 'some really wonderful things silks of all sorts beads watches rings yes even birds in cages just beauties'. Ashore, however, Annabella was less impressed: 'Its really not nice being among natives'.[59] Port Said, on the other hand, was more agreeable:

We went into a shop and purchased a few things such as sun hats, biscuits e*ct*. You would have laughed to seen the natives. They were most polite and bowed and smiled something awful. The Egyptian goods were exceptionally good and cheap as well. They simply ran through the streets after us with all their wares. They also come on board the liner with such a lot of it.[60]

This was then followed by a stop at Aden which Annabella found 'looks all right from the harbour very like Egypt in some ways. We can see the camels walking along the streets from where we are.'[61]

Other passengers were also observed and judged, in both written and oral testimony. Kathleen Lamberti was especially entranced with passengers on the *Celtic*, particularly the Arran Islanders who she assessed looked more Spanish than Irish:

We would get out on the deck and there were a lot of Irish there that we thought really they were not Irish because they never spoke English, they spoke Gaelic. They came from the Arran Islands. They do speak Gaelic there and they were tall, oh they were about 6 foot near 7 foot, and they had all the spun clothes you know ... They had all their own breads, all their own food, piles of it, and they'd

57 *Shaw Savill Handbook*, p. 39.
58 'The Ideal Route', in NMM, Ephemera Collections, Shaw Savill.
59 Shipboard journal of Annabella Sinclair, extract dated 19 April 1929.
60 *Ibid.*, extract dated 23 April 1929.
61 *Ibid.*, extract dated April 1929.

8 Lorna Carter on board the *Atlantis*, 1951

congregate in a corner of the boat and eat all day long and talk all day long to themselves but they didn't mix with us and they were really Irish.[62]

Annabella Sinclair also made comparisons between other nationalities and her Orkney origins in her contemporaneous diary: 'We have met quite a few Australians. They seem very like our own people.'[63] Familiarity was also

---

62 Interview with Kathleen Lamberti.
63 Shipboard journal of Annabella Sinclair, extract dated 16 April 1929.

found among those whose origins were closer to home: 'There are Scotch people here English and Irish. The Irish seem very like the Orkney people in their ways.'[64] For many migrants, the voyage out was the first time they encountered other migrants from their homelands and other ethnic groups. That such interaction would continue in their new settlements meant that initial stereotypes and prejudices would either be continually reinforced or altered over the duration of their lives. By contrast, English migrants would already have had more exposure to other groups given England's history as an immigrant destination.

Close encounters with other migrants were sometimes alarming. Anne Walsh, for instance, felt deeply threatened by an unwanted attempt at seduction:

One night, a man scared me. He was an Englishman, and he was all dressed up fancy. And every day he'd stare at me. And he had - this night he came over to me, and he said, 'Dolly, Dolly, I want you to come up on deck tonight, about nine o'clock.' 'For what?' He said, 'I want to tell you stories.' Well, he told a story to himself, 'cause I didn't go on deck. Although I didn't know too much about men, but I knew enough to keep away from him.[65]

Lorna Carter, meanwhile, documented the petty thieving occurring as her journey neared its end:

We have been told that a lot of pinching goes on during this last week of the voyage, so I'm leaving nowt lying about, not that I did before. When we had that long stay at Fremantle and weren't allowed to take sterling ashore, I wondered where to hide my extra money. My brown case <u>could</u> be broken into. I had to cash a cheque before going, changed £3 into Aussie money, so had about £3 left. Me [*word illegible*] thought as Sherlock Holmes would have done! and I ended up by emptying out my Andrew's Liver Salts, [*erased:* and] put the money int' bottom of tin and returned the salts – O.K. - you think I'm daft – I know – but you should see some of the types on board – and I mean females – dresses etc have gone already.[66]

Having endured extremes of boredom and entertainment during the voyage migrants were thrilled to finally spot land. This was particularly the case for those who had survived stormy passages. After the tempest endured by Kathleen Lamberti and her fellow passengers, sighting the Statue of Liberty generated a rapturous response: 'Everybody cheering and shouting and waving, oh yes, but the glorious part was to get your foot on the soil.'[67]

64 *Ibid.*, extract dated 17 April 1929.
65 Interview with Anne Walsh.
66 Lorna Carter (*Atlantis*) to her parents (Oban), continuation of letter 1, 22 September 1951, in ATL.
67 Interview with Kathleen Lamberti.

Likewise Della Gleckel, who had left Tuam, County Galway, for New York in 1925 aged just 14, recollected her emotions as the ship approached New York: 'I saw buildings. Oh, we were ecstatic. We were just so excited. And when you saw Ellis Island, I think you had to come through that way to have the respect for Ellis Island.'[68]

A rather more subdued encounter with land appeared in Lorna Carter's letters home as her vessel drew close to Wellington in 1951:

And now we are just crawling along passing time until our appointed time of arrival which is 6pm this evening and we are on the Cook Strait. I see away on the starboard side mountains just like our coast and snow capped peaks in the distance. I just feel that I'm sailing home from Kyle to Mallaig and I've got the feeling that I'm going to love this [*word illegible*] land.[69]

Clearly after days or weeks at sea, the sighting of land was an immense event. Yet such relief was tinged with anxiety as migrants prepared to leave a sphere they had grown accustomed to in order to engage with life in their new homeland.

Conclusion

By blending personal and official versions of departure from home and shipboard life, this chapter emphasises the fruitfulness of such a methodology. Though some discrepancies exist between the differing forms of evidence, overall they demonstrate the subtleties, nuances, and complex arrangements associated with voyages transporting millions of migrants from Old to New Worlds. In general, the testimonies reveal that there was a collective experience of the voyage out, typified by encounters with storms, other nationalities, and novel events. There are, however, some clear differences. First, in relation to the destinations to which migrants gravitated, the journey to the United States was relatively short and there were few organised activities on board ship. Those destined for Australasia, on the other hand, spent approximately six weeks at sea and shipping companies made an effort to ensure the passage was as pleasant as possible. Varied entertainments and exotic stopovers added to the appeal of the passage. Personal accounts also give a vivid insight into the changing process of migration from the early to middle twentieth century as technological improvements and competition continued to alter the size, speed, and comfort of ships. The major change was the revolution in providing improved facilities for all classes of travellers.

Second, the main contrast between Irish and Scottish migrants is a degree

---

68 Interview with Della Gleckel.
69 Lorna Carter (*Atlantis*) to her parents (Oban), Sunday afternoon 1951, in ATL.

of naivety among Irish migrants who seemingly had little experience of life at sea. While the same could be said of Scottish migrants, their testimonies at least reveal a familiarity with the shipping service, perhaps on account of their origins in strong shipbuilding areas in the west of Scotland. A further difference worth highlighting is the contrasts discernible when taking a gendered approach to the voyage out. Unmarried (and sometimes married) migrants were not only segregated in their sleeping quarters according to their gender, but female migrants were also subjected to attempts at seduction, a familiar aspect of the nineteenth-century passage. By contrast with the voyage experience in the nineteenth century, however, female migrants in all classes could interact with male passengers on a less regulated, restricted basis.

Being betwixt and between two worlds, though, did not automatically result in the abandonment of factors such as class. Many ships still had class divisions, and the crew held a measure of authority. Unlike the nineteenth century, however, the transitional phase was more relaxed, with migrants rarely commenting on issues of power, control, and discipline. Instead, they were alert to encountering new sights, sounds, and smells. This transformative period left them well disposed to cope with the challenges that lay before them. From the outset then, migration was a dislocating undertaking. In stressing their ability to address such transformations, however, migrants were establishing themselves as stoic and resolute, attributes further emphasised in discussions of their initial encounters with new homelands. The contrasts and disturbances they encountered during the voyage were inevitably rehearsed in years to follow as migrants recounted their great transition from origin to destination. Repetition of these memories served to emphasise their fortitude. It seems unlikely, though, that these iconic stories were blown out of proportion. Instead, their recollections seem to have survived the test of time because of the immense emotions and events associated with such a transformative episode in their life history. The uncertainty experienced by migrants before and during their journey abroad would be replicated upon arrival. As the following chapter highlights, confusion and disruption characterised initial impressions of their new land.

5

'The land of opportunity': Ellis Island and New York

Catherine English (née Hannon) was born on 15 February 1900 near Bella-vary, County Mayo, the daughter of John Hannon and Bridget McEvey. Her father died when Catherine was about four or five years of age, and she was raised by her mother, siblings, and a network of aunts and uncles. In 1924 at 24 years of age Catherine travelled to New York, where three of her sisters had already settled. At the time of recording her memories, Catherine was 91 years old.[1]

Paul Sigrist: Can you describe Ellis Island to me? What did it look like to you?

Catherine English: It, to me, it was like cages, you know, and they brought you just like you'd see a bunch of cattle going in and they brought you in on those, I think they had, like, it must be iron boards or something and there might be maybe the width of the kitchen and two could walk in and then they put you, they had sections, like, for the different countries, the ones that could speak English and the one that couldn't speak English and they put them in there but I wasn't long in there at all.

Paul Sigrist: Was it crowded there?

Catherine English: It was, oh yes.

Paul Sigrist: How did you feel being an English speaking person with people who didn't speak English?

Catherine English: Oh yes, coz I was so sorry for them. I was so sorry for them and then the inspectors that I saw there, but this boat was a different boat than ours, the boat that brought it in from Ireland. As a matter of fact we had no foreign people. The only foreign people we had was, I think, Hungarian. We had a few Hungarian people but they had to, they left from England and then they came, the boat came around to Queenstown. But what I didn't like, I was listening, they'd holler at them and, you know, that they weren't human beings. That I didn't like at all. So then they put us through, when I gave the papers that I took the tests and everything and then to see my vaccinations and all that stuff they let me out and put me in a room and then they brought in my sisters.

Paul Sigrist: What was that like, seeing your sisters?

Catherine English: Oh, of course I cried. I cried and cried when I saw them.

...

1 Interview with Catherine English by Paul Sigrist, recorded 19 September 1991, EIOHP, EI Series 91.

Paul Sigrist: So where did they bring you? Where did you spend your first night in America?

Catherine English: I spent it with my sister on 63rd Street and Third Avenue.

Paul Sigrist: What was New York like for you? Coz you'd been to Dublin so you've seen a big city.

Catherine English: You know, I don't know what it was, why I got this idea when I got off the tender and we got out and we took a train and it seems there were children coming from school and they were so sloppy looking and I did say where, and I thought they were orphans or something and they looked so dirty. I had visions of beautiful ribbons on their hair and, see, we were, I had uniforms and that uniform had to come off as soon as you came in from school. And you washed your own uniform and you pressed it and everything. Oh I, there was nothing that I didn't do that I had to do, that I had to do.

Paul Sigrist: But the Americans looked sloppy?

Catherine English: But they were so and the kids they didn't have uniforms or anything and I thought then we got out at, I think we came up to 63rd Street and then the streets were so dirty. Garbage all round the place and I couldn't get over it. I had thought America, I couldn't get here fast enough that everything was so beautiful and clean and all of this. But it, I soon broke in with the whole thing.

Paul Sigrist: So talk to me a little bit about those first couple of days in America. What did you do?

Catherine English: Well, cousins came to see me and they took me up to Ridgwood and we went by train out to Ridgwood. I thought I'd never get there. I thought you could walk every place like we did in Ireland. You walked miles and miles and I thought we'd never get there.

A major aspect of the immigration experience is the extent to which the new environment measured up to previous expectations. This is a constant theme in the personal testimonies of Irish and Scottish migrants as first impressions were an important stage in the complicated process of adjustment to a life away from home. First impressions, for instance, were dependent upon the images that migrants had of the destinations to which they gravitated. Did these initial encounters match the images migrants held of their destinations prior to arrival discussed in Chapter 2? Did prosperity and decorum suffuse recollections? Migrants also adjusted to society by evaluating aspects of the United States with their place of origin. In making these comparisons, Irish and Scottish migrants were explicitly and implicitly judging their own cultures, thereby providing insight into factors that may have played a part in their resolve to migrate. They were therefore frequently reinforcing or questioning their decision to leave home. Recollection of the contrasts confronted serves not only to explain their initial adjustment to city life, but also to assess their current interpretations of society. Many migrants, for instance, specified how their experiences differed from the arrivals of late twentieth-century newcomers to the United States. By undertaking comparisons migrants also reveal something of their identities. As Alastair Thomson put it, 'Migrant oral testimony – in which narrators describe the process of learning to live in a new world, the collisions between old and new ways, and the forging of new understandings of self and society – offers evidence about the changing nature and complex meanings of identity in the migrant experience.'[2]

In exploring these issues, this chapter suggests that first impressions remained vivid in a migrant's mind, as they can be classified as ongoing events, in which a migrant was continually confronted with repeat experiences.[3] Encountering traffic in New York, for instance, was experienced on a regular basis, but it was frequently the initial encounter with traffic that remained in a migrant's mind. So too did first tastes of novel foods provide a lingering impression, along with lasting amazement at the sheer architectural structure of New York. As a consequence, migrants articulated many specific details, including sights, sounds, and feelings connected with such observations. Naturally, the most vivid contrasts were encountered during the early days of settlement. Overall, the chapter argues that by comparing the new land with the old, and gradually accepting the benefits offered by the New World, migrants overcame an initial sense of dislocation and, occasionally, disappointment. Their first impression of the United States, however, was not an experience that they would repeat, or wish to replicate. It was their processing through Ellis Island and initial encounter with New York, the third element of incorporation in their rite of passage.[4] This chapter begins by charting that initial experience, following the migrant from ship to the processing station and the world that they encountered there, before moving to consider the contrasts they discerned between life at home and abroad.

Ellis Island

Interviewed in 1996, 60 years after her arrival, Mary Jo Lenney of Scotch-fort, County Mayo, summarised the procedure at Ellis Island as follows: 'I remember going into the port and they, American citizens, were allowed off first and then we were the immigrants and we had to stay. And I remember my Aunt Barbara on the pier and we could wave to her. And they said you have to

2 Alastair Thomson, 'Moving stories: oral history and migration studies', *Oral History*, 27:1 (1999), p. 35.
3 This is suggested by David B. Pillemer, *Momentous Events, Vivid Memories* (Cambridge and London: Harvard University Press, 1998), p. 3.
4 Arnold van Genepp, *Rites of Passage*, translated by Monika B. Vizedom and Gabrielle L. Caffee, with an introduction by Solon T. Kimball (London: Routledge and Kegan Paul, 1960), p. 21.

9 'An island of tears': Ellis Island

go to Ellis Island.' Mary Jo continued, describing being taken by bus 'from the dock to Ellis Island' where 'they had huge benches so you'd sit on the bench. I can still see myself sitting on the bench and then you had to go through a routine of examinations and it took a long time'.[5] The assessments included a written test and a medical inspection.

Of all the procedures undergone on Ellis Island, the testimonies reveal that the medical examination was almost universally recalled with horror, and this is presumably what accounts for one third of Irish and Scots categorising their experience at Ellis Island in negative terms. While 17 per cent had apparent difficulty remembering much of their experience, a further 17 per cent described events at Ellis Island without clarifying their feelings. Another 17 per cent did not discuss the experience. For many migrants, then, their first encounters with officials in the United States resulted in an image of their new homeland as intrusive and repressive. The agency which had marked their departure from home was suddenly counteracted by the powerlessness they felt at the hands of immigration officials. According to Stirling milliner Mary Dunn, who arrived as an 18-year-old in July 1923 on board the *Assyria*: 'Well, we got stripped to the waist, I know that. And they went through your hair and plugged in your ears and up your nose and in your mouth'.[6] Other migrants mentioned similar details, and contrasted this with what they perceived were

5 Interview with Mary Jo Lenney by Paul Sigrist, recorded 21 August 1996, EIOHP, EI Series 793.
6 Interview with Mary Dunn by Dana Gumb, recorded 23 January 1986, EIOHP, AKRF Series 127.

lax procedures operating in the 1990s. Maisie Pedersen of Greenock, who left in 1924 aged 18, recalled: 'Well, they examined your eyes, they examined under your feet, oh yeah, you went through some examination, your heart and your eye, everything, before they let you off. That's one thing I can't understand people coming in now. They can just come in from other countries no examination, no nothing.'[7] In similar vein, Sarah McQuinn of Dromore West, County Sligo, puzzled as a 95-year-old: 'Well they didn't treat us very good. They combed, fine combed our hair. They were so strict but they had to be, I guess, and I wish they were today. I wish they were today as strict as they were then. Things would have been much better for the United States.'[8] Ann Nelson of Bathgate, Scotland, was aged seven when she migrated and 73 years later she described her family's experience: 'These two nurses came and said "strip", all of us, that was three, two kids and three adults and we had to strip off all our clothes. We stood there like jaybirds [*laughs*] ... I suppose they were going to disinfect our clothes because they gave us gowns'.[9] Likewise, fellow Catholic Agnes Schilling from Motherwell remarked: 'The thing that I do remember was that they took all my clothes off and made me shower and wrapped all my beautiful clothes in a duffel bag which hurt so much to see them being rolled up, you know, put in a duffel bag and then I don't remember seeing them again till the day I was leaving.'[10]

One of the most distressing testimonies about the physical inspection on Ellis Island emerged from Anne Walsh. She had left County Cavan in 1922 at 14 years of age. In her seventies at the time of her interview, Anne attributed quarantine at Hoffman Island to the outbreak of disease on board ship. Hoffman Island was where migrants were quarantined if, on arrival at Ellis Island, they were found to be carryng a contagious disease. The vulnerable teenager's distress and the humiliation of her situation at the processing station was unequivocally captured 64 years later:

Something broke out on the ship, and it was a skin disease. And, one nurse discovered it anyhow. Thank God I never got it. Anyone who wasn't a citizen - there was lots of Irish there that were going back and were citizens, and they could get off, they supplied them with a boat, or whatever it was, a conveyance, for the land. But we couldn't get off the ship. So they sent us to a place called Hoffman Island. And you had to go in a room and strip naked and I nearly died with embarrass-

7 Interview with Maisie Pedersen by Paul Sigrist, recorded 26 February 1994, EIOHP, EI Series 442.
8 Interview with Sarah McQuinn by Janet Levine, recorded 12 June 1996, EIOHP, EI Series 755.
9 Interview with Ann Nelson by Janet Levine, recorded 8 December 1996, EIOHP, EI Series 832.
10 Interview with Agnes Schilling by Janet Levine, recorded 16 June 1992, EIOHP, EI Series 172.

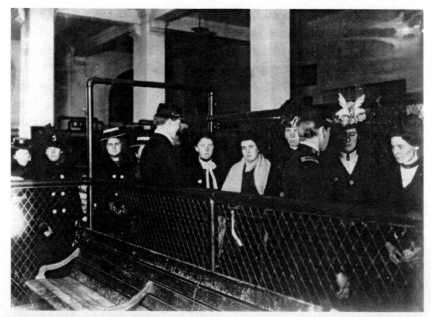

10 Irish women on Ellis Island

ment, strip naked, and the part of it was I have always during the years when I was younger menstruated very heavily and I was menstruating and they didn't give you napkins. So then they told us to stand in this room. It was a room that had no ceiling and they used hoses to hose us down and one nurse said, 'You poor little kid', she said to me, 'this is terrible.'[11]

While Anne Walsh's menstruation was a particularly gendered aspect of her experience at Ellis Island, male migrants were also subjected to physical scrutiny. The son of hotelkeepers at Urlingford, County Kilkenny, 16-year-old Patrick Henderson arrived in 1923. He related, 'We were ushered into a room and I haven't seen as many doctors around me since that I saw that day. We were stripped naked, the men in one area and the women that was pulled out in another area. We were stripped naked and the doctors come around us, each one examining different parts'.[12] Passing through the processing station two years later was 18-year-old Joseph Brady of Claddy, County Armagh. His testimony, gathered 70 years after the event, described: 'Then we were all lined up. I think the first thing we did was go through a doctor's examination and we had several doctors. One doctor listened to your heart another doctor

11 Interview with Anne Walsh by Nancy Dallett, recorded 26 June 1986, EIOHP, AKRF Series 200.
12 Interview with Patrick Henderson by Paul Sigrist, recorded 7 August 1994, EIOHP, EI Series 524.

your eyes and looked at your hands and looked at your hair to make sure your hair was clean.'[13] Glaswegian Joseph Delaney was also 18 when he landed at Ellis Island in 1922. He likewise indicated that males and females were segregated and had to strip before being medically examined. When asked what the physical examination involved, Joseph responded: 'Physical. Everything. Your heart, your head, your feet, your underwear, under your arm, oh yes and other parts too, the private parts of your body were all examined, if you'd any deadly diseases.'[14] Manny Steen, the orphan son of Dublin Jews, not only recounted his own inspection, but also chronicled the examination of females, perhaps gleaned from his sister Bertha who voyaged with him:

I think, frankly, the worst memory I have of Ellis Island was the physical because the doctors were seated at a long table with a basin full of potassium chloride and you had to stand in front of them, follow me? And they'd ask you and you had to reveal yourself. They gave you what we used to in the army they call short arm inspection, right there in front of everyone. I mean it wasn't private. You just had to, and the women had to open their bras and here, this was terrible. Remember these were immigrants from the very, reticent people and here, but nobody was lurking or watching. Looking back, I mean I can see that, but I was 19 and I was just as embarrassed as hell, you know. I had to open my trousers and they would check you for venereal disease or hernia or whatever they were looking for, I don't know, with the physical. I was a young buck, I was in good shape, you know, but just the same I thought this was very demeaning. Even then, I mean it's terrible for women, young girls, and everyone, you know, you had to line up in front and they, it wasn't personal. Looking back it wasn't personalised but nevertheless it's a very unpleasant memory and I didn't. It was years later years later I thought they didn't have to do it that way. There must have been some other way. But remember this was the height of immigration. They were coming in in their thousands. I mean the day I was there I said maybe three, four, five thousand. Who counts, you know what I mean? The place was jammed.[15]

Given the passing of time there are discrepancies among these accounts surrounding exactly what was inspected. Nevertheless, these testimonies serve as a stark reminder that these migrants never forgot how it felt to have their bodies publicly inspected. Furthermore, by overcoming such an invasive and often humiliating ordeal, and subsequently finding the words to relate the experience, migrants could envisage themselves as being conquerors of adversity. It is therefore unsurprising that many interviewees could recollect the intrica-

13 Interview with Joseph Brady by Paul Sigrist recorded 25 September 1995, EIOHP, EI Series 673.
14 Interview with Joseph Delaney by Dana Gumb, recorded 5 September 1985, EIOHP, AKRF Series 23.
15 Interview with Manny Steen by Paul Sigrist, recorded 22 March 1991, EIOHP, EI Series 33.

cies of their time on Ellis Island. Such stories, replete with shame, struggle, and sacrifice, set the scene for the remainder of the testimony in which the migrant typically survived the experience and went on to achieve a satisfactory and successful life in the United States. For some, however, the Ellis Island experience, particularly the medical examination, proved too traumatic and was not discussed. Mary Kelly, for example, stated that her experience was unpleasant and she flatly refused to talk about it.[16] Other migrants indicated that they could not recall their time on Ellis Island, perhaps evidence that they had suppressed their memories due to the trauma they had undergone there. Still others categorised it in such blunt terms as 'terrible', 'horrible', and 'couldn't get out of there fast enough'.[17] It was summarised most acutely by Thomas Allan, who arrived in 1927 at 9 years of age. In his words, it was an 'island of tears'.[18]

This general experience at Ellis Island, then, can be seen as what is referred to in much analytical literature as 'a site of memory'. This conceptualisation by Pierre Nora posits places and items as sparking acts of memory.[19] In many ways, though, Ellis Island can also be seen as 'a site of trauma'. That the time spent on Ellis Island was still considered disturbing many years later suggests that no further experience in the United States quite equalled this event in the lives of Irish and Scottish migrants. Indeed, subsequent encounters with American society, while challenging, were rarely discussed as negatively. While the testimonies reveal that a multiplicity of representations and experiences on Ellis Island exist, some common themes emerge from the varied recollections. For those migrants who wished to remember their time on Ellis Island, what did they choose to recall and what did these memories mean?

Encountering other nationalities was mentioned by many Irish and Scots who chose to portray themselves as explicitly different from other European newcomers. This was presumably undertaken to distinguish themselves from non-English-speaking migrants, for whom stringent entry regulations were implemented. Isabella Deeks, who arrived from Cathcart, Glasgow, in 1923, reported her mother saying, 'we're with all these foreigners', but not knowing

16 Interview with Mary Kelly by Paul Sigrist, recorded 10 September 1997, EIOHP, EI Series 936.
17 Interviews with Johanna Flaherty by Debra Allee, recorded 29 May 1986, EIOHP, AKRF Series, 182; Maisie Pedersen; Mary Margaret McGloin by Janet Levine, recorded 12 April 1994, EIOHP, EI Series 457; and David Saltman by Janet Levine, recorded 26 September 1991, EIOHP, EI Series 97.
18 Interview with Thomas Allan by Jean Kolva, recorded 16 July 1984, EIOHP, NPS Series 149.
19 Pierre Nora, 'Between memory and history', in Pierre Nora (ed.), *Realms of Memory: Rethinking the French Past*, Vol. 1: *Conflicts and Divisions* (New York: Columbia University Press, 1996), pp. 1–20.

why because she did not consider herself a foreigner.[20] In a similar, if some-what more extended, fashion Kathleen Lamberti of County Down, reminisced dejectedly:

I thought it was dreadful. We were put in rooms, you know, we had never had mixed with people who did not speak English and these people, I don't know what part of the world they came from, but boat, a boat load must have come in with all these people with little things tied around their head, little carpet bags, carrying them and they're talking in their own language and my mother sitting, you know, with the brood all around her, you know, saying, 'Why did we leave Ireland? Why did we come here? Listen to this.'

Kathleen went on to recount her aversion at being considered alien. When an official instructed the group, 'All foreigners follow me', the command was ignored. When it was repeated, 22-year-old Kathleen allegedly jumped to her feet in tears, responding, 'I'm not a foreigner, I'm Irish.' The official reacted kindly: 'I know my dear but you must follow me.' As Kathleen remembered, 'Oh that broke my heart anybody to call me a foreigner [*laughs*]. So we had to follow her and they lectured us you know about coming in to the country and what would you expect and all from the country.'[21]

Anne Craven, the daughter of a carpenter and nurse, arrived from County Offaly in 1925 and suddenly found herself being labelled German, as 'there was a lot of foreign people on that boat. You know there wasn't many, not that many Irish. It was mainly Greeks, Russians, and Polish people and I guess I looked a little German. I had very red cheeks at the time.'[22] Patrick Henderson of Urlingford, County Kilkenny, however, recalled explicit divisions between the different nationalities when he arrived in 1923, for English-speaking migrants were taken to one area and Germans to another.[23] Being among other nationalities proved frightening for many Irish and Scots, though this was perhaps amplified by the confined space at Ellis Island. Thomas Allan, for instance, described himself and his brother as 'scared kids' when they found themselves surrounded by people from other countries talking in different languages.[24] Even with a mother of German extraction, County Mayo migrant Mary Jo Lenney likewise stated, 'I remember just a great big room with all these people around and with their little suitcases and their bags and a lot of

20 Interview with Isabella Deeks by Janet Levine, recorded 30 April 1997, EIOHP, EI Series 869.
21 Interview with Kathleen Lamberti by Paul Sigrist, recorded 25 Feb 1994, EIOHP, EI Series 439.
22 Interview with Anne Craven by Paul Sigrist, recorded 2 October 1991, EIOHP, EI Series 102.
23 Interview with Patrick Henderson.
24 Interview with Thomas Allan.

poverty. That's all. It was very, very, very scary.'[25] Other migrants, however, reinforced official narratives of the United States as a melting pot. Coachbuilder's son John Will, who arrived from Cupar in 1924, asserted boldly, 'It was the melting pot for sure. There was people there from all walks and stratas of life'.[26]

These recollections indicate that Irish and Scottish migrants perceived themselves as separate from other European migrant groups. Though not explicitly denying a European identity, they were implicitly viewing themselves as having a common connection to the United States through a similar language and culture. In this way, Irish and Scottish migrants presumably saw themselves as continuing a strong tradition of migration to the United States from their respective homelands. As with the voyage out, Irish and Scottish migrants shared a broad sense of purpose.

If Irish and Scottish migrants perceived themselves as separate from other European groups arriving at Ellis Island, there was no escaping their similar confinement when suspicion fell upon the state of their health. Kathleen Lamberti described sleeping in 'Little wire cages. I see them yet. Everybody had a little cage and they took our lovely skirts our lovely plaids and fumigated them and ruined them. I'll never forget that. My mother said, "Oh my god what have we done? This is dreadful." We followed her like that man with the rats who followed him through England crying.' Kathleen was also separated from her brother for the medical inspection and when he returned she discovered he 'had some card pinned on him' indicating he had a disease of the heart. According to Kathleen, 'I took it off and put it in my pocket. There was never a word about that.'[27] In this way, Kathleen Lamberti discovered a sense of agency in the wake of powerlessness.

Generally, migrants with communicable diseases were placed in cages. Patrick Peak, an emigrant from Glasgow in 1921, was detained after authorities thought a mark on his youngest sibling was a communicable disease rather than a simple rash, as it was later discovered. As a result the family was confined for six days and ended up sleeping in a cage with bunks and blankets.[28] Thomas Allan of Tillypotrie was nine years of age in 1927 and because his brother contracted chickenpox they were quarantined for two days on the ship *Caledonia* and then at Ellis Island for about a week. Their father could not see them because of this quarantine, which Thomas described ruefully as a 'dismal experience'.[29] Ann Nelson of Bathgate was also quarantined at

25 Interview with Mary Jo Lenney.
26 Interview with John Will by Elysa Matsen, recorded 16 Sept 1994, EI Series 547.
27 Interview with Kathleen Lamberti.
28 Interview with Patrick Peak by Nancy Dallett, recorded 15 November 1985, EIOHP, AKRF series 84.
29 Interview with Thomas Allan.

11 Scottish children on Ellis Island

Hoffman Island because two younger siblings had contracted chickenpox in 1923 on the *Columbia*.[30] Agnes Schilling, who was 15 when she left Motherwell in 1922, spoke of her anxiety in the light of such knowledge: 'I was always afraid of Ellis Island. The stories, you know, that we heard and I was so afraid. What if they keep you in Ellis Island? They go through your hair looking for

30 Interview with Ann Nelson.

bugs and, you know, and my mother was always scaring me.' Such testimony was not unfounded for Agnes was found to have a possible disease in her eyes which took ten days to test; eventually, though, she was cleared and released.[31] Elizabeth Griffin of County Donegal was likewise detained in 1950 as an X-ray seemed to reveal a spot on her lung. It was, however, images of holy medals and scapulars that showed up on the X-ray, and she was released.[32]

Eventually, all migrants who passed the medical inspection were brought before a judge who interrogated them and supplied sustained patter about the United States. Among the questions directed to newcomers were why they wanted to come and who was going to claim them. Anne Walsh, who arrived in 1922, remembered being asked how old she was, what part of Ireland she was from, and what family she had in the United States.[33] Anne Quinn also depicted her mother being quizzed extensively as her father had suffered a stroke six years before the family's emigration: "'Was there anything really mentally wrong with my father?" Of course, there wasn't. And "would her family support her" and she said, "yes". "Who was claiming her?" Well she said, "her eldest son".'[34] James Joseph Walls, who arrived 1930 at 12 years of age from Belfast, lengthily narrated his interaction with officials questioning him on Ellis Island:

I had to go before these three, I don't know what you might call them, commissioners or what they were, but I can remember them very distinctly. They were on a sort of a dais, you know, and I'm looking up at them, you know, a little guy, right? And they asked me my name and where I came from and how old I was and a lot of elementary questions, you know, and then finally 'Why did you come to America?', you know, right? And I said, 'I came to America because I want to make good and I want to help my family', right? And then one of the men he said, 'James', he says, 'have you ever told a lie?' I said, 'Of course I've told a lie'. And he said, 'why?' And I said, 'Because at the particular time the circumstances required me to tell a lie', right? I said, 'It was not a lie to hurt anyone, it was a lie of convenience.'[35]

In responding to such questioning, some migrants highlighted their ingenuity. Such accounts were designed to showcase their ability in pulling a fast one over authorities who had the power to deny their entry into the United States. These stories also suggest that migrants were endeavouring to assert a sense

31 Interview with Agnes Schilling.
32 Interview with Elizabeth Griffin by Andrew Phillips, recorded 26 May 1989, EIOHP, DP Series 38.
33 Interview with Anne Walsh.
34 Interview with Anne Quinn by Dennis Cloutier and Peter Kaplan, recorded 8 December 1983, EIOHP, NPS Series 146.
35 Interview with James Joseph Walls by Janet Levine, recorded 20 July 1996, EIOHP, EI Series 771.

of power in an atmosphere designed to diminish their agency. Some migrants, such as Joseph Delaney, also remembered being lectured about the country and informed of what to expect.[36]

Following this process, migrants were claimed by their sponsor before proceeding to collect their luggage and venture forth into American society. They then had to proceed to their final destination. For many this meant further transportation by rail. Some would presumably have been aware of this from information in booklets such as the Cunard Canadian tract which supplied details of onward journeys. Canadian Pacific also claimed that its great advantage 'is that of combined steamship and railway services'.[37] Often this entailed a longer stay on Ellis Island, despite completion of the various procedures. As Mary Dunn related:

I think the reason we had to stay there that long was, maybe everybody didn't have to stay that long, it all depended on where they were going from New York, from the station, you know. But I know that, the train that I was assigned to was not leaving till nine o'clock at night and they couldn't send me any place else. They had to keep me on the island until it was time. Not only me, I mean, a lot of people, because a lot of people went on that train.[38]

A common element, then, for both Irish and Scottish migrants arriving in the United States through New York was their recollection of the Ellis Island experience. Such was the common thread of their testimonies focusing on such aspects as the medical examination and questioning by officials that a collective memory of the experience is discernible through the myriad subjective accounts. Such memories have not only been woven into the commemoration of the experience depicted by the Ellis Island Museum, but have also been reconstructed by migrants as a result of this collective imagery. Yet this collective representation is at odds with how some migrants viewed themselves, and reveals that there was not a shared identity of being a migrant which linked all migrant groups. John Will of Cupar, Fife, for instance, arrived in the United States in 1924. In his testimony he was critical of the contemporary representation of the Ellis Island experience, as it depicted 'downtrodden types and poorly dressed with bags on the top of their heads and stuff like that'. By contrast, John Will stressed that 'there was people like our family that were, you know, fairly decent type citizens in their education and background and appearance. You never got my father without a suit on. He dressed formally all the time.'[39]

36 Interview with Joseph Delaney.
37 'Canadian Pacific to Canada & USA Third Class', April 1926, p. 17, in NMM, Canadian Pacific Ephemera, Brochures (General) 1.
38 Interview with Mary Dunn.
39 Interview with John Will.

What, though, is the meaning of these representations of the Ellis Island experience? What particular function did remembering these details serve? Primarily, recounting their experiences enabled migrants to locate their stories in contrast with the procedure undergone by recent arrivals. They posited that their entrance into the United States was based on rigorous procedures and in their recollections they complained about the laxity afforded to recent newcomers. In emphasising the rigour and hardship that they endured at Ellis Island, these interviewees have created a stereotypical representation of their type of migrant as stoic and resolute in overcoming such initial hostility to settle successfully in the United States, without resorting to the welfare system. For instance, Jack Whitecross Carnegie of Dundee, in describing being claimed by his sponsor, rued that new migrants went into the United States to obtain state assistance. In 1996, a proud Carnegie stressed, 'It isn't like today. They come in today and they go on to welfare [*laughs*]. We never, we never were on welfare.'[40] The collective narrative of the examination process, questioning, and interaction with other foreigners was also emphasised in order to set themselves apart from recent migrants in the United States. As historian John Bodnar remarks in an essay on generational memory in a midwestern American town, 'memories [were] only partly based on encounters with historic events; they were also meant to be heard as contemporary discourses about value and authority.'[41]

In the final analysis of the Ellis Island experience, Mary Dunn's comment about the image and reality of the United States, the treatment received on Ellis Island, and eventual acceptance and happiness with life in the United States, encapsulates the experience of migration for many:

We had heard so many things about the United States, come to America and the gold and money grows on the trees and all this kind of stuff. And the land of opportunity. And I'm saying to myself, 'If this is the land of opportunity, is this the way they treat everybody when they come in?' You know. They really treated you like they didn't want you. These people that were examining you, you know. But I couldn't say that about people now because I've had a wonderful life in this country.[42]

Differences

As with Mary Dunn's snapshot, the testimony of other migrants likewise conveys that despite the trauma endured at Ellis Island, most migrants were satisfied with their subsequent life in the United States. A crucial part of this

40 Interview with Jack Whitecross Carnegie by Janet Levine, recorded 15 February 1996, EIOHP, EI Series 729.
41 John Bodnar, 'Generational memory in an American town', *Journal of Interdisciplinary History*, 26:4 (1996), p. 624.
42 Interview with Mary Dunn.

process of adjustment related to the initial contrasts identified between home and abroad once they left Ellis Island. The last part of this chapter explores these differences. It focuses specifically on the disparities that migrants identified, usually without prompting, when asked what initial contrasts they perceived between origin and destination. It is therefore linear contrasts (differences between origin and destination) that are considered in this chapter.

What sort of city, though, were they entering? Undeniably, New York was the biggest city in the United States, with a vast assortment of ethnicities. No work has yet been undertaken on the experiences of Scottish migrants in New York, even though the 1930 Census shows 67,623 Scots in the city. For the Irish, on the other hand, New York was historically *their* city. As one commentator put it, 'They controlled its government and politics, dominated construction and building, moved into the professions and managerial classes, and benefited, perhaps disproportionately, from the general prosperity of the times.'[43] While the inflow of Irish during the boom times of the 1920s continued this domination, the decades following the Great Depression witnessed a transformation in the ethnic composition of the city, in which the Irish were supplanted by Italian and Jewish migrants. While one third of New York's ethnic stock was Irish in 1880, this had fallen to one in ten by 1945.[44] Indeed, between 1910 and 1960 New York's Irish-born population fell by more than 100,000.[45]

For migrants arriving in the United States through Ellis Island, the processing station afforded them an opportunity to encounter several differences between home and abroad. Della Gleckel, for instance, declared she could remember her experience 'to a T':

First of all, I didn't think there was such a thing as a black person. I'd never seen anybody black in all of Ireland, like how much of Ireland had I seen, and there was no black people on our boat coming over and I'd never seen a black person. So when I got to Ellis Island this gal was about 5 foot 8, great big black woman, I can see her earrings now, they were real impressive earrings, large and dangling, and she wanted to give me a glass of milk and I thought, you know, I just can't

43 Chris McNickle, 'When New York was Irish, and after', in Ronald H. Bayor and Timothy J. Meagher (eds), *The New York Irish* (Baltimore and London: Johns Hopkins University Press, 1996), p. 337. For other accounts of the Irish in New York see Mary C. Kelly, *The Shamrock and the Lily: The New York Irish and the Creation of a Transatlantic Identity, 1845–1921* (New York: Peter Lang, 2005) and Linda Dowling Almeida, *Irish Immigrants in New York City, 1945–1995* (Bloomington and Indianapolis: Indiana University Press, 2001).
44 McNickle, 'When New York was Irish', p. 339.
45 Marion R. Casey, '"From the east side to the seaside": Irish Americans on the move in New York city', in Ronald H. Bayor and Timothy J. Meagher (eds), *The New York Irish* (Baltimore and London: Johns Hopkins University Press, 1996), p. 395.

imagine this person so I wouldn't take the milk. I just didn't take it because I was so puzzled as to know what the black person was. Isn't that amazing? And so then I saw my sisters and my uncle and my brother all of them were like a distance from the boat but I could see them and they were trying to tell me that they were missing one important paper to get me off. They didn't realise Immigration wanted this particular paper and they were telling me to call them. Well I had never seen a telephone and I had no idea and they're telling me that the phone was there like near me was like a wall phone and I saw it and, of course, they were trying their level best but I went in and I did take the receiver off the hook but I didn't know what to do with the rest and I said to them, 'I can't do it.'[46]

The first contrast mentioned by Della Gleckel, that of encounters with African-Americans, was echoed by other migrants arriving in the United States. Overall, however, the testimonies suggest that there was very little interaction between Irish and Scots and African-Americans. Instead, African-Americans were simply mentioned in context of being visually dissimilar. Elizabeth Dalbey of County Meath, who later took up domestic work for a Jewish family, explained how her relation 'took me on the subway to where she lived and I couldn't figure out the coloured people whatever. I'd never seen one before and they intrigued me [laughs]. I never seen a coloured person before.'[47] Allan Gunn, meanwhile, attempted to grapple with the interpretation of why his mother had taken her children to church and shunted them quickly out when she realised the congregation was entirely African-American: 'Now I don't know whether it was because she was afraid or whether it was because she didn't want to offend them, figured we were in the wrong place, but we had no experience with blacks. Where I lived we had no blacks … It wasn't because we were biased, coz we didn't know anything about them.'[48]

By contrast, Irish and Scottish migrants did specify interacting with other ethnic groups in the United States, especially Italians. In doing so, some emphasised that they had not been labelled a 'greenhorn'. As Ann Nelson, daughter of a Bathgate coalminer, so aptly categorised her Bayown community in New Jersey, 'We had German, Irish, Scotch, Jewish, Swedish, all mixed up in this little neighbourhood and who's gonna call who a greenhorn? [laughs].'[49] Others acknowledged being called a 'greenhorn' but took that in their stride. Curiously, there is little in these personal accounts to suggest that these Irish and Scottish newcomers lived in conflict with other groups such

46 Interview with Della Gleckel by Paul Sigrist, recorded 2 May 1995, EIOHP, EI Series 611.
47 Interview with Elizabeth Dalbey by Paul Sigrist, recorded 29 August 1995, EIOHP, EI Series 662.
48 Interview with Allan Gunn.
49 Interview with Ann Nelson.

as the Germans, Jews, and Italians.[50] Rather, as will be seen, recollections of enmity predominantly emanated from those arriving as youngsters and being subjected to hostility by American children. Despite these encounters Irish and Scottish migrants were still most strongly tied to their own ethnic groups, a theme that will be discussed in Chapters 6 and 7.

The second contrast from Della Gleckel's statement relates to the technological differences confronting her in the United States, such as telephones and the availability of electricity, compared with gas lamps back home. Other migrants likewise referred to these disparities. Having been reared in County Mayo, surrounded by mountains and lakes, Julia Carmody emphasised use of the telephone because people allegedly liked to listen to her talking.[51] As for electricity, Paisley-born Anne Quinn reported, 'We didn't have electricity when we left Scotland and here we had electricity and that was fabulous, you know, flick a switch and the light comes on and, you know, we, we just loved that.'[52]

Perhaps the greatest technological contrast for migrants was the subway system in New York. Bridget Jones of Castlefrench, County Galway, recalled her first encounter with animated amusement:

Oh New York was very exciting to me. When I was coming home from Ellis Island on the subway I was very slow and I remember, oh I'll always remember this, my aunt got into the subway ahead of me and I had the big suitcase, I was carrying the big suitcase, and I was afraid to get into this into the subway car and a man took the suitcase out of my hand and he just pushed it in and pushed me in with it [*laughs*]. It was really funny.[53]

Allan Gunn, a young Scots lad, remembered: 'It was scary when we first rode in the subway ... To go way underground and the noise. I think the noise scared us more than anything ... and we wondered how do you know where you're going underground, you know, how do you know where you're going and how you're going to get there?'[54] Maisie Pedersen of Greenock was similarly perplexed by the subway system:

Well, what I couldn't understand at first was the subway. They had to take me, my friend's son had to take me back and forth for my job when I worked for three months on 56th Street. What I couldn't remember was the subway. We'd come off one train and get on the other and both trains were going the same direction. I

50 For an alternative depiction see Ronald H. Bayor, *Neighbors in Conflict: The Irish, Germans, Jews, and Italians of New York City, 1929–1941* (Urbana and Chicago: University of Illinois Press, 1988, 2nd edn).
51 Interview with Julia Carmody by Paul Sigrist, recorded 18 July 1996, EI Series 767.
52 Interview with Anne Quinn.
53 Interview with Bridget Jones by Margo Nash, recorded 15 November 1974, EIOHP, NPS Series 78.
54 Interview with Allan Gunn.

said, 'why do we have to get off this train?' When you get off the local you get on to the express, you know. We weren't used to that in Scotland, you know.[55]

Occasionally, migrants recalled their first encounters with the subway in the 1920s with contemporary conditions in mind. According to Kathleen Lamberti, 'In those days it was lovely because there was a conductor on every train on every department, compartment there, and it was only five cents and you could, well, up until lately you could have been on that subway at any time of the day or night and no one bothered you ... You're afraid now to go out to the post office up the block there.'[56] For migrants arriving in later decades, such technology was also impressive. John Joe Gallogly conveyed his fascination with the railroad system, recalling 'the train ride was great. I never was on a train as fast as the one from New York to Boston to Rhode Island. It was a great ride.'[57] Such a situation was a great novelty for the second eldest child of a small farmer in County Leitrim. These descriptions not only highlighted the sophisticated technology of New York, but also conjured up images of technologically backward homelands.

The size of the city and its buildings also seemed technologically innovative to migrants. Upon her arrival in 1924, Maisie Pedersen was astonished at how large New York was, a feature reiterated by John Joe Gallogly, who arrived 28 years later: 'I couldn't get over the height of the buildings and before we took a cab to the railway station we walked a good bit because I was still curious and I had a creak in my neck looking up at the buildings, you know'.[58] On the other hand, Johanna Flaherty of Castlewest, County Limerick, initially felt New York in 1923 to be 'terrifying, those large buildings it seemed like they were just about to close in on you. But I got used to it very fast. I liked it.'[59]

For those with experiences of cities in Ireland and Scotland, the contrast of New York seemingly proved less startling. Kathleen Lamberti explained, 'It wasn't a shock to us because we were coming from a city and Belfast in those days, those days was a very flourishing city.'[60] Likewise, Paul O'Dwyer, the youngest of 11 children from a country village in County Mayo, found New York in 1925 'a very strange place. It wasn't that the buildings were big. I'd seen big buildings before. Nothing the size of that but some how or another there was a different style about them.'[61] Similarly, for one migrant from Limerick

---

55 Interview with Maisie Pedersen.
56 Interview with Kathleen Lamberti.
57 Interview with John Joe Gallogly by Janet Levine, recorded 6 March 2001, EIOHP, EI series 1194.
58 Interview with Maisie Pedersen; interview with John Joe Gallogly.
59 Interview with Johanna Flaherty.
60 Interview with Kathleen Lamberti.
61 Interview with Paul O'Dwyer by Paul Sigrist, recorded 17 July 1993, EIOHP, EI Series 362.

city, New York was disappointing: 'Well I knew that the buildings, you know, they looked high. They were six stories. Terrible. And they were very crude.'[62] Michael Jordan went on to explain, 'the lavatories were out in the yards. We had to go out in the cold and everything at that time.'[63]

A further difference recognised by migrants was the intensity of movement of both people and traffic. Many migrants recollected people rushing around, 'hollering' and 'screaming'. That the city contained in a small space a population in 1920 of 5,620,048 that climbed to 7,891,957 in 1950 was a profound contrast to life at home.[64] The accompanying speed and pace of life proved to be a formidable contrast. For John Joe Gallogly of County Leitrim, New York in the early 1950s was a world of difference from his rural townland of Drumran:

It's scary even though I was 26 years of age going probably on 15 because I never was in Dublin or never was any place. I was out of the woods, you know, so it was scary back in those days, you know, but anyway I met my two uncles at the ship, they met me at the ship, and they said, 'Well this is America.' And everybody was running, everybody was running. I said, 'What's everybody in a hurry for?' And they said, 'This is America' [*laughs*].[65]

As most migrants were familiar with cars back in their homelands, it was the volume of traffic, rather than the novelty of automobiles, that perplexed them. Patrick Henderson of County Kilkenny had clear memories of 'dodging in and out of cars which I wasn't used to that kind of traffic and then it was mostly cabs. I was scared even crossing the street.'[66] Discussing her journey to her sister's flat, Della Gleckel was likewise terrified: 'So in the cab coming up the most traffic I had ever seen was a car at a funeral, you know, in the town. They would have one car to carry the coffin and all the funerals, by the way, were led with a white horse – that was really impressive. So I'd say "Oh, oh, you're gonna get killed." I was a wreck in that cab coming up.'[67]

While certain districts of the homelands were also congested, the relaxed pace of life at their origins was a far cry from the intensity of New York and its environs. How were the other elements of society perceived?

62 Interview with Michael Jordan by Paul Sigrist, recorded 19 October 1993, EIOHP, EI Series 397.
63 *Ibid.*
64 Figures cited in David M. Ellis, James A. Frost, Harold C. Syrett, and Harry J. Carman, *A History of New York State* (Ithaca, NY: Cornell University Press, 1967, revised edn, 1st pub. 1957), table 8, p. 461.
65 Interview with John Joe Gallogly.
66 Interview with Patrick Henderson.
67 Interview with Della Gleckel.

Food, climate, and clothing

Food, too, proved to be a further illuminating contrast in destinations to which migrants gravitated. Though many Irish and Scottish migrants had been introduced to new foods on board ship, it was only after arrival that they confronted America's full range of gastronomical delights. In the United States teabags, hotdogs, pizzas, peaches, melons, and ice cream were all novelties, along with white sliced bread and spinach. Corn on the cob was also considered an American food, with many pointing out that back in the homelands corn was considered appropriate only for livestock consumption. According to Scotswoman Anne Quinn:

Food-wise I didn't see all that much difference. White sliced bread, yes, that was something that we did not have in Scotland. As for fruits, peaches, I don't recall peaches or melons. They may have had them but we never had them. Oranges, they used to call them jaffas … I don't ever recall spinach as a British vegetable. To me that's strictly American. But cabbage, Brussels sprouts, which I abhor, and string beans to me were an American vegetable.[68]

Irish migrants also had intriguing anecdotes about novelty foods to relay. Kathleen Lamberti reminisced about her first encounter with pizza supplied by her uncle: 'We looked at that and he said, "This is pizza pie" and mother said, "Oh what is that? It's dreadful looking stuff. It's awful." He was very disappointed. When he got his back turned we threw it out.'[69] Other foods were more enticing. Joseph Brady of County Armagh who arrived in 1925 stated, 'I had had ice cream, of course, but I never had a ice cream soda, I never had a sundae and, of course, now being in America and because I had some money when I came here I had money to go in and get an ice cream soda. That's one of the things that stuck in my mind.'[70]

Johanna Flaherty of Castlewest, County Limerick, was struck by two main contrasts relating to food, and these were related back to her experiences in Ireland. The first was in connection with the train ride she made from Ellis Island to her aunt's house:

I looked around and I saw everybody on the train was chewing. They would chew and chew and I couldn't imagine, how come that everybody's chewing and nobody's putting anything in their mouth, what are they eating? So two days later I learned what it was: chewing gum. But I wouldn't dare ask my aunt, I wouldn't make believe I was that stupid, that I didn't know what they [*laughs*], what they were chewing.

68 Interview with Anne Quinn.
69 Interview with Kathleen Lamberti.
70 Interview with Joseph Brady.

The first meal Johanna had in the United States also provoked stringent comment as well as conveying the ongoing importance of a staple Irish diet: 'When my aunt cooked the dinner on Saturday after we came back from Ellis Island she cooked about, I think there was four, four, or five of us at the table, she cooked about eight or ten potatoes and I loved her but, oh gosh, she must be stingy because when we cook potatoes in Ireland we cook a great big tray of potatoes.' Johanna also recalled consuming a hot dog and thinking 'Oh gosh what is this? I would call it a sausage but they would, kept calling them hot dogs.'[71] John Joe Gallogly was puzzled when his uncle ordered a hot dog with onions and mustard.[72] Food was clearly alien and the imprint lasted long in migrants' minds.

The weather was a further subject of discussion that migrants alluded to as being a major contrast with life at home. Mary Jo Lenney claimed, 'I'd never seen that much snow. It was snowing and it was bitter cold, bitter cold.' She further elucidated, 'it doesn't get that cold in Ireland at all, you know, it's kind of a moderate temperature. It never gets, once in a while it does but not that cold it usually stays in the 40s and 50s whereas here it gets subzero.'[73] Indeed most migrants emphasised the extremes of stifling summers and fierce winters in the United States. According to Patrick Peak, who grew up in Glasgow:

Like every kid it's an adventure, you know, and you look forward to it especially, of course, the snowstorm. We must have landed in New Bedford in October and, of course, in Scotland you don't get too much snow, it's more like, except up in the Highlands, you know, but down in Lowland Scotland you might get half an inch or an inch but it would be gone the next day because your weather was so mild, you know, … that first winter I used to chip ice out of the sink … it was so different from the old country.

When Patrick experienced extremes of heat that summer the consequences caused immense discomfort:

I get the worse sunburn I ever had in my life because over in Scotland, like I said, the climate is mild. The people over there just go out and don't lie on the beach for hours at a time, you know, if they go for a swim and they're in and out. Down in New Bedford there's two or three beaches and I remember that first summer being light skinned. Oh my god, I can still feel that sun and I had blisters. I didn't get over that for about a month.[74]

Occasionally, a differing climate propelled migrants to undertake novel activities. As Allan Gunn remembered jokingly, 'The first time we got a lot of

71 Interview with Johanna Flaherty.
72 Interview with John Joe Gallogly.
73 Interview with Mary Jo Lenney.
74 Interview with Patrick Peak.

snow somebody showed me a sled because I'd never seen a sled before … And I had it upside down. I thought you sat inside and you held on to the rails.'[75] In retrospect, the climate of the homelands for some must have been a pleasant memory compared with the spectacular fluctuations of the New World.

Clothing was also raised as a topic of discussion in connection with the climate. Those who arrived as children, such as Monkstown migrant James Gleeson, were more inclined to disclose how their clothing set them apart from other people in New York:

We came in March and confirmation was in June at St Luke's Church in the Bronx on 38th Street in the Bronx. I was a candidate for confirmation and so I got dressed up with a straw hat and short pants and off I went to be confirmed and, of course, that greenhorn was really I guess what you could really call us in those days. My mother thought it was all right to be dressed like that but I didn't think so.

James Gleeson's comment arose from the fact that whereas in Ireland he had worn 'shorts', in New York 'kids my age then wore long pants and I was razzed continually by the other young fellows my own age in this country but that passed.'[76]

His testimony echoes that of young Scotsman John Will, who reveals how powerful clothing was when tied to identity and discrimination:

Then this brings us again to an interesting story. We arrive in Los Angeles and the first Sunday rolls around. It's traditional in Scotland that you dress up your young kids for Sunday school. Dressing up in Scotland means wearing a kilt. And seven years old and my mother dresses me up in my kilt or I put it on I guess and off I go down the street three or four blocks to the Presbyterian church. Needless to say this was a riot. The American kids had never seen anything like this and we went through all the routines that you get kidded about kilts like, you know, what's a kilt, what do you wear around your, all that kind of stuff. I might add that that was the first and last time that I wore a kilt. End of that one.[77]

Intriguingly, migrants focused on social and cultural contrasts related to day-to-day practicalities rather than differences connected to broader social structures such as economic, political, and religious elements. While this does not imply that migrants were not influenced by such contrasts at a broader level, they concentrated instead on memories with strong visual and sensory elements. In many ways, then, these recollections produce a model of society, of what contrasts were deemed most significant to migrants. These divergences also provide an alternative interpretation of Irish and Scottish

75 Interview with Allan Gunn.
76 Interview with James Gleeson by Janet Levine, recorded 15 April 1993, EIOHP, EI Series 277.
77 Interview with John Will.

migration history. Whereas migration is often posited in economic terms, the contrasts identified by Irish and Scottish migrants show that a wider range of factors such as climate and daily essentials like food were important in their mindset. It is also striking that these migrants, in reminiscing, failed to acknowledge longing for any aspect of their homeland, except their family and friends. They did not, for instance, express despair at missing Ireland's rustic simplicity, its less extreme climate, or its slow pace of life. Even if the United States did not deliver the untold wealth that images of it suggested prior to migration, migrants found benefits at other levels. That they could happily rather than miserably reflect on such discrepancies between image and reality years later suggests they were satisfied with life in their new homelands at the time of recording their memories. Had their experience been downbeat it is unlikely that they would wish to revisit the past.

Conclusion

These reminiscences reveal that there was little difference between Irish and Scottish migrants, male and female, child and adult, in relation to their initial settlement in the United States. Many experienced trauma at Ellis Island; all focused on similar recollections when asked to identify initial contrasts between life at home and abroad. The discrepancies that they acknowledged were also consistent across time. Migrants arriving in the 1950s were perplexed with the same contrasts between home and abroad that had struck newcomers arriving in the 1920s. In encountering dissimilar elements, migrants responded in three ways: quizzically, silently, and embarrassedly. Yet their naivety was recalled with humour rather than bitterness, suggesting that they were not subject to harshness or hostility from established residents. From diverse representations of the past, then, a common thread can be discerned.

In comparing the Old and New Worlds the majority of migrants were endeavouring to come to grips with the disruption that their move had generated. Their contrasts also generated insight into contemporary conditions in the New World, particularly in relation to the entry of recent newcomers, and declining safety in the city. What contrasts, however, can be drawn between the experience of Irish and Scottish migrants in the United States and those entering Canada, Australia, and New Zealand? How did they cope with the act of incorporation in the post-liminal phase of their rite of passage?

6

'It just isn't home': entering the British World

Ernest Younger of Tillicoultry arrived in Toronto, Canada, on 7 September 1924. For the next fifteen years he wrote to his family and 155 letters survive. He made several trips home. The following snippets from his voluminous sequence of letters mention a number of comparisons that he distinguished between life at home and abroad.[1]

12 April 1925
Gosh what a lot of Jews there are here & Italians (Dagoes they are called), Greeks Chinese & niggers, all sorts & sizes anything but British, but they all have quarters of their own, thank the Lord.

10 May 1925
I don't think I have seen a sheep (except as mutton) since I came here, so that shows what a handicap the city children are under. They cannot visualise what a sheep is like except from pictures. That applies to all farm animals except the horse.

3 May 1925
I bought a new hat last week, Canadian style, & its just tip top. It's a sort of gray with a black band quite nice & $4. I hate parting with money for personal adornment. However it's got to be done. Everybody is so well dressed here. One doesn't like to be left in the cold, & here, if anywhere, it pays to be smart & it pays, as I have found out, to be willing.

10 May 1925
The climate here seems to agree with me, & chances are big here, compared with home.

20 September 1925
There seems to be quite a few motor accidents at home just now, according to the papers you send. The motor traffic seems to be getting pretty heavy over there, but it has a long way to go before it can come up to this country.

8 November 1925
You were asking if this place is better than home, well it isn't. Lots of freedom, good eats etc but it just isn't home, although it is the next best.

15 November 1925
The trouble in this country is that every job is rushed through as fast as possible, sort of hunger & a burst style & when the job is finished [*erased:* the] naturally,

---

1 Ernest Younger's correspondence is in NLS, Acc. 9407/1–4.

12 Betty, Mrs Sowler, Mrs Cameron, Mr Sowler, and Ernest Younger at Jackson's Point, 11 May 1930

the men are laid off, & you can't blame the employer. He can't pay men for doing nothing, & competition is keen.

28 February 1926
A fire lends a cheery atmosphere to a room, & last winter it seemed funny to me that there were no fires in the houses, but one soon becomes accustomed to this want, as the houses are kept very cosy with the furnaces, which heat the entire house, but there is no doubt as to the cheerfulness of a goodly fire, as long as the fire is in the grate.

20 June 1926
Going along this road reminds one of the beautiful roads at home, & except for the heavy traffic, it is a typical Old Country highway & is named the Hamilton Highway.

1 February 1931
I notice in the paper yesterday where snow shovelling & general cleaning up of the snow is giving employment to about six thousand men so that will give you an idea just how many men are out of work in the city & there are lots who don't go in for snow shovelling.

30 July 1935
Berries have been quite plentiful here this year, but the flavour cannot come up to Old Country standards. Of course you can't tell the folks here that, they think there's no berries like theirs.

Ernest Younger's encounter with Toronto in the early 1920s to mid-1930s covers many of the concerns of this chapter, primarily the differences perceived between origin and destination in such vital matters as environment, employment, and housing. As he observed, 'it just isn't home', a penetrating comment given the traditional assumption that British migrants would find the dominions familiar.[2] This chapter focuses on the contrasts that migrants found in their British World destinations. It not only explores the divergences between the various points of settlement in the British World and between Irish and Scottish experiences, but also enables comparisons to be made with the encounters migrants had in the United States, examined in the preceding chapter. The disparities gleaned by migrants were not only the outcome of their own background and mentalities, but were also the result of the differing structure, politically, economically, and socially, of the societies they encountered. This chapter also enables a number of methodological issues to be explored, primarily the contrasts between divergent forms of testimony, including contemporary written accounts and retrospective oral and written interviews.

The initial transition

In the 1920s two-thirds of Irish migrants went to the United States, while a similar proportion of British migrants went to Canada and Australia, the Scots contributing two-thirds of the British outflow.[3] Apart from these changing demographics, a fundamental contrast between migration to the United States and Australasia related to the voyage experience and initial arrival. Whereas Scots and Irish travelling to the United States journeyed in just over a week and were subjected to rigorous scrutiny at Ellis Island, the passage to Australia and New Zealand took approximately six weeks and the arrival process was rarely presented in such harrowing terms. The arrival process was also the biggest contrast between the United States and Canada as destinations for Irish and Scots migrants. The major complaint of those arriving in Australasia centred instead around the difficulties associated with accommodation on arrival, a major factor in generating such discontent.[4] This arose largely from

2 See Stephen Constantine, 'British emigration to the Empire-Commonwealth since 1880: from overseas settlement to diaspora?', *Journal of Imperial and Commonwealth History*, 31:2 (2003), pp. 16–35.
3 Eric Richards, *Britannia's Children: Emigration from England, Scotland, Wales, and Ireland Since 1600* (London and New York: Hambledon and London, 2004), p. 236.
4 For analysis of this see chapter 5 in A. James Hammerton and Alistair Thomson, *Ten Pound Poms: Australia's Invisible Migrants. A Life History of Postwar British Emigration to Australia* (Manchester: Manchester University Press, 2005).

government promises to assisted migrants of hostel lodging subsequently found to be woefully deficient. Major grievances included a lack of privacy, substandard food, and infuriating neighbours.[5] Such frankness surrounding criticism of Australia and New Zealand by newcomers contributed to the 'whingeing Pom' label universally attached to British migrants, irrespective of their country of origin. As James Hammerton and Alastair Thomson have argued, however, the stereotype has concealed 'the validity of complaints about hostel conditions'.[6]

Voicing criticism of the dominion's deficiencies not only resulted in disparaging labels attached to migrants, but was also counteracted by challenges from locals. Christina Lovatt, a typist from Glasgow who arrived in Wellington in March 1951, portrayed the defensive reaction of her host society and her own response to ultimatums directed at her:

We were surprised at the anti-immigrant feeling from the locals. People were friendly, kind and helpful to us personally, but they kept asking us how we liked New Zealand and if we said anything like 'found something different or strange about it' they quickly responded by saying things like, 'you chose to come here, don't criticise it – go back to where you came from if you don't like it.' We found this quite bewildering, we didn't mean to be critical we were just commenting on differences because similarities were very common and obvious. We soon learned to praise something – anything![7]

The timing of Christina Lovatt's arrival coincided with a volatile period involving confrontation between the government and 20,000 waterside workers. As James Belich has indicated in his general history, though not the supreme industrial battle in New Zealand, the Waterfront Dispute of 1951 was 'the greatest civil disturbance between the Depression riots of 1932 and the Springbok tour protests of 1981'.[8] Combined with high rates of immigration, tensions were increasingly rife, presumably exacerbated by the involvement of shipping companies, responsible for transporting migrants, in the conflict.[9]

Migrants were, however, retrospectively forthcoming with the contrasts, positive and negative, that they identified between origin and destination. In alternating between favourable and downbeat comparisons of their homeland, it must be emphasised that such contrasts were shaped not only by their recollections, but also by the changes to society that they discerned since first

5 *Ibid.*, p. 178.
6 *Ibid.*, p. 184.
7 Christina Lovatt, BAIQ 157.
8 James Belich, *Paradise Reforged: A History of the New Zealanders from the 1880s to the Year 2000* (Auckland: Penguin, 2001), p. 300.
9 Anna Green, 'The shipping companies and '51', in David Grant (ed.), *The Big Blue: Snapshots of the 1951 Waterfront Lockout* (Christchurch: Canterbury University Press, 2004), pp. 109–14.

arriving. Such comparisons proved significant in facilitating the adjustment of migrants. Similarities with home could make the transition easier, as did disparity that favoured conditions in the destination over those in the country of origin. What elements of life abroad in the British World did migrants find different between home and settlement?

Part of the transition to new societies took place on the journey out. Propaganda campaigns, for instance, uniformly emphasised the abundant opportunities available throughout the British World. High living standards, widespread employment opportunities, and a temperate climate were all propounded by officials.[10] But as migrants soon discovered, the information proffered could prove erroneous. As Aberdonian Anne Anderson stated of her voyage on the *Captain Cook* to New Zealand, 'We had had lectures on the ship – mainly about how similar NZ was to the UK but it would have been better if the information had been more realistic because expectations would have been different.'[11] While such information was generally not disseminated on ships to the United States because of the short distance involved, migrants seeking American shores also held distorted impressions, as outlined in Chapter 2. This glaring disparity between expectations and reality in New Zealand was frequently voiced. George Nicholson, a schoolteacher from Belfast who arrived at Wellington in September 1952, described arriving in a howling southerly. 'Where was the tropical paradise we were told about. Badly misled by rep. from N.Z. House', he lamented.[12] On the other hand, fellow Belfast migrant Thomas Brown, who voyaged two years earlier, considered the advice he received beneficial:

On the good ship 'Atlantis' we had a number of lectures to explain about life in N.Z. and one piece of advice which made a strong impression on me was, 'There are 2½ million people in NZ and there is only one of you, so it would be much easier for you to change your ways' good advice which I followed, I refused to join the Irish Club, Settlers Club or the R.S.A. and I never once mentioned 'Back-Ome'.[13]

Such discrepancies, however, were largely the result of advertising campaigns. Migrants who drew on the knowledge of family and friends already settled abroad could expect to receive more accurate information, though this was not always so as we will see in the following chapter.

10 See, for example, *Prospects of Migration to New Zealand* (London, 1957), in NAW, New Zealand Prospects of Settlement, L1 22/2/1, and Hon F. Hackett, 'Post-war Immigration in New Zealand', 13 July 1960, in NAW, Advertising and Publicity, L1 22/2/14.
11 Anne Anderson, BAIQ 001.
12 George Nicholson, BAIQ 191.
13 Thomas Brown, BAIQ 028.

Environmental contrasts

Among the first contrasts that migrants discerned between origin and destination were environmental oddities. Just as migrants arriving at New York caught glimpses of the Statue of Liberty and New York's skyscrapers, so too did migrants bound for the British World capture a preview of their new land. Not surprisingly, the contrasts specified between home and abroad depended on the origin and destination of migrants. Evelyn Duncan, for instance, had clearly been left breathless after her arrival at Wellington in 1958: 'I loved it from the first moment we could see land. It was a brilliant day – the sky was so blue, the hills were brilliant yellow (I discovered later that it was gorse in bloom!) and the green seemed <u>so</u> green after five weeks at sea! I was amazed at all the coloured roofs and, then, seeing the houses, too, were coloured I realised how grey my homeland was.'[14] Evelyn's comment is instructive given her origins in Helensburgh, a coastal resort town that she clearly perceived as being as dreary and colourless as major urban centres in Scotland.

Lorna Carter likewise arrived in Wellington in the 1950s, from the Scottish seaport of Oban. She relished her first impressions of the city's surroundings, gleaned from the ship, but primarily because she considered the landscape familiar, rather than dissimilar, to that which she had left behind. She wrote wistfully at the time, 'I see away on the starboard side mountains just like our coast and snow capped peaks in the distance. I just feel that I'm sailing home from Kyle to Mallaig and I've got the feeling that I'm going to love this [*word illegible*] land.'[15] Two years later, after some time touring New Zealand, Lorna Carter was more alert to the differences between the environments in the two countries. Travelling through the South Island and having passed through the Eglinton and Hollyford Valleys, she drew comparisons between these mountain ranges and those in the Scottish Highlands: 'There was snow on the mountains and the air was keen. It reminded me of the hielans a bit, but the mountains are very much higher – one we passed was nearly 8000 Mt Talbot.'[16] A few days later Lorna jocularly added, 'We went up the Routeburn Valley from the head of the lake in open buses and on either side there were these gigantic mountains. He pointed out the smallest and it was as high as Ben Cruachan!!'[17] The spaciousness of New Zealand was also mentioned by those intrigued with the absence of people and traffic.[18]

14 Evelyn Duncan, BAIQ 063.
15 Lorna Carter (Wellington) to her parents (Oban), October 1951, in ATL, Carter family letters, MS-Papers-7377.
16 *Ibid.*, 1 April 1953.
17 *Ibid.*, 5 April 1953. All letters in the Carter collection not attributed to ATL were kindly supplied by Lorna Ross.
18 BAIQ 013, 100, 160, 179, 261, 271.

The climate was a major environmental contrast, particularly in the light of the widespread publicity, which advertised that 'no great extremes of tempera- ture are experienced' in New Zealand.[19] In the correspondence that Lorna Carter sent to her parents back in Oban, Scotland, she frequently commented on New Zealand's climate. She noted wryly in 1952, 'The weather has been its usual sunny self all this week and this morning we had frost – N.Z variety – I had to be told about it!!'[20] A week earlier she reported, 'I notice the winter mornings here. It is pitch black when you waken at 6.45am, then the sun liter- ally pops up and it is bright daylight at 7am. I notice it more in the mornings than I do when it sets. It doesn't seem so quick going down. It gets dark about 5.30pm just now.'[21] This contrast of the shorter days in New Zealand was echoed in an interview recorded with Lorna half a decade after her sojourn in New Zealand. She testified how during summer the sun went down at 8.30pm, while in Scotland summer evenings stayed light until at least 10pm and the sun rose again between 3 and 4am.[22] By 1953, a year and a half after her arrival, Lorna declared: 'The sun out here is so much more dazzling that I haven't quite got used to it – I mean on a sunny day you can't stand and have a photo taken as your eyes all screw up and water like blazes if you have sun glasses off for more than 2 ticks.'[23] This last verdict would prove especially impressive to her family in Oban, receiving it as they would have done in the midst of a Scottish winter. Lorna's preoccupation with the New Zealand climate was presumably also due to aspects surrounding her decision to migrate.

Such was the importance of the climate to assisted migrants in New Zealand that 66 per cent of respondents referred to it, though admittedly it was one of the suggested topics of discussion. While 15 per cent either found the climate too hot or too cold, the majority were favourably impressed. In some cases this was because New Zealand's climate compared so positively with the previous summer at the point of origin: 'after a typical "Irish Summer" I thought I had arrived in heaven', explained an enthusiastic Thomas Brown of Belfast.[24] Others simply drew contrasts between home and destination, with James McLachlan of Glasgow reckoning, 'much better than Scotland, the snow is on the right place up on the Alps'.[25] Only one migrant confessed to missing 'the dramatic change to the countryside in spring in Scotland'.[26]

19 *Prospects of Migration to New Zealand* (London, 1957), p. 11, in NAW, New Zealand Prospects of Settlement, L1 22/2/1.
20 Lorna Carter (Wellington) to her parents (Oban), 14 May 1952.
21 *Ibid.*, 7 May 1952.
22 Interview with Lorna Ross by Angela McCarthy, recorded 24 February 2003.
23 Lorna Carter (Wellington) to her parents (Oban), 14 January 1953.
24 Thomas Brown, BAIQ 028.
25 James McLachlan, BAIQ 172.
26 David Gilchrist, BAIQ 099.

Migrants arriving in Australia likewise reflected on environmental contrasts which deviated substantially not only from their homeland, but also from New Zealand and Canada. An extremely arid climate and the presence of poisonous wildlife were the two main indicators of this disparity. A scorched Sydney landscape proved particularly appalling to Ena Hughes, who had left a farm at Augher, County Tyrone: 'My first impressions were your bare trees, those bare trunks. They looked so dry and so poor after leaving our fir trees and that, that I just couldn't understand how people admired gum trees. I'll never forget the first few looks at them. I thought they were just so miserable looking things.' Ena also elaborated on Australia's insect and reptilian inhabitants:

I can always remember people telling us to mind the spiders and I thought, 'What on earth, what's wrong with spiders?', you know, because we hadn't any poisonous spiders you see and to see these people scared of spiders I couldn't understand it. But we were terribly scared of snakes and I can remember looking when we came to Australia making sure looking in the bed and under the bed and all round the bed in Sydney [*laughing*] to ensure there were no snakes.[27]

In this way, while the climate in the United States and the British World was alien to migrants, the most positive accounts were confined to New Zealand. Canada, Australia, and the United States possessed extremes of climate that posed greater challenges.

Housing and technology

Just as migrants were influenced by images of superior weather conditions in Australasia, so too did they expect quality housing, a major topic in migrant testimony. In the New Zealand context, it was not so much the condition of houses that migrants recalled, as their flamboyant colours and construction from timber. Typical in this respect was Patrick Joseph Sweeney, who described 'Funny wooden houses perched on the sides of hills painted all different colours'.[28] Such constructions were a far cry from houses in Ireland and Scotland built from stone. Others pointed out the challenges posed by the infamous quarter-acre section. Thomas Brown from Belfast commented, 'Having lived all my life in "Terraced Houses" where neighbours are a fairly

27 Interview with Ena Hughes by Bronwyn Hughes, recorded 1987, in OHC NLA, NSW Bicentennial Oral History Project, Oral TRC 2279/8.
28 Patrick Josephy Sweeney, BAIQ 240. See also BAIQ 041, 063, 157, 173, 178, 213, 219, 230, 271, 278. By contrast, German migrants discussed housing in relation to how cold they were in winter. See Brigitte Bönisch-Brednich, *Keeping a Low Profile: An Oral History of German Immigration to New Zealand* (Wellington: Victoria University Press, 2002), p. 42.

close knit group, the "¼ acre" syndrome set me back a bit. After 10 years in one house I only knew the immediate neighbours on either side.'[29] Comments such as this are intriguing, for they fail to indicate the impediments many migrants encountered in securing housing, a condition which official organisations were aware of.[30] Some newcomers to Christchurch likewise experienced difficulty interacting with fellow inhabitants. For George Michie of Foveran in Aberdeenshire, it was the character of the city rather than the housing pattern which deserved criticism: 'We found the people very hard to get to know in Christchurch as it is a typical English city.'[31] Luckier was Elizabeth Meyer who settled further south in Otago, emphasising that 'Dunedin being a Scottish city, it was like being home, everyone you talked to was of Scottish descent, or so it seemed. Living on a street where everyone was a new immigrant we tended to socialise a lot together.'[32] These stereotypes still exist today.

As for the technology available in such houses, perspectives differed. Aberdeen typist Anne Anderson recalled her surprise at discovering that 'some so called upmarket suburbs in Auckland only had night soil collection & of course in the country – I mean on some farms it was a dry closet or longdrop or the flush toilet was outside either down the garden or off the back porch.'[33] Meanwhile, Doreen Wilkinson had to visit an outside toilet at Rotowaro, a stark contrast from the family home in Scotland which contained a flush toilet. Spiders and wetas were frequently encountered on such excursions.[34] Other migrants were impressed by the facilities available, including 'electricity for lighting and cooking as we only had kerosene lamps and open fires'. Elizabeth Harris went on to express her amazement at the availability of hot and cold water rather than carrying it from a well or river. Her appreciation presumably arose from remembering a harsher lifestyle in Enniskillen, County Fermanagh. She judged, 'Everything here was so convenient it was like a holiday for me.'[35]

If migrants expressed some ambivalence towards the housing situation which existed in the 1950s, newcomers of the 1920s almost universally complained about the quality of housing that they confronted. Jim Comerford, who narrated his family's arrival at Sydney in the early 1920s, outlined

29 Thomas Brown, BAIQ 028.
30 See, for instance, Hon. F. Hackett, 'Post-war immigration in New Zealand', 13 July 1960, in NAW, Advertising and Publicity, L1 22/2/14; *Prospects of Migration to New Zealand*, p. 27.
31 George Michie, BAIQ 178.
32 Elizabeth Meyer, BAIQ 177.
33 Anne Anderson, BAIQ 001.
34 Interview with Doreen Wilkinson by Sarah Smith, recorded 1995, in HCL, OH0253.
35 Elizabeth Harris, BAIQ 107.

a number of living arrangements pursued by the family. The first house in which they settled was 'shocking. Unpainted, two room bach place with a back verandah, no water of its own, a dry toilet, no electric light, and I remember my mother saying to my father, "If I could get back on the boat now I'd go straight home." Sparsely furnished. It was a real miner's bach.' The family swiftly moved to a four-roomed house that featured electricity, water supply, and verandahs at the front and rear of the house. The relocation signified a substantial change in the adjustment of Jim Comerford's mother: 'It was a marked improvement and had a marked affect on my mother's outlook. Because after the better than normal standards we had had in Scotland we were at the bottom of the heap in that horrible bach and to move from that into a house that was even better than the one we lived in in Scotland quite clearly had its beneficial effect on her outlook.' Nevertheless, Jim Comerford's mother held ambitions that the family would own a house of their own. To obtain this, the family moved again to a dilapidated house in order to conserve financial resources. The accommodation was deplorable: 'No verandah, unpainted, had running water but no electric light. Again we had to fall back on the kerosene lamps. Millions of cockroaches in it that took the place over the first night we lived there and she was appalled.'[36] The presence of insects, of course, was common to all migrants, irrespective of their time of arrival.

The situation in Canada also proved less appealing, but for other reasons. As Mary MacIver of Lewis divulged, 'You rented a flat from a private family who were buying a home, and you rented the upstairs. You had maybe three rooms, or two rooms, and that's how everybody lived.'[37] Despite this situation, few migrants in Canada appear to have experienced serious difficulties obtaining accommodation, primarily because companies they were contracted to made such provision available.[38] Migrants in New Zealand and Australia, on the other hand, were more likely to encounter difficulties securing housing.

Some features, then, were universally shocking to migrants, irrespective of their year of arrival, for many migrants were emigrating from urban districts in which such facilities were standard. Those that were impressed tended to be Irish migrants leaving rural agricultural districts. This is not surprising when considering a letter sent home to County Armagh from Wanganui in 1924 by Brigid Dawson. In it Brigid made extensive comparisons between the ease of daily life in New Zealand compared with Northern Ireland:

36 Interview with Jim Comerford by Marjorie Biggins, recorded 15 May 1987, in OHC NLA, NSW Bicentennial Oral History Project, Oral TRC 2301/54.
37 Transcript of interview with Mary MacIver in Jim Wilkie, *Metagama: A Journey from Lewis to the New World* (Edinburgh: Birlinn, 1987 and 2000), p. 129.
38 'Canadian immigration', c.1950, p. 6, in NAW, Canada – Policy and General, 1947–61, L1 22/1/138.

13 'I said it was like a "Western" town': Lambton Quay, Wellington (c.1951)

You would never have to wash the chairs or Tables in a lifetime and the Floors are all polished and carpets so there is no slavery or work only to cook and wash and the clothes are never dirty for washing like at home. The most of the people just steeps them in the Boiler with washing powder the call easy Monday so the next morning the[y] light the fire and boils them and when the[y] are taken out they are perfect. No scrubbing whatever for they are not dirty but I give mine a wee touch. It will be a miracle to me Ellen if I get in the remainder of my life like this. No worry or trouble about crops or how they will be saved or hens or eggs or Turkeys or not wet feet like going across Craigs fields. I am surprised at myself and the Comfort I have.[39]

The town of Wanganui also proved delightful to Brigid Dawson. She described how 'Ladies go riding horses along the Beach. The Trams come to the very edge of it. Motor cars are lined up in dozens.'[40] As with the housing situation, however, verdicts on towns and technology depended to a large extent on the background of migrants. Those emerging from urban districts in Scotland and Ireland, for instance, expressed disbelief at the 'cowboy-like' environment that they encountered in many Antipodean towns, such as Wellington:

My first impression of N.Z. was Lambton Quay on a Sunday afternoon. It was absolutely deserted. One could have shot a rifle in the street and you wouldn't have hit anybody. I also thought it was like an American West Town as the shops all had these verandahs over their doors & windows which came right out over the

39 Brigid Dawson (Wanganui) to her sister Ellen Quinn (Armagh), 30 July 1924. This letter was kindly provided by Joan Leonard.
40 *Ibid.*

pavements and then there were these bike stands (I didn't know that's what they were at the time) which I thought looked like hitching rails to tie a horse up to as seen in the movies.[41]

Farms also differed. Some were astonished at the smallness of farms, others at the large number of stock.[42] Still others were astounded to see 'horses to muster sheep' and in one case 'Farmers rounding sheep & cattle in BMW's & Jaguars'.[43]

For many migrants this encounter with new realities proved particularly troubling, especially in the testimonies of those migrating as children in the 1920s. It was less their own adjustment to the peculiar conditions that they mentioned than that of their mother. As Trudie Lloyd put it so bluntly, 'Coming out here was a shocker.' She explained, 'Poor mother it was simply dreadful for her', but Trudie maintained that she never complained.[44] Likewise, Isabella Peat stated how Puponga proved to be 'a dreadful shock for my mother', who had no conception of the living conditions awaiting the family. Back in Scotland they hailed from the market town of Strathaven in Lanarkshire where ordinary amenities were provided.[45] In Australia, by contrast, the nature of settlement meant that certain provisions were supplied. Jim Comerford pointed out that whereas the co-operative called to the house in Australia, that did not happen in Scotland:

You put in an order each week to the co-operative. It was delivered without any extra charge and none of those services were ever available to the women in Scotland and I never discussed it with mother. Had I been a housewife that came out from the conditions in Scotland and Geordie land where they baked their own bloody bread, I'd have thought this was paradise and it was doubly beneficial to my mother who detested the heat of this country that she didn't have to make long jaunts up to the main business centre in Kurri to get loaded up with all of these goods that were then delivered to the house for her.[46]

A child migrant's concern with the adjustment of their mother may have been the result of the nature of the family's migration. While women could and did have a say in the decision to migrate, often they subordinated their own wishes to that of their husband. Their adjustment to new societies was therefore probably a paramount element in the family's decision to remain

41 Catherine Graham, BAIQ 100.
42 BAIQ 001, 099, 135.
43 BAIQ 271, 219.
44 Interview with Trudie Lloyd by Judith Fyfe, recorded 20 April 1990, in ATL OHC, Women's Division Federated Farmers of NZ (Inc) Oral History Project, OHC-0115.
45 Interview with Walter and Isabella Solly by Rosie Little, recorded 16–20 August 1985, in ATL OHC, Nelson and Golden Bay Oral History Project, OHC-0053.
46 Interview with Jim Comerford.

14 'Sydney is a <u>real</u> city, and I felt a bit of a country cousin coming from N.Z.': Sydney (c.1953)

abroad, and perhaps their initial dislike of life abroad meant an uncertain future, which remained etched in a child's mind.

Technological contrasts between home and abroad continued to be made throughout the century and were frequently mentioned in relation to transportation. Outlining her family's arrival at Wellington in 1946, Doreen Wilkinson remembered 'we had to come up to Huntly on the train. What a miserable journey that was. Long, slow, of course the carriages they weren't as nice as the trains in UK.' Ruminating further she disclosed, 'We'd done a lot of travelling by train in UK just even to do visiting because my mother and father lived on one side of the Firth of Forth and all her family where she'd been brought up were on the other side so you know there quite a bit of toing and froing so a lot of it was done by train and of course the train here was just no comparison at all.'[47] George Smith from Dumbarton was equally negative, conveying his astonishment at the slowness of 'express' trains, and the lack of comfort: 'a terrible trip to Wellington on the railway "express" that took fourteen hours, the sight of people getting pillows at Auckland railway station and wondering what they were for, until I got on the train and sat on the hard wooden seats. Ouch!!'[48] Other migrants recalled how old the cars were, the poor road conditions, and 'atrocious driving habits'.[49]

For those Scots leaving highly urban and industrial towns and cities, New Zealand and Australia in all decades proved primitive by contrast with home.

47 Interview with Doreen Wilkinson.
48 George Smith, BAIQ 230.
49 BAIQ 178, 240, 219, 271.

In part this may reflect their origins in urban areas and eventual settlement abroad in rural districts. It is also likely that Scottish expectations were higher as a result of improvements in technology occurring throughout Britain in the twentieth century. Or it may be that by focusing on negative conditions in Australasia migrants were emphasising the resilience of their families in choosing to stay rather than leave. Whatever the explanation, their reactions to everyday technology in New Zealand and Australia clearly differed from the encounters experienced by Irish and Scottish migrants arriving in the USA in all decades, who found the technological contrast of New York astounding, vibrant, and advanced.

By contrast, migrants from rural Ireland and the Highlands of Scotland were more likely to be bewildered by the conditions that they encountered. Mary MacIver of Lewis, pretending to be conversant with the novel technology she encountered when arriving in Toronto in the 1920s, acknowledged, 'I hadn't been out of the island before I came here. I hadn't seen a train, I hadn't seen electricity and although there had been a bus from Ness and a bus from Point, I was never in them. I thought, well, I'm going to pretend as if I know all about this, and that's what I did.'[50] Meanwhile, Donald 'Tulag' MacLeod recalled having to learn to operate a milking machine, not having seen one before. His recollections were also shaped by contemporary innovations: 'They hadn't got anything like the modern machines that they have today'.[51] He soon abandoned milking, however, and went commercial fishing. With the lakes frozen in winter Donald crossed to Detroit and ended up working for General Motors.

Employment and recreation

While generally discussed very little by migrants in their motives for migration, employment was a major factor in any decision to move abroad. Again, the lure of better employment opportunities and working conditions featured in the propaganda tracts of the British dominions. Publicity for New Zealand stressed wages and hours, while agriculture and domestic service were promoted for Canada.[52] How did migrants report their working conditions in New Zealand? Interestingly, 36 per cent of assisted migrants mentioned matters about work in their questionnaires, even though this was not cited as a possible area of discussion. Despite some dissenting voices which felt working conditions and wages were not as favourable as the UK, most responses

50 Transcript of interview with Mary MacIver in Wilkie, *Metagama*, p. 128.
51 Transcript of interview with Donald 'Tulag' MacLeod, in *ibid.*, pp. 103–4.
52 See *Prospects of Migration to New Zealand*, pp. 16, 31–7; *White Star-Dominion Line: Facts About Canada*, (c.1924), pp. 2–6, in NMM, White Star Ephemera.

emphasised the amount of work offered, the greater technology available for electrical trades, and the opportunities to pursue alternative employment.[53]

On 30 September 1951 the ship *Atlantis* docked in Wellington. That year the Wellington region received 1,058 assisted migrants, while throughout the duration of the scheme most newcomers also went to the district with one third of 52,000 assisted workers sent there.[54] Those who travelled on board the *Atlantis* mirrored the New Zealand government's intention to attract industrial rather than agricultural migrants. According to an Australian newspaper account copied by Lorna Carter and sent home, the *Atlantis* carried 873 migrants including nurses, carpenters, labourers, and public service employees.[55] Lorna was among the latter. As she wrote after arrival, 'All we Public Service Commission folk had to assemble in the Social Security Blding at 9am this morning. There were about 100 of us and we each had to be interviewed and allocated a job.' As a result of Lorna's typing skills, her position was altered from clerical writer to typist and she was appointed to the Geological Survey Department. Her salary was to commence at £391 per annum.[56] The letters Lorna sent back to her family in Scotland during her two-year stint in New Zealand frequently comment on employment conditions in New Zealand. She also recollected such differences in her interview. Work hours also differed. In Scotland Lorna recalled toiling from 9am until 1pm with an hour for lunch, then from 2pm till 5 or 5.30pm. She also laboured Saturday mornings. In New Zealand, by contrast, she worked a five-day week from 8am until 4pm.

Many migrants considered work conditions in New Zealand superior, though this naturally depended on the type of occupation pursued. David Mackie, a miner from West Calder, emigrated in 1923 at 23 years of age. Comparing mining conditions in Scotland with New Zealand, David revealed that in New Zealand 'money was better and conditions were better because in New Zealand we had the baths. In Scotland we never had the baths in those days.'[57] Farmers were also appreciative of the abundance of land in New Zealand. According to Sister Laboure, whose father worked dairy farms in both Ireland and New Zealand, 'In Ireland the farms are so small.'[58] Meanwhile,

53 BAIQ 041, 157, 206, 065, 278, 213, 126, 135, 219, 240, 271, 173, 160, 115, 212, 075, 013.

54 Megan Hutching, *Long Journey for Sevenpence: Assisted Immigration to New Zealand from the United Kingdom, 1947–1975* (Wellington: Victoria University Press, 1999), pp. 126, 128.

55 Lorna Carter (*Atlantis*) to her parents (Oban), 20 September 1951, in ATL.

56 Lorna Carter (Wellington) to her parents (Oban), 30 September 1951, in ATL.

57 Interview with David Mackie by Jamie Mackay, recorded 25 February 1992, in ATL OHC, Huntly Coalfields Oral History Project, OHC-0020.

58 Interview with Sister Mary Catherine Laboure McAleese by Jacqueline Gallagher, recorded 19–26 October 1993, in ATL OHC, Reading, Writing and Rosaries: Life Stories of Seven Dominican Nuns, OHC-0554.

Donald 'Tulag' MacLeod specified the innovations in milking that he found in Canada in the 1920s: 'There were 50 milking cows and I learned to run the milking machine – I'd never seen one before'.[59] These impressions contrasted with that of fellow Scot Sydney Samuels, who arrived in Australia in 1933 to find conditions appalling: 'When I landed in Australia I was horrified. The Depression was actually worse in Australia when I landed than I'd left in Scotland. There were people starving, [*word unclear*], queues, kitchens, derelicts sleeping in parks. It was horrific.'[60]

For Mary MacIver, the promise of work in Canada was well founded, and her testimony contains intriguing comments about contemporary opportunities. She told how:

The girls could always get work ... all we knew was housework, anyway! And you had a lovely room to yourself and good food. The wage was only about $40 a month, but, anyway, you had a bathroom to yourself, and the girls didn't do badly here at all. We had every Sunday off, and a Wednesday afternoon. They didn't have all the convenience that they have today. Instead of going and buying a carton of bleach like they do today, we had to boil the clothes on a two-ring burner, down in the basement.[61]

By contrast, those working in agricultural occupations were hampered by the rigours of the Canadian climate, which caused seasonal unemployment.

Not surprisingly, many accounts mention the wages that were available throughout the dominions. For Irish migrants like James Killeen, wages were a novelty: 'Went out to Fortification sawmill about the 6th January. Wages were 13 shillings per day. It was the first time that I worked for wages.'[62] Brigid Dawson also revealed the luxury afforded by the good salary her husband earned in Wanganui compared with County Armagh: 'we have more money that we [*erased:* call] can call our own than ever we had on our big farm in Camly.'[63] The contrasting income between Canada and the United States proved attractive in luring migrants south. According to Donald 'Tulag' MacLeod, 'they were only makin' $50 a month on the Canadian boats, while in this country they were gettin' $75, and a $100 for an able seaman. So the wage also was an incentive to cross the border.'[64]

With a regular wage migrants could either save or spend, and one of the

59 Interview with Donald 'Tulag' MacLeod, cited in Wilkie, *Metagama*, p. 103.
60 Interview with Sydney Samuels by Sarah Dalton, recorded 13 February 1990, ACL, Glen Innes Oral History Project, 90-OH-012/1-2.
61 Transcript of interview with Mary MacIver, in Wilkie, *Metagama*, p. 126.
62 Interview with James Killeen by Madeline McGilvray, recorded 13 April 1999, in ATL OHC, Southland Oral History Project, OHC-0464.
63 Brigid Dawson to her sister Ellen Quinn, 1924.
64 Interview with Donald 'Tulag' MacLeod, cited in Wilkie, *Metagama*, p. 101.

many areas upon which they outlaid their money was food. Indeed, a quarter of assisted migrants in New Zealand chose to comment on the variety and cheapness of food.[65] As Dorothy Batcheler remarked, 'I was amazed how cheap the bread, milk and meat were and how people seemed to waste a lot of bread by throwing out "stale" bread to the birds. Saveloys, silverbeet, chinese gooseberries, tree tomatoes, pavlovas and finely sliced lettuce salad were all new experiences and very good.'[66] Lorna Carter also recollected the profusion of butter in New Zealand during her temporary sojourn there in the early 1950s: 'There's no such thing as margarine or cooking flour. Everything was butter … Coming from a place that had been rationed to a wee bit of butter a week I thought it was such a waste'.[67] Cheap food in New Zealand in the 1960s was also fundamental, as Ann Crutchley explained in a series of reflections: 'I didn't realise butter was so cheap in New Zealand or I would have asked for butter'; 'I was really, really thrilled because the meat was so cheap'; 'In Ireland where I would have bought just a, maybe a couple of chops here I was able to buy a whole leg of lamb for about the same price.'[68]

These accounts show that a major contrast between migrants arriving in the United States compared with Australasia concerned their encounters with food. Whereas Irish and Scottish migrants in the United States recollected being wary and critical of many new foods they sampled, migrants in New Zealand were more receptive to the range of exotic foods that they encountered. This is not to say that migrants were not bemused at cultural contrasts they found, such as the cuts of meat. George Michie of Aberdeenshire explained, 'When going to a butcher's shop it took a wee while to get used to the different cuts of meat, as we very seldom seen mutton or lamb at home mostly beef'.[69]

Hard earned cash was also spent on drink, the circumstances in which it was consumed being recalled with both disbelief and disdain for those in New Zealand. Irish and Scottish migrants, accustomed to regular drinking hours and accessible places to drink, found the archaic drinking laws astounding, with the six o'clock swill mentioned by 53 per cent of Scottish and Irish assisted migrants.[70] Many respondents were disgusted at the practice. Anne Anderson from Aberdeenshire, a registered nurse, was presumably influenced

65 BAIQ 001, 013, 075, 099, 173, 178, 206, 213, 261, 271.
66 Dorothy Batcheler, BAIQ 013.
67 Interview with Lorna Ross.
68 Interview with Annie and Bob Crutchley by Megan Hutching, recorded 27 February 1998, in ATL OHC, 1998 New Zealand Citizenship Oral History Project, OHC-0421.
69 George Michie, BAIQ 178.
70 BAIQ 001, 007, 028, 042, 060, 065, 099, 100, 107, 115, 135, 137, 165, 172, 173, 177, 178, 179, 194, 206, 208, 219, 230, 261, 271.

to a degree by her profession, when she admitted, 'the six o'clock swill appalled me – not that I was in bars but the drunks were very much in evidence – vomiting in gutters etc & when I did look into a bar was disgusted at the décor & surroundings in some.'[71] Others, such as Kenneth Ward from Bridge of Allan, compared conditions with those found back home: 'had seen drunks rarely in UK but saw them regularly here – businessmen in suits staggering around, quite unbelievable.'[72] Belfast-born James McMeekin, a technician, also 'felt the 6 o'clock closing was a bit antiquated, and strange to see people carrying flagans of beer home. In Ireland during the 1950s we did not bring drink home. I could not get used to the large beer halls (pubs) in N.Z as we were used to small pubs in Ireland, well placed for easy walking.'[73] The situation lingered until 1967.

The early closure of bars in New Zealand and poor nightlife generated recognition in official publicity that 'to a settler coming from a large metropolitan city, New Zealand city life will probably seem dull.'[74] Some leisure facilities did, however, exist. Other entertainment pursuits, apart from eating and drinking, included visits to the cinema. Archibald Prentice from Alexandria in Dunbartonshire concluded, 'In Christchurch a visit to the cinema was a great improvement to a similar visit in the U.K. One did not have to breathe in cigarette smoke and put up with people moving in and out of their seats during the film, but if one wanted to have a meal in a restaurant before or after the cinema then you were in for a disap[p]ointment.'[75] The lack of facilities in the evening also provoked comment from other migrants. Reflecting on her imminent return home to Scotland, Lorna Carter informed her parents, 'I'm just itching to get in a nice restaurant with clean silver and nicely served food – and to go to a decent theatre. There is just nothing like that out here. Perhaps it will come. They are only 100 years old.'[76]

Other contrasts discerned by Lorna Carter between New Zealand and Scotland favoured her new residence. In December 1951 she reported, 'It is so easy to shop here, plenty of everything ... Folks out here say how difficult it is to shop – so little to choose from! If they only knew, but the[y] won't believe it when I say how well off they are.'[77] By July 1953, however, Lorna remarked, 'I see a letter in the paper today complaining about the shoes out here. If only one of the firms from home sent out a few of their expert shoemakers they'd

71 Anne Anderson, BAIQ 001.
72 Kenneth Ward, BAIQ 261.
73 James McMeekin, BAIQ 173.
74 *Prospects of Migration to New Zealand*, p. 29.
75 Archibald Prentice, BAIQ 212.
76 Lorna Carter (Wellington) to her parents (Oban), 16 July 1953.
77 *Ibid.*, 12 December 1951.

make a fortune.'[78] Such comments, quite apart from revealing the superiority of British goods and services, also indicate that Lorna missed elements of life in Britain. Other migrants also commented on shopping facilities, presumably spurred on by guidance in the questionnaire concerning shop opening hours. There was a rough balance between those who savoured late Friday shopping and weekend closures, and those who found the lack of shopping facilities difficult to adjust to.

Cultural contrasts

Encountering novel cultural traditions also set migrant newcomers apart, including the term 'bringing a plate'. Elizabeth Meyer, a knitwear hand-sewer of Hawick, 'found the term bring a plate when invited to a party quite quaint, especially as it wasn't explained we had to put some food on it'.[79] Similar memories about this New Zealand phrase were predominantly recounted with humour, whereas recollections by German migrants cited the situation as a 'female, shame-filled rite of passage into the culture of New Zealand hospitality'.[80] Yet throughout the testimonies of Scots and Irish it is the humour of these everyday cultural contrasts that is emphasised. Indeed, the New Zealand dialect amused a number of respondents. Dorothy Batcheler of Kirkcaldy found 'the NZ vocabulary a bit odd at first – words like duchess, hottie, jandals, scuffs, batch, "take a plate" etc'.[81] In similar vein, Harold Armstrong of Selkirk, who arrived at Wellington in January 1963, considered, 'The NZ dialect was rather strange (still is)'. He remarked that 'Slang was difficult to follow ie my cousins visited and being from farming stock were talking about cockies, jokers and the like, we had to tell them we couldn't follow their conversation.'[82] Migrants, too, could perplex the locals: 'Everything was different and with my Irish accent I had to repeat everything I said just about.'[83] Despite such reactions, Irish and Scottish migrants were less prone to the difficulties and cultural misunderstandings experienced by non-English-speaking foreign groups, such as German migrants.[84]

Despite these contrasts, more than half of assisted migrants overwhelmingly emphasised the friendliness and hospitality of New Zealanders.[85] Typical was Elizabeth Harris, who 'found the people were so very friendly and helpful

78 *Ibid.*, 11 July 1953.
79 Elizabeth Meyer, BAIQ 177.
80 Bönisch-Brednich, *Keeping a Low Profile*, p. 179.
81 Dorothy Batcheler, BAIQ 013.
82 Harold Armstrong, BAIQ 007.
83 Sylvia Nicholson, BAIQ 192.
84 Bönisch-Brednich, *Keeping a Low Profile*, pp. 162–82.
85 BAIQ 001, 063, 065, 066, 099, 107, 115, 135, 137, 140, 157, 160, 179, 192, 193, 206, 208, 213, 219, 230, 240, 261, 263, 271.

15 'Here's a Haka – kids style': Maori children (c.1952)

to us. People brought us all sorts of things like food, clothes and furniture as we were struggling. It was really great.'[86] This verdict was also expressed years earlier, in the mid-1920s. Bringing to mind the atmosphere in County Armagh, Brigid Dawson told her sister, 'We would be a good while in Ireland before anyone would come to see if we wanted money or anything. This is the sort of the people in New Zealand and if you got to a house the[y] will not let you go without something.'[87] The only complaint made was the tendency of New Zealanders to resist criticism.[88]

Participating in cultural continuities and contrasts also raises the issue of interactions with other ethnic and national groups. The distinguishable component of the New Zealand population was Maori and many migrants were divided with their impressions. Some were afraid of Maori, while others found them difficult to understand.[89] Others made fast friendships.[90] Still others commented on what they perceived to be good race relations. According to Trudie Lloyd, Maori–Pakeha relations were 'very good' and she found them nice and was fond of them. Others claimed, 'I was also not aware of any racist overtones in those days and felt that Maori and Pakeha were on much better terms than they are today.'[91] Generally, migrants seemed to recollect good race relations in New Zealand. Possibly this was in contrast to

86 Elizabeth Harris, BAIQ 107.
87 Brigid Dawson to her sister Ellen Quinn, 1924.
88 BAIQ 015, 157, 208, 212.
89 BAIQ 042, 099.
90 BAIQ 107, 135, 137.
91 Catherine Graham, BAIQ 100.

contemporary knowledge at the time of their interviews of other destinations in which indigenous populations were perceived to be treated worse. It might also reflect contemporary racial tensions in the late 1990s when the interviews were conducted. Or it may simply mirror migrants' irregular interaction with and knowledge of Maori prior to the latter's increasing relocation to urban areas in the later twentieth century. Between 1945 and 1966, for instance, the Maori presence in the urban population rose from 26 per cent to 62 per cent and by 1986 had reached 83 per cent.[92]

Other correspondents specified that they made Maori aware of similarities with Ireland and Scotland. Andrew Rae of West Calder who came to NZ in 1948 aged 21 recalled that his grandfather was an orator. He then spoke of telling Maori 'You don't have the sole rights of speaking oratory or being the only oppressed country ever in the whole world.' He went on to discuss problems in Scotland and Ireland in connection with land holdings and social development.[93] John Gallagher, meanwhile, likened Ireland and the north of Scotland to Maori, stressing that language is culture: 'If you lose your language you lose your identity.'[94]

Little comment is made in the testimony from Canada and Australia about migrant interactions with other ethnicities there, though Donald 'Tulag' MacLeod did comment that 'I saw the first black man in St John', before referring to a settlement of 'descendants of slaves' at North and South Buxton.[95]

A sense of freedom also prevailed in some testimonies. Migrants highlighted various activities that could be pursued in New Zealand which were restricted at home. As James McMeekin of Belfast remembered, 'I liked the opportunities to go skiing, shooting and fishing. These were rather eletist back home and I felt it was wonderful that they were open to everyone in N.Z.'[96] Robert Paton of Ferryden, Montrose, arrived in August 1954 and declared:

there was a feeling of freedom, which I think most immigrants had. Lack of family constraints, removal from the 'class' structure in Britain, the feeling you could do 'almost anything you wanted to do'. I went to hear the NZ S.O. I went to live theatre, things that were not available locally in Scotland. I was able to participate in lots of activities here while they may have been available in Scotland in NZ you were asked to join, encouraged to take part. A lot of this was to make up the numbers (I suspect).[97]

92 Belich, *Paradise Reforged*, p. 471.
93 Interview with Andrew Rae by Robert Paton, recorded 9 December 1991, in ATL OHC, Labour Movement Oral History Project, OHC-0056.
94 Interview with John Gallagher by Robert Paton, recorded 1 September 1993, in ATL OHC, Labour Movement Oral History Project – Part II, OHC-0059.
95 Transcript of interview with Donald 'Tulag' MacLeod in Wilkie, *Metagama*, pp. 102–4.
96 James McMeekin, BAIQ 173.
97 Robert Paton, BAIQ 206.

Former inequalities were therefore viewed as non-existent in New Zealand. As well as freedom, equality was also stressed. A number of migrants commented on the lack of a class structure, that 'everyone was equal no matter who you were.'[98]

Overall, migrants provided summaries of their life abroad that overwhelmingly favoured their new homeland. Donald 'Tulag' MacLeod 'liked Canada. It wasn't that different from my native island. And there was no crime. You could leave your doors unlocked at that time.'[99] In similar vein, fellow Lewis migrant Mary MacIver reported, 'If your door was not locked at night in those days you didn't have to worry. Toronto was called "Toronto the Good", but it's not like that today, of course.'[100] This perception of safety was also prevalent in New Zealand for some migrants. One Irishman found New Zealand harmless compared with Northern Ireland, while another found it more secure in earlier years than currently: 'Safer to walk the streets and didn't have to worry about locking everything up the way we have to do now.'[101] Another, Thomas Brown, from Belfast wrote, 'N.Z. certainly has changed since the 50's and 60's. My biggest impression (and difference) of N.Z. when I arrived was safety & peace of mind ... you walked the streets at night, put something down and expect it to be there when you returned, rarely lock your doors, leave your car on the street! But after nearly 43 years its still "Godzone" to me!'[102] Such juxtapositions therefore reflected the development as well as differences in various British World societies.

What is intriguing in the analysis of questionnaires conducted with Irish and Scottish migrants in New Zealand is the conception of what they missed. As cultural anthropologist Brigitte Bönisch-Brednich has posited for German migrants in New Zealand, conceptualising first impressions also entailed establishing what was absent. Germans missed changes of the season, history, their family, music, theatre, and culture.[103] While Irish and Scottish respondents also yearned for some of these elements, the vast majority, 53 per cent, simply stated that they pined for their family and friends.[104]

98 Elizabeth Meyer, BAIQ 177.
99 Transcript of interview with Donald 'Tulag' MacLeod, in Wilkie, *Metagama*, p. 101.
100 Transcript of interview with Mary MacIver, in *ibid.*, p. 128.
101 BAIQ 173, 264.
102 Thomas Brown, BAIQ 028.
103 Bönisch-Brednich, *Keeping a Low Profile*, p. 239.
104 BAIQ 007, 013, 028, 042, 065, 066, 075, 107, 115, 135, 160, 165, 173, 177, 178, 179, 192, 193, 212, 213, 230, 261, 263, 264, 278.

Conclusion

Out of these diverse representations of the past a common thread can be discerned. The majority of migrants in comparing the Old and New Worlds were attempting to come to grips with the disruption that their move had generated. Their contrasts also supplied insight into contemporary conditions in the New World. For those migrants in New Zealand, the somewhat antiquated society they had entered had technologically developed. Race relations, volatile in the later twentieth century, were viewed in a happier light. The freedoms that New Zealand offered were seen to have continued and the achievements of the second generation compensated for the upheavals migrants had undergone.

A significant difference between the British World destinations and the United States related to the type of image circulating about the competing destinations prior to a migrant leaving home. As outlined in Chapter 2, migrants who went to Australasia typically recalled factors such as the climate being a major consideration, while for those choosing the United States its image of prosperity was critical. Indeed, in migrant testimonies the appeal of the United States, mythically, symbolically, and in reality, eclipsed the images associated with other competing destinations. Yet the reality, as this chapter highlighted, did not always live up to the myth, particularly as many elements contradicted what they had been told through propaganda campaigns. That they could happily rather than miserably reflect on such disappointments years later entails a sense of satisfaction with life in their new homelands at the time of recording their memories. Had their experience been negative it is unlikely that they would wish to revisit the past.

Utilising written questionnaires with assisted migrants to New Zealand offers a useful contrast with those oral interviews conducted with Irish and Scots moving to the United States. From a methodological angle, the first impressions that migrants in New Zealand recalled were not subject to ongoing influence from the interviewer. Instead, the questionnaire merely asked for their first impressions and cited some examples such as people, land, shops, licensing hours, shop opening hours, and weather, which migrants could develop at length. That migrants chose to reflect on areas of interest outside these themes reveals the importance of their first impressions. Housing, work, accents, and food were also discussed. Perhaps the most significant element in facilitating adjustment, however, was the presence of family and friends as the following chapter reveals.

7

'A crony of my own type': personal and group networks

Lorna Carter was born in August 1923 to Englishman Harry Carter and Scots-woman Catherine MacDougall. Lorna was raised in Oban on the west coast of Scotland and in 1941 joined the Wrens. In 1951 she emigrated to New Zealand on board the *Atlantis*, claiming the complimentary passage that was available to ex-service personnel. Upon arrival she was housed by her mother's relations and Lorna spent the next three years in New Zealand, writing to her parents usually at least once a week. It is from this voluminous collection of 136 letters that the following extracts are taken.[1]

2 October 1951
I went down a path lined on either side with freisias, primroses, bluebells, daffo-dils, tulips and every other spring flower you can think of with most gorgeous perfume, in the front door of this big wooden house and there were Effie & Guy. She is small and thin. Bill is very like her. Guy is tall and thin and both are great fun and Effie is just as you thought she would be easy going with a twinkle in her eye and Guy is great fun too. We had a cup of tea & a blether & then I was shown my room. It is one of the boys. It's a bit bigger than our back bedroom has two lots of [*word illegible*] paned windows, a fireplace, large wardrobe, dressing table and window seats arranged like so [*drawing*]. There's a light over the bed, and head phones, which the boys had and I can listen to the wireless [*word illegible*] time!! I came down and we blethered again.

25 May 1952
I am going to write to Marjory now and then I hope to do a few more. I hope she'll like it out here – the hostel is a good bit out of the city but she'll have to go flat hunting when she gets here, and find a place of her own – I don't think she'll think getting up at 6am each morning much fun, however, we'll watch and see. I should be able to meet her on the ship when she arrives. It seems a wee way off yet but the time will soon fly – wont she be lucky if she gets on the Captain Cook from Glasgow – no trekking down to Southampton, much less bother.

27 Sept 1952
I knew he was Scots but not where he hailed from – and believe it or not – he comes from Greenock ... He's been out 4 years and was in Edinburgh before he

---

1 The letters Lorna wrote during her voyage to New Zealand are deposited in ATL while the remainder of the correspondence is in the author's possession and is reproduced with permission of Lorna Ross.

came – what next do you think!! Out of all the churches in Wgton I have to go to this one and find a pal of our Flo'.

14 Sept 1952

By this time I'd twigged that he was from the Hielans somewhere – he'd got to the stage of saying have a sweetie – well no Newzealander would say that – they talk about 'Lollies'. So says I 'where do you come from? And says he 'Scotland' and says I 'Stornoway?' and he nearly dropped. He did come from Stornoway too – poor soul wanted to know if I spoke Gaelic – he 'chust wished he could speak the English as well as he could the gaelic'. He couldn't understand how I came from Oban.

Migrants such as Lorna Carter moved in tightly defined networks of family and friends which assisted the processes of migration and settlement abroad.[2] Such networks frequently offered newcomers practical support, and social and emotional nourishment. Networks were also conduits of communication, and expatriates could influence their transnational connections at home by supplying advice and information about the day-to-day living in their new destination of choice. These informal networks were comprised of both family and friends, and in this way kin and local attachments proved substantially more important in the processes of migration and settlement than a broad affiliation to Ireland or Scotland. This is amply demonstrated through the emphasis Lorna Carter put on linking friends and acquaintances with partic-ular localities in Scotland. The chapter begins by assessing the origins, devel-opment, and operation of these informal personal networks for Irish and Scottish migrants.

The existence of networks

As seen, contrast between their homeland and new country of settlement was one of the main aspects of settlement concerning Irish and Scottish migrants.

2 There is a strong international literature focusing on the role of networks in the process of migration. See Monica Boyd, 'Family and personal networks in international migration: recent developments and new agendas', *International Migration Review*, 23:3 (1989), pp. 638–70; Douglas S. Massey, Joaquín Arango, Graeme Hugo, Ali Kouaouci, Adela Pellegrino, and J. Edward Taylor, 'Theories of international migration: a review and appraisal', *Population and Development Review*, 19:3 (1993), pp. 431–66; Leslie Page Moch, 'Networks among Bretons? The evidence for Paris, 1875–1925', *Continuity and Change*, 18:3 (2003), pp. 431–55; and Charles Tilly, 'Transplanted networks', in Virginia Yans-McLaughlin (ed.), *Immigration Reconsidered: History, Sociology, and Politics* (New York and Oxford: Oxford University Press, 1990), pp. 79–95. For Scottish networks see Angela McCarthy (ed.), *A Global Clan: Scottish Migrant Networks and Identities Since the Eighteenth Century* (London and New York: Tauris Academic Studies, 2006) and for Irish networks see the articles in *Immigrants and Minorities*, 23:2–3 (2005).

This was especially important, for settlers frequently provided intending migrants at home with impressions, positive and negative, of their new homeland. As Ann Crutchley of Belfast best explained it, 'My family had followed us here … I think I had written such glowing accounts of New Zealand'.[3] It is not known, though, whether her family considered her impressions accurate after their arrival. Other migrants were especially wary about encouraging their connections from home to settle abroad, particularly during times of economic downturn. Responding to his parents' request for information in advance of an intending migrant's relocation to Toronto in the mid–1920s, Ernest Younger suggested, 'I don't think it would be advisable at the present time. Work isn't too plentiful & there are a lot of men walking the streets, but I'll gather as much reliable information as I can get, & write him.'[4]

The desire to be joined by friends and family from home is well documented. In the letters sent by Lorna Carter from New Zealand to Scotland in the early 1950s, the young sojourner wrote to her parents, 'a crony of my own type would just make life out here. You can't blether the same to a Kiwi girl.'[5] Lorna's correspondence reveals that two intimate friends were giving an immense amount of attention to the possibility of emigration. According to Lorna, 'Margie says that Betty takes spasms of filling in papers and not [*erased:* to] sending them in!! but thinks that she may make for N.Z. next year.'[6] While Betty remained in Scotland, Marjory's potential for migration seemed more promising. As Lorna determinedly informed her parents, 'I will write to Marjory and give her the gen. The "Captain Cook" is pretty crowded for deck space, but they don't have more than 6 berth cabins, so she'll be allright. It is a case of suiting yourself to the occasion – so I'll give her the low down.'[7] Later that month Lorna's correspondence with her parents, cited in the extracts at the beginning of this chapter, indicated that Marjory's voyage out seemed imminent, yet she failed to make the trip to New Zealand. Lorna was particularly aggrieved at this outcome: 'I had a letter from Marjorie & she has postponed coming out – really!! She has waited so long that now she is going to see her mother settled in the new house. She'll miss the boat alltogether if she doesn't watch because they are cutting down immigrants and probably will from now on.'[8] Indeed, that same month, September 1952, the

3 Interview with Annie and Bob Crutchley by Megan Hutching, recorded 27 February 1998, in ATL OHC, 1998 New Zealand Citizenship Oral History Project, OHC-0421.
4 Ernest Younger (Toronto) to his parents (Tillicoultry), 15 November 1925, in NLS, Acc. 9407/1.
5 Lorna Carter (Wellington) to her parents (Oban), 14 January 1953.
6 *Ibid.*, 24 June 1952.
7 *Ibid.*, 10 May 1952.
8 *Ibid.*, 27 September 1952.

government reduced the assisted migrant inflow to New Zealand from 7,500 to 5,000 per year.[9]

The desire to have friends join her also arose in an interview conducted with Lorna more than half a century after her emigration: 'I tried to get lots of them to come but no they never did.' The full extent of this, however, is not contained in Lorna Carter's letters, presumably because she wrote direct to the individuals concerned, rather than mentioning them in letters to her parents. When quizzed as to why these contacts stayed in Scotland, Lorna reckoned that 'They were frightened to leave home ... A lot of them had parents that would say you can't go. In those days you had to do what you were told.' Besides this implicit verdict on such parent–child relations in Scottish society, Lorna further elaborated, 'Some parents think their children should be there all the time, you know. They wouldn't let go.' Lorna Carter's testimony is revealing not only in its discussion of the collective involvement in the decision to migrate, but also in considering reasons for staying rather than leaving, an issue rarely considered by scholars of migration. As for Lorna, her migration to New Zealand was facilitated by her mother's cousin, who supplied accommodation upon her arrival.[10]

For many intending migrants, the information and assistance offered by their migrant networks before and after the decision to migrate had been made was considerable. As Bob Crutchley explained of his move to New Zealand from Belfast:

Well, I corresponded with an uncle of mine who lived in Johnsonville, another brother of my father's who had been out here since before the first war, and my uncle Leonard or Len and corresponded with him and decided we'd come out and stay with him for a few days till we get a job, a house. In the meantime my uncle Len died so we still corresponded with his daughter my cousin and that's why we came to Johnsonville.[11]

Yet, family connections could also give inaccurate advice: 'We were told we must bring a sewing machine because they're impossible to get in New Zealand which we found and we were told not to bring a washing machine and we found the direct opposite when we got here.' As Ann Crutchley further rued, 'we were ill-advised'.[12] Lorna Carter revealed similar misleading recommendations: 'My cousin in Wellington said bring your tweed suits. She said it gets very cold here. I duly took my tweed suits, costumes they called them

9 Megan Hutching, *Long Journey for Sevenpence: Assisted Immigration to New Zealand from the United Kingdom, 1947–1975* (Wellington: Victoria University Press, 1999), p. 65.
10 Interview with Lorna Ross by Angela McCarthy, recorded 24 February 2003.
11 Interview with the Crutchleys.
12 *Ibid.*

in those days and I think I wore them once. Their winters were like our summers.'[13] Such matters, though, were relatively minor.

The presence abroad of family and friends, then, should not be underestimated in any consideration of twentieth-century Irish and Scottish migration. Such movements raise the question of when cycles of departure begin. Clearly Irish and Scottish migrations were continuums based on the unrelenting involvement of personal networks so that heavy twentieth-century flows were facilitated by a familial infrastructure that was firmly established by departures prior to 1914. In what ways, though, did such networks develop and what functions and operations did they provide?

Quite apart from encouraging their close family and friends to migrate, or supplying financial assistance with the fare or acting as sponsors, networks proved vital after arrival. The existence of such networks is clearly demonstrated in its most basic form through general mention made by interviewees. In New Zealand, for instance, several Scottish migrants referred to the extent of their expatriate connections. Robert Paton said, 'As you can imagine most of our friends and acquaintances that we've made over the years have been immigrant couples.'[14] In similar terminology Doreen Wilkinson indicated, 'Coming from overseas we had a lot of overseas visitors and you did a lot of visiting and everybody kept in touch with their friends from overseas'.[15] Irish migrants were just as inclined to maintain these connections. According to Sister Laboure, 'Our house in New Zealand became, more or less, the hub of quite a number of Irish people who came out. Some came out with us, some came out later, but our house was always open house'.[16]

These networks are also discernible in contemporary written data, which demonstrates the daily encounters between expatriates. Ernest Younger migrated to Toronto in the early 1920s and initially boarded with a fellow Tillicoultrian. His voluminous correspondence documents his widespread interaction with other Scots, particularly those from his native Tillicoultry. As he commented in July 1925 of a close friend, 'Her house is quite a meeting place for Tillicoultronians, who are now Torontonians.'[17] Indeed at Christmas

13 Interview with Lorna Ross.
14 Interview with Robert Paton by Joyce Paton, recorded 1982–84, in ATL OHC, Hawkes Bay Oral History Project, OHC-0438.
15 Interview with Doreen Wilkinson, recorded by Sarah Smith, 1995, in HCL, OH0253.
16 Interview with Sister Mary Catherine Laboure McAleese by Jacqueline Gallagher, recorded 19–26 October 1993, in ATL OHC, Reading, Writing and Rosaries: Life Stories of Seven Dominican Nuns, OHC-0554.
17 Ernest Younger (Toronto) to his parents (Tillicoultry), 26 July 1925, NLS, Acc. 9407/1.

that year 'The guests were all Tilly people.'[18] The social dimension to these connections was also evident. Cards, movies, car tours, dinners, dances, picnics, fishing, miniature golf, bowling, and bridge all featured as pursuits engaged in by these social networks. Nostalgic conversation was also undertaken: 'I went back to work yesterday afternoon but Bill Howieson came in & there was nothing done. We talked of Tilly, Devonside & Coalsnaughton & had many a laugh over his reminisinces.'[19] There was, however, a downside to such proximity with these expatriates, with Ernest lamenting, 'I was sorry to hear that Adam Keir had got into trouble, but I hope the gossip doesn't follow him over here, but I suppose it will as there are so many Tilly folks here, altogether too bad.'[20] This remark indicates that close connections could generate conflict as well as co-operation. In addition, it is possible that local connections only proved significant after settlement abroad. As Ernest contemplated, 'It is curious how few people in Tilly really [k]new who I was.'[21]

The practical functions of networks

The most significant roles played by family and friends abroad included, first, the assistance given to newcomers in connection with accommodation. This embraced both national groups, both sexes, all destinations, and all time periods. In Australia in the 1920s, for instance, Ena Hughes reported that 'People came from Ireland and they always came to my mother's. They still laugh about it some of them. They always came there and she liked to keep them without charging them until they got a job. So mother had people continuously coming and staying there.'[22] Doreen Wilkinson, meanwhile, elaborated on her father's connections with New Zealand which the family took advantage of after arriving at Huntly in the 1950s: 'He had an auntie there and we went and stayed with his auntie and lived with them for 10 months before we got a house of our own'.[23]

Despite the shorter distance to Canada and the United States from Ireland and Scotland, ethnic connections there likewise proved crucial. Mary MacIver remembered that in the 1920s, 'When I arrived in Toronto, I came to friends here, and this man who was a great friend of my father, and I had their address. A Lewisman, and his wife was from Tiree, and I stayed with

18 *Ibid.*, 27 December 1925, NLS, Acc. 9407/1.
19 *Ibid.*, 5 April 1925, NLS, Acc. 9407/1.
20 *Ibid.*, 26 May 1930, NLS, Acc. 9407/3.
21 *Ibid.*, 25 May 1925, NLS, Acc. 9407/1.
22 Interview with Ena Hughes by Bronwyn Hughes, recorded 1987, in OHC NLA, NSW Bicentennial Oral History Project, Oral TRC 2279/8.
23 Interview with Doreen Wilkinson.

them for two or three days while I went looking for work.'[24] Male migrants also made firm use of these social ties. When having to acquire new lodgings Ernest Younger informed his parents, 'I have had several offers of board from neigbors, one being Mrs McCallum, Mrs Hardie's sister.'[25] On another occasion Ernest disclosed that fellow Tillicoultrian and neighbour 'Mrs Yeo has rented her flat to a Scotch lady & her two daughters'.[26]

Scottish migrants to the United States likewise utilised family and friends for accommodation. Maisie Pedersen of Greenock followed her friend and friend's family to the United States, initially residing with them in New York.[27] Even when families had fathers already settled in the United States, it was often other family members who supplied housing assistance. Isabella Deeks's family stayed with an uncle for a couple of weeks after being reunited.[28] William McGuire's parents, meanwhile, had both been in the United States, when his mother came back and took the children there in 1928 to live for a time with an aunt and uncle.[29] Anne Quinn also had two sisters and three brothers in the United States and 'They all had jobs, were working, and they had taken an apartment for us and had it furnished.'[30] Originally from Cupar in Fife, John Will and his family left in 1924 and stayed with a maternal aunt before moving on to Los Angeles, where their sponsor, his mother's second cousin, lived. Once in Los Angeles they lodged with their sponsor, Alexander Munro, for several weeks.[31] Clearly this extended conceptualisation of kinship meant that intending migrants had a greater chance of securing support from their relatives already settled abroad.

Despite the assistance provided by established networks of family and friends abroad, some evidence suggests that these early connections faded in significance after arrival. Anne Quinn, for instance, mentioned that her parents had met newly arrived neighbours from Scotland and her mother

---

24 Transcript of interview with Mary MacIver in Jim Wilkie, *Metagama: A Journey from Lewis to the New World* (Edinburgh: Birlinn, 1987 and 2001), p. 126.

25 Ernest Younger (Toronto) to his parents (Tillicoultry), 2 March 1930, NLS, Acc. 9407/3.

26 *Ibid.*, 26 October 1930, NLS, Acc. 9407/3.

27 Interview with Maisie Pedersen by Paul Sigrist, recorded 26 February 1994, EIOHP, EI Series 442.

28 Interview with Isabella Deeks by Janet Levine, recorded 30 April 1997, EIOHP, EI Series 869.

29 Interview with William McGuire by Kate Moore, recorded 30 July 1994, EIOHP, KM Series 77.

30 Interview with Anne Quinn by Dennis Cloutier and Peter Kaplan, recorded 8 December 1983, EIOHP, NPS Series 146.

31 Interview with John Will by Elysa Matsen, recorded 16 September 1994, EIOHP, EI Series 547.

helped the husband get an apartment and set it up for them, you know. She was a much younger woman than my mother but they were quite friendly. And things like that happen, the friendship kind of trailed off, you know, and we didn't see an awful lot of them after that. Because she, you know, they made new friends of their own. By this time my mother had made other friends also. And the families, you know, had all their own friends by this time.[32]

Motherwell-born Agnes Schilling, on the other hand, claimed she had no relatives in the United States when she migrated there in 1922 at 15 years of age. Yet she had friends who visited her throughout her ten-day stay on Ellis Island. They eventually took Agnes to their home in Newark, New Jersey. Despite the initial absence of family in the United States, Agnes's brother joined her two months later and they were then joined by a sister, a feature typical of several testimonies. Agnes Schilling's sister worked for a family at Montclare in New Jersey and through them Agnes obtained employment with a judge's family.[33]

Irish migrants also participated this way. Limerick-born Michael Jordan deliberated over the practicalities associated with his family's reunion:

Well we told them that when we have a job once we had a job we'd get our money together and we would take them out that was the main thing. And I said to my brothers at that time I'm going to, we're not going to be paying rent for the rest of our lives here I says, I'm going to buy a house. We're going to buy houses. So I said we'll pool our money together and we'll buy a house eventually but it took a good while because the Depression came but that's what I wrote. I wrote and I said, 'We'll take you out when we can, when we're working together, we'll do the right thing', and that's what we done.[34]

James Gleeson of Monkstown, County Cork, also recalled that his father and brothers, the forerunners of the family migration, 'lived with an aunt, my mother's sister. She had a couple of rooms that she rent out to them.' The family were reunited in 1927, with James later observing, 'We moved several times in the period of time that I lived in the Bronx. It was certainly a difference from the way we were forced to live over in Ireland.'[35]

The son of a teacher in County Mayo, Paul O'Dwyer, on the other hand, stayed with his brothers in boarding houses, which were characterised by a strong Irish ethos:

32 Interview with Anne Quinn.
33 Interview with Agnes Schilling by Janet Levine, recorded 16 June 1992, EIOHP, EI Series 172.
34 Interview with Michael Jordan by Paul Sigrist, recorded 19 October 1993, EIOHP, EI Series 397.
35 Interview with James Gleeson by Janet Levine, recorded 15 April 1993, EIOHP, EI Series 277.

There were several neighbourhoods but if you were staying in Manhattan you would stay on the Upper West Side and you would live in a boarding house for the most part and there would be an Irish woman would cook your meals and take care of your sleeping quarters and look after you in the fashion and make certain that you didn't have a woman in the room and that was, that qualified her to take care of my mother's son and that was the situation.

Indeed, between 1920 and 1930 Irish movement within New York was at its zenith. This increased mobility saw a resulting shift from previous concentrations in Manhattan and Brooklyn to residence in Bronx and Queens. Such movement was undertaken not solely for upward mobility but also for practical reasons and reflected advances in housing and transportation.[36]

O'Dwyer also pointed out the Irish involvement in the work situation in New York, in which natives from Ireland 'made up practically all the grocery clerks. They were taken in, they had enough education to be able to add up and subtract and what not so they fitted into that and they worked for Irish grocers, Butler Brothers, Reeves Brothers, who would have 20–30–40 stores. They would hire these greenhorns and would pay a fair price by comparison to what was the going rate at that time.'[37]

While Paul O'Dwyer mentioned the assistance offered by established migrants in New York to those of the same ethnicity, other migrants reveal that it was their close family and friends who aided their employment chances, rather than Irishness in a broad sense. For instance, after his arrival in 1924 Limerick-born Michael Jordan initially obtained work at Bloomingdale's but upon learning of his wages of $12 to $15 a week his brother, 'said, "Don't bother I'll get you a better job in the express, 60 cents an hour", so it amounted to a lot more. And I went to that job, the express, and I worked as a clerk labourer there'.[38] A brother's intervention also secured Joseph Brady a position in the subway system.[39] Irish women likewise proved instrumental in assisting their kinsfolk find work. Mary McGloin of Bellavary, County Mayo, claimed after her arrival in 1922, 'my sister came round here and I took her to the telephone company and they wouldn't take her because she had a brogue so I got the job.' She also declared, 'I was, you know, willing to

36 See Marion R. Casey, '"From the east side to the seaside": Irish Americans on the move in New York city', in Ronald H. Bayor and Timothy J. Meagher (eds), *The New York Irish* (Baltimore and London: Johns Hopkins University Press, 1996), pp. 395, 397. In 1910 88 per cent of Irish lived in Manhattan and Brooklyn while by 1960 half of all Irish lived in the Bronx and Queens.

37 Interview with Paul O'Dwyer by Paul Sigrist, recorded 17 July 1993, EIOHP, EI Series 362.

38 Interview with Michael Jordan.

39 Interview with Joseph Brady by Paul Sigrist recorded 25 September 1995, EIOHP, EI Series 673.

take a chance. I brought in the short time, I brought my father out, I brought all of my brothers out, I helped bring them out, that's what, got them jobs ... my mother didn't go to work, she stayed home but she did a lot of work around you know the house and everything'.[40] As well as the residential moves already noted, between 1910 and 1930 the Irish also experienced occupational advances.[41]

Irish migrants were not unique in this regard. Many Scottish newcomers also drew upon their connections to obtain work, the second critical practical function that networks performed. The son of a streetcar conductor, Allan Gunn recalled that a neighbour 'had a job lined up for my father if he was interested'.[42] Mary Dunn, meanwhile, was encouraged to migrate to the United States by her maternal aunts. After arrival she took the train to Buffalo and from there continued on to her relations in Pennsylvania. She later recollected, 'I got in contact with some of my Scottish friends that lived in Youngstown, Ohio, and they said, "Come over to Youngstown" because there are a lot of wealthy people that had big homes and you got more so I got a job then at $15 a week.'[43] Meanwhile, Joseph Delaney's uncle Jim McDaid secured him a job.[44]

In Canada, evidence shows that Ernest Younger recognised his ability to offer assistance to newcomers: 'I was surprised to see that Sinclair Malcolm had sailed for Canada. I wish I had known sooner, because I know what it means to arrive here, knowing no one, although I wasn't like that, I was lucky ... Perhaps I could help him find a job'.[45] Ernest's comment is insightful in the absence of direct testimony concerning his own move to Canada for it clearly alludes to the fact that his relocation was assisted by those he knew already settled in Toronto. Ernest also provided vital assistance to natives of Scotland beyond his home town of Tillicoultry: 'The family two doors below Mrs Yeo have had pretty hard luck. The husband has only worked about four weeks this year. He was in hospital for about three months & hasn't been so very strong since but like hundreds of others he just can't get a job & they are broke. He

40 Interview with Mary Margaret McGloin by Janet Levine, recorded 12 April 1994, EIOHP, EI Series 457.
41 Chris McNickle, 'When New York was Irish, and after', in Bayor and Meagher (eds), *The New York Irish*, p. 343.
42 Interview with Allan Gunn by Paul E. Sigrist Jr., recorded 20 June 1992, EIOHP, EI Series 179.
43 Interview with Mary Dunn by Dana Gumb, recorded 23 January 1986, EIOHP, AKRF Series 127.
44 Interview with Joseph Delaney by Dana Gumb, recorded 5 September 1985, EIOHP, AKRF Series 23.
45 Ernest Younger (Toronto) to his parents (Tillicoultry), 19 July 1925, NLS, Acc. 9407/1.

is a Scotsman & I have helped him a little, so have some of the neighbours.'[46] In some cases, then, simply being a Scottish expatriate mattered almost as much as being close family and friends, though a personal connection was still required.

Ernest Younger's letters also reveal the encouragement that he received from his contacts to financially improve his situation. In April 1925, for instance, he notified his parents, 'I had another letter from Bobby Nicholson urging me to go to the States, but I don't think I'll move in a great hurry. He was saying I could command from $30 to $40 a week there.'[47] Interviews show that many migrants moved from Canada to the United States, frequently assisted by their connections. According to Angus MacDonald, 'To get into the States, you had to have $200 pocket money, and $8.40 for head tax. We went in two at a time because we didn't have enough money for all of us to come over. When two got in legally, one of us went back with the money for the next two.'[48]

As these examples demonstrate, networks based on close durable connections with family and friends were instrumental in the process of settlement. This network of informal personal ties not only drew upon family members already in the United States, such as brothers, sisters, cousins, aunts, uncles, and in-laws, but also upon friends derived from specific localities in Scotland and Ireland. Kinship ties and intimate friendships based on local origins and work affiliations were of considerably more importance than a broad identification with their homelands. In what other ways were local connections discernible through personal testimonies?

Neighbourhood linkages

Contemporary written sources convey the most extensive documentation of local connections among migrants abroad, with individuals frequently located in their specific place of origin. In the Scottish-Canadian context, J. M. Bumsted has commented on the paucity of the label 'British' in reference 'to customs, culture or the nationality of one's friends and neighbours', highlighting instead the propensity of Scottish correspondents to refer to local or national origins.[49] Scottish letter-writers and diarists in the twentieth century also took this approach. Again, the testimony reveals that such migrant

46 *Ibid.*, 8 December 1930, NLS, Acc. 9407/3.
47 *Ibid.*, 19 April 1925, NLS, Acc. 9407/1.
48 Transcript of interview with Angus MacDonald, in Wilkie, *Metagama*, p. 114.
49 J. M. Bumsted, 'Scottishness and Britishness in Canada, 1790–1914', in Marjory Harper and Michael E. Vance (eds), *Myth, Migration and the Making of Memory: Scotia and Nova Scotia, c.1700–1990* (Halifax and Edinburgh: Fernwood Publishing and John Donald Publishers, 1999), p. 102.

networks operated beyond Canada, and were an integral aspect of Lowland as well as Highland adjustment. In part, migrants' extensive commentary on the social activities they pursued with other expatriates suggests that strong communal bonds helped reinforce their sense of national and ethnic identities. Again, such contact can be viewed as both private and public depending on the observer.

As mentioned, one of the most sustained commentators on ongoing contact with his local connections from home was Ernest Younger. Having migrated to Toronto in the early 1920s, Ernest wrote frequently about his social world, which was inhabited to a large degree by fellow Scots, especially those from his native Tillicoultry. As we saw above, writing of one acquaintance he revealed, 'Her house is quite a meeting place for Tillicoultronians, who are now Torontonians.'[50] This comment is important, for it shows local, rather than national, identifiers in both Scotland and Canada. Ernest also specified the local links of Scottish acquaintances whom he met through work and church which stretched to encompass other localities. 'The new draftsman is Scotch from Dunoon. His people came over here when he was about the size of ten cents (one year old)', he revealed in 1925.[51] The following year he told of 'Another young fellow, just two weeks out from the Old Country, started in the office the other day, from Motherwell this time.'[52] As for Jean Ford, chosen to be Miss Toronto, Ernest remarked, 'I understand she, or at least her people come from Edinburgh so that is rather gratifying to us Scotch folks, if it is the case.'[53] And in early 1931 Ernest announced, 'I was at church last night with Jack Ross. The minister was a Scotsman from Fifeshire, who had been in West Kilbride for fifteen years.'[54]

Local origins in Scotland were clearly crucial for Scottish migrants throughout the British World. Indeed, the correspondence of Lorna Carter in New Zealand in the 1950s likewise testifies to this geographical belonging. In documenting the range of Scottish individuals she met in New Zealand, Lorna frequently pointed to their local origins. During a tour of New Zealand, Lorna discussed, 'an old boy on the trip who came from Tarbert and he'd been back home in Scotland for 5 months recently – 5 months too long he said – a miserable existence nowadays!! He was an old sourpuss, but I've met more Scots than ever before.'[55] Another Scot Lorna met was 'from a wee

50 Ernest Younger (Toronto) to his parents (Tillicoultry), 26 July 1925, NLS, Acc. 9407/1.
51 *Ibid.*, 19 April 1925, NLS, Acc. 9407/1.
52 *Ibid.*, 6 June 1926, NLS, Acc. 9407/2.
53 *Ibid.*, 15 August 1926, NLS, Acc. 9407/2.
54 *Ibid.*, 19 January 1931, NLS, Acc. 9407/4.
55 Lorna Carter (Wellington) to her parents (Oban), 2 November 1952.

village near Strathmore near Dundee and he's as Scots as if he'd never left'.[56] These examples highlight that neighbourhood rather than regional or national origins were of fundamental importance in communications between Scots at home and abroad. Local proximity rather than a broad national identifier was of great significance for many Scots when communicating with their transnational connections.

The shipboard diary of Annabella Sinclair, a native of Onziebust on the island of Wyre, Orkney, likewise reflects such linkages. Voyaging to Australia in 1929, Annabella reported striking up an acquaintance with two girls from Glasgow. Furthermore, upon arrival in Adelaide, Australia, she divulged, 'Guy and me went ashore a walk and went into a shop to get some fruit so who did we meet there but a Kirkwall chap. Shearer to name. He came on board and visited us in the evening and we had a nice talk together. He had heard beforehand that we were on our way so news soon travels.'[57] Documenting such connections was presumably undertaken to reassure family and friends at home that the settlements Scots found themselves in were familiar and welcoming. They also point to the powerful role of physical location in Scottish society.

Apart from drawing attention to the local origins of their expatriate acquaintances, Scots also emphasised local attachments in their allusions to other nationalities. As Annabella Sinclair reported in 1929: 'We have met quite a few Australians on board. They seem very like our own people.'[58] That Annabella meant a local rather than national similarity is evident from her further declaration, 'the real Australians are all right Just like the Weir folk very homely.'[59] This specific linkage was also ascribed to Irish migrants on board: 'The Irish seem very like the Orkney people in their ways.'[60]

The absence of written testimony from Irish migrants contained in this study hinders a comparable analysis. Certainly there is little discussion in oral interviews that neighbourhood was prioritised over broader ethnic allegiances, and this applies to both Irish and Scots. The available testimony, then, provides a methodological impasse in relation to this issue for the Irish, though systematic examination of personal letters sent by Irish migrants throughout the nineteenth century, in which strong local ties were discussed and maintained, is suggestive that such bonds operated in a similar manner in the twentieth

56 *Ibid.*, 5 April 1953.
57 Shipboard journal of Annabella Sinclair, 1929, OA, D1/118. Extract dated 25 May 1929.
58 *Ibid.*, 16 April 1929.
59 *Ibid.*, 18 May 1929.
60 *Ibid.*, 17 May 1929.

century.[61] More unearthing of material, however, is required to systematically pursue this avenue of enquiry.

Associational Culture

A further component that reveals the importance of local attachments among Scots is the existence and operation of Scottish societies. One of the more extensive accounts emerges from Angus Macdonald, a native of North Uist who moved to New South Wales, Australia, in 1929. Angus was asked to discuss his involvement with Scottish societies in Sydney. He explained, 'There were a lot of Scottish societies in them days. There was a Highland Society. They had a big building in Phillip Street.' Angus recounted that 'I joined the High-land Society when I first came to Australia … We used to hold our gathering at the Showground every year. It was a big affair them days. And at that time they had a Scottish concert. See they had the Highland concert at the Town Hall on New Year's night.' The leading Scottish society in New South Wales before the Second World War, the Highland Society, as Angus MacDonald testified, perpetuated the maintenance of Scottish culture through its dances, which 'were every week, different places. You'd go to a dance every Saturday night … Scottish dances. Scottish mostly. Strip the willow on the high gates, and Reelin', square dances.'[62] As well as the recreational function of Scottish societies in Sydney, these formal associations also facilitated more practical endeavours; Angus, for instance, met his wife through the Highland society.[63] Eventually Angus departed the organisation due to its being too costly, thereby providing some support for claims that Scotland's 'national, regional and clan societies were often élite clubs'.[64] Consequently, vigorous affirma-tion of symbolic Scottishness through society involvement could depend on the economic resources of participants. Other factors may also account for the Highland Society's decline after the Second World War including a

---

61 See David Fitzpatrick, *Oceans of Consolation: Personal Accounts of Irish Migration to Australia* (Cork: Cork University Press, 1995); Angela McCarthy, *Irish Migrants in New Zealand, 1840–1937: 'The Desired Haven'* (Woodbridge: Boydell Press, 2005).

62 Interview with Angus Macdonald by Paula Hamilton, recorded 1 September 1987, in OHC NLA, NSW Bicentennial Oral History Project, Oral TRC 2301/137.

63 Due to high levels of emigration to Australia in the 1920s, 25 per cent of Scottish grooms and 28 per cent of Scottish brides married endogamously. Prior to that the figures were approximately 16 per cent and 28 per cent. See D. Lucas, 'Scottish immigration, 1861–1945', in James Jupp (ed.), *The Australian People: An Encyclopedia of the Nation, Its People and Their Origins* (Cambridge: Cambridge University Press, 2001), p. 668.

64 Marjory Harper, *Adventurers and Exiles: The Great Scottish Exodus* (London: Profile Books, 2003), p. 372.

16 The Blue Lake Highland Pipe Band, 1938

conservative elderly leadership and settlement of migrants in Sydney's outer suburbs.[65]

Although Angus Macdonald joined the Highland Society, he also indicated that a vast array of Scottish societies existed in the suburbs. The naming of these societies, however, did not echo their Scottish origins, but took their identifiers from the Australian suburb that they served. As Angus meticulously summarised, 'See different districts had their own. There was, oh Lakemba Scottish, Bankstown Scottish, Marrickville Scottish ... there was Dulwich Hill Scottish too. They were Marrickville Scottish, I think. And there was Petersham.'[66] These examples show a blending of origin and destination and suggest expatriate willingness to integrate with settler society.

Intriguingly, Angus Macdonald was recollecting events taking place in the 1920s and 1930s, decades that brought enough Scots to Australia to ensure that, by 1933, they supplied the largest proportion of the non–Australian-born population that they would reach: 14.7 per cent.[67] It was also a period in which Australia's foreign-born population was still heavily dominated by settlers of combined British and Irish origins (see Appendix 8), with the Scottish inflow twice as large as the English one relative to their homeland populations.[68] The

65 Irene Bain, 'Post-war Scottish immigration', in Jupp (ed.), *The Australian People*, p. 671.
66 Interview with Angus Macdonald.
67 Lucas, 'Scottish immigration', p. 666.
68 *Ibid.*

British ethos of Australasia therefore enabled a range of Scottish identities to be expressed in a positive rather than defensive manner. Unlike other ethnic groups, articulation of aspects of Scottishness was not viewed as a failure to integrate into Australasian society. Nor were Scots perceived by their Antipodean host societies as being problematic. Indeed, by 1947 there was a profusion of Scottish societies and Highland pipe bands in Australia. Out of almost 200 associations, 56 societies were in New South Wales.[69] Jim Comerford was another in Australia who commented on the profusion of Scottish societies in New South Wales: 'Well there was a Scots club in Kurri run regular social functions, dances. There was a Caledonian club. They had a cross-fertilisation of members but they were rivals and there was a Burns club.'[70]

Concerning her involvement in Scottish events in New Zealand, Lorna Carter indicated that she maintained her Scottishness 'by going to anything Scottish that was on in the town' including a Highland Games event at Masterton.[71] Lorna could not confirm, though, whether or not there was a Scottish society in Wellington, yet her letters reveal there was. She went, for instance, to 'listen to a concert by the Scots' Society'. That same night, 'Another lady sang – a soprano – I had heard her at the Burns Club. There were also three one act plays, all done by Scotties.'[72]

What accounts for this divergence between Lorna's oral and written testimony? Possibly Lorna may simply have felt more Scottish abroad and her social interactions with other Scots presumably amplified this. On the other hand, Lorna may have been deliberately reassuring her parents of her ongoing affiliation towards her homeland, thereby counteracting any possible fears they may have had that she would remain overseas. Once back in Scotland there was no emotional or practical requirement for Lorna to express her Scottishness, which led to it being diluted further through the years. Then again, in her interview Lorna may have been predominantly concerned with attempting to recall external and public expressions of Scottishness, so visible in twentieth-century Scotland, rather than her internal sense of being Scottish.[73] Lorna's sense of cultural Scottishness also incorporated a number of 'reinvented' physical manifestations of Scottish national identity.[74]

69 *Ibid.*, p. 668.
70 Interview with Jim Comerford by Marjorie Biggins, recorded 15 May 1987, in OHC NLA, NSW Bicentennial Oral History Project, Oral TRC 2301/54.
71 Interview with Lorna Ross.
72 Lorna Carter (Wellington) to her parents (Oban), 19 July 1952.
73 Analysis of Lorna's written and oral accounts are discussed extensively in Angela McCarthy, 'Personal letters, oral testimony, and Scottish migration to New Zealand in the 1950s: the case of Lorna Carter', *Immigrants and Minorities*, 23:1 (2005), pp. 59–79.
74 For summaries of this 'reinvention' of Scottishness see T. M. Devine, 'The invention of Scotland', in David Dickson, Seán Duffy, Cathal Ó Háinle and Ian Campbell Ross

The migrant narratives so far discussed shows that Scottish societies in Australia emphasised a local dimension, with clubs often named according to Australian suburbs. The testimony of Highland migrants in the United States, by contrast, conveys a sense of regional identity, named not according to their destinations, but their origins. This is particularly the case with recollections emanating from migrants of Lewis and suggests that a strong sense of island identities and belonging prevailed. Their accounts, however, have been taken from published transcripts and it is unclear whether their reminiscences were in response to focused questions or whether they were instructed to muse at length on various themes. Despite this difficulty in establishing under what circumstances discussion of the local and national consciousness of these Lewis men and women emerged, the testimony is critical for any examination of Scottish ethnic societies abroad.

Murdo MacLean, who sailed from Liverpool to Montreal in 1929, attested, 'We had a Lewis Society in Montreal. We rented a hall on Saturday nights and had a ceilidh.'[75] Dòmhnall Chrut revealed a more inclusive Society, which nevertheless had the same aim: 'There was a Gaelic Society [*in Canada*] and every month we'd meet up, sing songs and have a dance.'[76] Meanwhile, Mary MacIver, a native of Upper Garrabost, migrated to Toronto in 1927 to join her brother. She discussed the inundation of Lewis migrants in the city and provided a lengthy account of the activities of the Lewis society. Her recollection also documents the existence of other Scottish associations in Toronto which not only expressed regional origins in Scotland, but the degree of co-operation between the clubs, a situation which might reflect Lowland and Highland hybridisation. For instance, there were at least 50 Highland and Gaelic societies in Glasgow during the eighteenth to early twentieth centuries.[77] Some Lewis migrants in Toronto, then, may have moved to Canada via Glasgow where they were imbued with forms of association practised by Gaels in urban areas of Scotland. Such a possibility reveals the need for sensitivity when dividing 'Highland' and 'Lowland' at the expense of exploring the symbiosis between these two cultural descriptors of twentieth-century Scottishness. As Mary recollected:

The Lewis Society met once a month on a Saturday night. They had it in the Ketchum Hall, right opposite the church on Devonport Road. They had like a

---

(eds), *Ireland and Scotland: Nation, Region, Identity. A Record of the TCD Conference September 2000* (Dublin: A. & A. Farmar, 2001), pp. 18–24; T. M. Devine, *The Scottish Nation, 1700–2000* (London: Penguin, 1999) especially ch. 11 and pp. 285–98.

75 Transcript of interview with Murdo M. MacLean in Wilkie, *Metagama*, p. 155.

76 Transcript of interview with Dòmhnall Chrut in CEN, Emigration folder.

77 Charles W. J. Withers, *Urban Highlanders: Highland-Lowland Migration and Urban Gaelic Culture, 1700–1900* (East Linton: Tuckwell Press, 1998), p. 186, Table 6.1.

concert first, and the dancing after that. Of course, we had to be out before twelve. There were good Gaelic singers here, those days. We used just to get up and sing this and sing that, and sing together. We used to have a cup of tea, and we were the first society in Toronto who started to give you the potatoes and salt herring in the winter time. We made a special night and everybody came from the Caithness Society and the Skye Association … and we used to make big money on that![78]

By contrast with reminiscences, the voluminous series of letters from Ernest Younger sent from Toronto between 1925 and 1938 reveals the failure of Tillicoultry connections to establish an official society for natives of his home town. As Ernest wrote in October 1925: 'Geo. Speedie talked again of forming a Tillicoultry Club, to meet 2 or 3 times a year, but that was about as far as it got'.[79] Possibly Ernest's connections preferred the more informal gatherings that took place, such events being catalogued regularly in his missives. Such accounts were presumably documented in order to reassure his parents of the Scottish network surrounding him, thereby aiding his settlement. Although the Younger letters indicate that Ernest maintained informal links with Tillicoultry connections in Toronto, there is no mention of his regular attendance at Scottish society events.

Despite their sustained presence in the United States, examination of Scottish settlement there in the nineteenth and twentieth centuries is also a glaring omission in studies of the Scots abroad. In a chapter on migrant identity in her valuable comparative overview of Scottish migration, Marjory Harper has indicated that Scottishness was far more visible in Canada than the United States, in part because a melting pot policy in the United States obscured the visibility of groups like the Scots.[80] Harper writes: 'The decline of many of the symbols of ethnicity in the early twentieth century suggests that the preservation of Scottish identity was also generational, at least in the United States, where by the 1920s the once thriving Scottish immigrant press had disappeared and only two Highland Games remained.'[81] Such a conclusion, though, not only excludes the interior sense of Scottishness articulated by many migrants, but also fails to acknowledge that if the press and Highland games had almost been extinguished in the 1920s, societies continued to prosper, at least according to migrant testimony.

One particularly illuminating meditation on a multitude of Scottish societies saturating New York was supplied by Norman 'Broxy' MacKenzie, a native of Habost, who sailed on the *Canada* for Ontario in 1924. He spent

78 Transcript of interview with Mary MacIver in Wilkie, *Metagama*, p. 127.
79 Ernest Younger (Toronto) to his parents (Tillicoultry), 11 October 1925, NLS, Acc. 9407/1.
80 Harper, *Adventurers and Exiles*, p. 369.
81 *Ibid.*, p. 372.

time in Buffalo before moving to New York where he encountered an array of associations:

In the 'thirties, the Lewis Society was going on up in Harlem. At eight o'clock on a Saturday night – nobody bothered you – the girls who worked as domestics would go up there to the hall. There were four Scottish societies met in that hall – Lewis, Lewis and Skye, the Celtic Society and the New York Gaelic Society – and they all got together on a Saturday night. Maybe 400 Scottish people in New York, congregating in Harlem, for a dance.[82]

His comment provides an intriguing depiction of Harlem, for the 1920s saw the African-American presence there rise 115 per cent, while the overall population declined as other ethnic groups moved to the Bronx, Brooklyn, and Queens.[83] MacKenzie's statement that there were no disturbances, however, presumably reflects contemporary concerns at the time of his interview in 1980 relating to violent incidents in the neighbourhood of Harlem. Mary Ann MacDonald from Tong on Lewis, who arrived in New York in 1921, likewise mentioned attending in New York 'the Lewis or Skye Association dances, and I remember there was a yearly event in Brooklyn'.[84]

Migrants from Lewis resident elsewhere in the United States also provided evidence of the existence of Lewis societies. According to Norman 'Broxy' MacKenzie, 'They started a Lewis Society in Buffalo and I'm sure there would be 200 Lewis people there.'[85] This was reiterated by Dòmhnall Chrut, who left on the *Metagama* in April 1923 at twenty years of age: 'There was another society in Buffalo when I was there … There are only six members now. When I was there, there were forty.'[86] Seonaidh Shiurra also departed Stornoway on the *Metagama* destined for Canada. After a period of time there he went to several cities in the United States, all containing Scottish clubs: 'We had a society there in Buffalo. We had another one in Cleveland – [the] Lewis Society – and one in Detroit as well. There was one in nearly every town there, and we met once a week. If there was no cèilidh, there would be a party or something.'[87] Just as Dòmhnall Chrut specified the decline in membership among the Scottish society in Buffalo, he also pointed to the falling away of Lewis members in the Cleveland and Detroit clubs. On his time in Cleveland in 1923 and 1924 he remarked, 'There was a Lewis Society. They

82 Transcript of interview with Norman 'Broxy' MacKenzie, in Wilkie, *Metagama*, pp. 148–9.
83 Gilbert Osofsky, *Harlem: The Making of a Ghetto. Negro New York, 1890–1930* (New York: Harper & Row, 1971, 2nd edn; 1st pub. 1963), pp. 128–9.
84 Transcript of interview with Mary Ann MacDonald, in Wilkie, *Metagama*, p. 139.
85 Transcript of interview with Norman 'Broxy' MacKenzie, in *Ibid.*, p. 146.
86 Transcript of interview with Dòmhnall Chrut in CEN, Emigration folder.
87 Transcript of interview with Seonaidh Shiurra [John Macdonald], in *ibid.*

tell me that there is only one Lewisman [left] in Cleveland nowadays. There were around 60 then.'[88] Chrut also revealed, 'We had a big society in Detroit ... Hundreds attended the Lewis Society in Detroit at that time. There are not many [?societies] left now save the one in Detroit, it's still pretty good.'[89] These testimonies reveal that the decline of Scottish societies needs to be redated, as many clubs were still thriving in the 1920s. This is not surprising given the vast influx of Scots into the USA during that decade. They also show that societies were not simply benevolent organisations like the St Andrews Society, but associations which more often than not had a local or regional ethnic, rather than national, emphasis.

Helen Hansen, a native of Queensferry, south of Edinburgh, went to Gary, Indiana, in 1923 with her mother and sister to join their father, who had migrated the year before. Chronicling her migration and settlement decades later in 1989, Helen conveyed her family's involvement in the 'regular Scotch colony' of Gary, including membership for Scottish men in the Clan MacNeill and women's participation in the Daughters of Scotia:

We belonged to a Scottish clan and they had meetings every two weeks or some-thing and they used to have the dances and the bagpipes and do the Scotch dancing and stuff like that. We used to like to go ... The meetings were every two weeks but the dances were like on a Saturday night and we had a good time.[90]

Mary Dunn, meanwhile, left Stirling in 1923 at eighteen years of age on the *Assyria*. An Episcopalian, she went to Pennsylvania and later told, 'I was going back and forth to Youngstown to Scottish gatherings and dances and that was where I met my husband.' In providing Mary with an introduction to her husband, formal ethnic associations clearly offered practical as well as social dimensions, thus mirroring the functions that they provided in Australia.[91]

Jack Whitecross Carnegie, a native of Dundee, emigrated in 1921 on the *Columbia* with his mother and siblings to join his father, who had settled in Patterson, New Jersey. While Jack's father was active in the Scottish Caledonian Club as a football trainer, his Protestant mother, half Irish, 'belonged to a Caledonian club, Daughters of Scotia, and they were, they used to meet every month down at Patterson ... and she liked to do the Irish jig'.[92] As with Jim Comerford and Patrick Peak, both of Irish Catholic descent, Jack's testimony

---

88 Transcript of interview with Dòmhnall Chrut in *ibid*.
89 *Ibid*.
90 Interview with Helen Hansen by Andrew Phillips, recorded 30 August 1989, EIOHP, DP Series 46.
91 Interview with Mary Dunn.
92 Interview with Jack Whitecross Carnegie by Janet Levine, recorded 15 February 1996, EIOHP, EI Series 729.

shows the adoption of Scottish cultural practices by other ethnic groups. As one contemporary put it, 'the Irishman in Scotland, as elsewhere, takes on the colour of his surroundings, and in two or three generations becomes more Scottish than the Scot.'[93] Indeed, for the individuals in this study, the religious fracture in Scotland failed to make any difference concerning a sense of Scottishness.

Unlike the dearth of discussion in testimonies about Irish societies throughout the British World, more evidence emanates from Irish migrants in the United States concerning their participation in ethnic societies. Unlike Scottish societies, however, these tend to be less focused on local origins, though by 1930 there were societies representing all Irish counties in New York.[94] Bridget Jones of Castlefrench, County Galway, left home as a 19-year-old in 1923. As well as attending the local Catholic church and Rosary society, Bridget also claimed to frequent an Irish musicians' club in Brooklyn in which music, dancing, and drinking brought migrants together. She also stated that there was no political activity in the clubs she frequented.[95] Another who left Ireland that same year and who stressed her regular attendance at a number of Irish cultural events was Johanna Flaherty of Castlewest, County Limerick. She attended 'anything Irish' including feishes and concerts, as well as being a participant in Irish step dancing.[96] Bridget McNulty, another emigrant from 1923, left Cashel in County Tipperary and remembered that in New York, 'we went to dances, not too many. The dances in Ireland last all night long, it's not like here. They last all night … Oh yes, everybody, you at the dance were from Ireland. And you meet a lot of nice friends.'[97] Anne Craven, who had left Kings County in 1925 at 18 years of age certainly claimed to have attended many Irish dances, which she stressed counteracted feelings of loneliness and homesickness.[98]

Some Irish migrants, such as Michael Jordan from Limerick who left in 1924, claimed not to have had much contact initially with fellow expatriates 'until we start reading the papers we see where there's entertainment and we usually went to Irish dance halls that's where we made our acquaintance with

93 'Scotland for the Scottish Race', *Scotsman*, 22 May 1923, p. 11, online at http://archive.scotsman.com (accessed February 2006).

94 John T. Ridge, 'Irish county societies in New York, 1880–1914', in Bayor and Meagher (eds.), *The New York Irish*, p. 300.

95 Interview with Bridget Jones by Margo Nash, recorded 15 November 1974, EIOHP, NPS Series 78.

96 Interview with Johanna Flaherty by Debra Allee, recorded 29 May 1986, EIOHP, AKRF Series, 182.

97 Interview with Brigid McNulty by Janet Levine, recorded 24 November 1998, EIOHP, EI Series 1029.

98 Interview with Anne Craven by Paul Sigrist, recorded 2 October 1991, EIOHP, EI Series 102.

17 Queensland Irish Association Float, c.1935

Irish people'. He continued by emphasising the importance of cultural and sporting events:

Well I went with this friend of mine and was in the Army. I met his sister on the ship. I got in touch with him I said, 'We'll go to a dance, Irish dance', so we used to go. We were just looking and dancing. We were too crude to start but eventually we got into it and we went into the different dance halls and we met the girls there and that's how we usually get married, you know, your own people ... At that time they were doing something very much similar to the dancing in Ireland in those days jigs and reels and hornpipes that was the main dances at them times. We went to the park, there was a sports park in Long Island, Long Island City, near Long Island, yes, Long Island City Gaelic Park. They had sportsmen there and meetings there and every Sunday there was games there so we went there and they had a big platform where they would dance before or sing before the games would start so what they had these fiddlers and accordion players and they all played, they came there, but they used to, we used to pay them because you'd ask a girl to dance, you'd pay maybe 25 cents.[99]

One of the most extensive commentators on the activities of the Irish in New York was John Joe Gallogly who left Ballinamore, County Leitrim, in the early 1950s, 'the lost decade'. This period of intensified emigration from

99 Interview with Michael Jordan by Paul Sigrist.

Ireland in the twentieth century has contributed to the term 'vanishing Irish'. It is difficult to determine from personal testimony alone, however, if this was a period in which a vibrant associational culture existed.[100] Gallogly's testimony certainly points to concentrated pockets of Irish migrants in various areas of the eastern United States. He described 'going to visit Irish people in New York ... and we would pick up some people and we would go from New York to the Catskills Mountains, Upper New York State. They call it the Irish Alps. There were more Irish people up in East Durham, New York, than I ever knew in Ireland and I played football, I played Irish football'.

Extending his recollection, Gallogly revealed the participation of these Irish newcomers in work and church:

There was probably 300 Irish people. I know a lot of Irish girls and men who had come out in the late 40s and 50s coz I came in '52 see and those were the years when there was a lot of emigration because of hard times in Ireland, you know, and we helped each other because we worked together and some of them were in the contracting business or had little businesses going so we would work for them, you know, and we always, we were always making extra money. We were hustling, you know. It was a good community and, of course, we always went to church also. We were good church supporters.

In a further comment he discussed the ethnic rivalries that existed between the Irish and British clubs and the attacks on symbolic identifiers of Britishness:

The Irish community in Providence was great. They had their own club there, an Irish club, and it was right beside the British Club and some of the Irish men after they would have a few drinks they would want to go down to the British Club and pull down the Union Jack [*chuckles*] and put up an Irish flag [*laughs*] so we got thrown out of there a few times. A couple of times we got put in the paddy wagon but we never caused any problem, we never caused any problem or broke anything. So I never forget one night the cops picked us up and they put us in the back of the paddy wagon and they took us around the corner and gave us a lecture because most of them were Irish and they said 'Get out of here and don't go back there again' [*laughs*].[101]

Quite apart from establishing the extent of such societies abroad, these testimonies demonstrate that Irish and Scottish national societies were

100 Work on the Irish in 1950s New York suggests that there was a strong cultural element at this time. See Linda Dowling Almeida, 'A great time to be in America: the Irish in post-Second World War New York City', in Dermot Keogh, Finbarr O'Shea, and Carmel Quinlan (eds), *The Lost Decade: Ireland in the 1950s* (Cork: Mercier Press, 2004), p. 214.

101 Interview with John Joe Gallogly, by Janet Levine, recorded 6 March 2001, EIOHP, EI Series 1194.

predominantly recreational, rather than political in function. These societies also became increasingly important after initial settlement. By providing newcomers with opportunities to meet, Scottish and Irish societies played an important social function in migrant adjustment abroad.

Conclusion

This chapter reveals that personal testimonies allow important insight into the way ordinary migrants constituted and articulated their networks. For migrants, personal ethnic networks served significant practical purposes in their migration and settlement patterns, directing them to certain destinations, providing assistance with housing and work, and access to social events. It was these functions, rather than the influence of ethnic networks on social and economic mobility, that were more readily expressed in the testimony. In facilitating newcomers, there was little difference between Irish and Scottish migrants in all destinations concerning the ways in which they encouraged family and friends to join them, and provided vital assistance upon arrival. These informal personal networks were primarily composed of family and friends known to newcomers, though in some cases the origins of such ties stretched back to earlier generations. The chapter therefore highlights the essential role of a broadly defined family network in the process of migration and initial settlement. Yet these connections were most critical prior to and immediately after arrival, whereas ethnic societies became increasingly important after their initial settlement.[102] By providing newcomers with opportunities to meet, societies played an important social function in migrant adjustment abroad.

Where differences exist, however, is in relation to their attachment to a local identity exhibited through acquaintances and societies. The absence of such issues for Irish migrants is most probably the result of the source materials utilised. These issues appear, for instance, most dominantly in the written word of Scottish migrants, a source which has remained undiscovered and untapped for Irish migrants. Of course, we need to bear in mind the climate in which these declarations arose and this chapter has been valuable in this respect by revealing the range of Scottish local identities that emerged not solely from direct questioning in interviews about identities, but also in unmediated contemporary communications. Of course, these written materials likewise need to be treated with caution, for migrants could be emphasising their identities for advantageous reasons, but nevertheless they still reveal that such local ties mattered for migrants.

102 See Angela McCarthy, 'Ethnic networks and identities among interwar Scottish migrants in North America', in McCarthy (ed.), *A Global Clan*, pp. 203–26.

A further difference relates to the destinations in which migrants settled, particularly in connection with the Scots. Indeed, for Scots in North America it is the frequent reference to Scottish societies which stands out when compared with stories of their associates settling elsewhere. Accounting for this might be the timing of their arrival. Whereas testimony for the Scots arriving in the United States is centred on the inter-war period, existing testimonies from their compatriots in Australasia arose mainly from those voyaging after the Second World War. Another factor is the nature of their settlement abroad. While these Scottish migrants in the United States tended to settle in populated urban areas, Scots in Australia were more likely to have a geographical scattering in suburban areas, a feature which Jim Hammerton insists 'inclined against ethnic concentration; such dispersal was not congenial to the fostering of cultural nationalism'.[103]

In examining the articulation of network ties this chapter has blended exterior/institutional and interior/personal worlds. In doing so it reveals the self-profession of tight local connections. Irish and Scots conceptualised their affiliations in practical terms as both societies and expatriate ties to certain localities ensured that migrants could benefit socially and materially from these connections. The perpetuation and maintenance of these distinctive ethnic ties performed a central role in the expression of a cultural identity. While migrants did not always hold an overarching sense of national identity, many did, and as we will see in the following chapter a general sense of Irishness and Scottishness could coexist with more intimate bonds.

103 A. James Hammerton, '"We're not Poms": the shifting identities of post-war Scottish migrants to Australia', in *ibid.*, p. 229.

8

'Jigs and reels and hornpipes': identity, culture, and belonging

Jim Comerford was born on 9 September 1913 at Glencraig, Fifeshire. His mother was also born in Fifeshire while his father was born at Blantyre, Lanarkshire, the son of a migrant from County Waterford, Ireland. In 1921 Jim's father, a miner, moved to Australia and was followed the next year by the remainder of the family. Jim Comerford recorded his recollections at Newcastle, Australia, in May 1987 when he was 73 years old.[1]

Jim Comerford: The trip out here was fascinating … And of course for the first time in my brief life I was meeting people who weren't Scots. English, Welsh, plenty of other Scots and some Australians and to my mother's disgust I was speaking Australian before I got off the ship instead of Scots doric.
Marjorie Biggins: What's Scots doric?
Jim Comerford: That's the Scots idiom which I'm sorry I ever gave away. It's a beautiful way of speaking.
…
Marjorie Biggins: What sort of pattern of eating did she bring with her from Scotland?
Jim Comerford: Big meals, big miner's meals. There'd be meat and vegetables, not grills but plenty of Scottish soups, stews, lashings of vegetables mainly grown by my father. He was a terrific gardener too. Always a sweet, pudding as it was called by the Scots.
…
Marjorie Biggins: Did you truly have a Highland stag?
Jim Comerford: Oh, my word we did. There had to be something Scottish in the house. There was the kitchen with its open fireplace, settee, table, chairs, and more pictures on the wall of Ben Lomond, Loch Lomond …

I've often heard both my parents speak about the Australian kids as being spoilt by their parents, answering back, giving cheek and so on. Well, if that was true my brother and I certainly were not Australianised. It wasn't as though we were kept under the thumb. We could read what we liked. We were permitted to go to any moving pictures that we liked but we were pretty strictly controlled.
Marjorie Biggins: What about by your father?
Jim Comerford: Less by him than by my mother. My mother was the head of the

1 Interview with Jim Comerford by Marjorie Biggins, recorded 15 May 1987, in OHC NLA, NSW Bicentennial Oral History Project, Oral TRC 2301/54.

household in every way. My father went to work. He provided for us. He mixed with his chums as he called them. Made his three nights a week trips to the local library, attended these miners meetings. Took part in the only one thing I can remember. He was one of the foundation committee members of the Kurri Kurri Pipe Band but he kept to himself and while he would discipline us if the occasion required most of our upbringing was left to my mother.

Marjorie Biggins: Well, let's look at everybody's leisure. Your father's leisure some of the things you've said. He played the pipes.

Jim Comerford: No he didn't. He played the accordion beautifully. So did mother. But no he didn't play the pipes but a crowd of Scots people got together and decided the place wasn't a place without a pipe band and decided to set the pipe band up and father was on the committee of it which in retrospect surprises me that he even went that far.

Marjorie Biggins: Because he was so shy?

Jim Comerford: Yes.

…

Marjorie Biggins: What sort of religion was the family?

Jim Comerford: There was no religion. … Not anti-religious in the pagan sense but anti-religious out of reasoning but I suppose a lot of religious families would have no better moral standards than existed in our home. Mother came from a strong religious background, the Kirk of Scotland, and my father came from very strong Catholic background. Might be one of the reasons he came out here. My paternal grandmother, she had shelves all round her kitchen and they were all bloody bottles of River Jordan water and then you couldn't poke a stick at. Anybody wanted two bob would arrive at her door with a bottle of water from the Jordan and she's so intensely Catholic that, well that's the kind of thing that she went in for. My grandfather had abandoned religion but he was very tolerant about his wife's and grandmother's strong affinity with it. During the 1929/30 coal lockout there were relief soup kitchens for the school kids of the miners involved and my father was a helper and he took the food down to the Catholic school at Kurri one day and one of the nuns said, 'Comerford, that's a very Irish name.' And he told her yes, that his father had been Irish and she wanted to know if he was a Catholic. He said, 'Well, he had been.' And she said, 'Well, why aren't you a Catholic now?' 'Well, I've read my way out of it.' And she didn't argue with him, she just said, 'Well, a lot of people have read their way into it too.' And that summarised it. Very intense reader. He'd read his way out of the church. But he used to get angry. Now there a load of cheap talk. There was a book out, *The Confessions of Morai Monk.* It was allegedly the confessions of a Catholic nun all about the sex orgies and that used to get him angry because you know he branded that sensationalism and that was a slur on women that he had a terrific amount of respect for although he didn't believe in their religious practice.

Marjorie Biggins: Were you aware that there was much conflict in the twenties in Kurri between Catholics and Protestants?

Jim Comerford: No, there wasn't out here. There had been in Scotland. The Catholic school was opposite our public school in Scotland and very often by mutual consent we'd meet in the road and get stuck into each other and that was so bloody stupid. You see the Irish troubles were on while I lived over there and that split Scotland right down the middle. And I've heard father and mother and the Johnsons, Johnny Conway, and others that used to come to our house talk about an incident in Lochore that two Black and Tans came back after they were demobilised, turned up to resume their work at the local mines, and the miners held them head first down the shaft by the ankles and told them that if ever they came back they'd let go the next time. And that was repeated on the pit top at Richmond Main one morning in 1928 and all the kids together and this commotion started before the whistle blew and of course you rushed to the middle of it to see what was going on, a big crowd of men shouting and this Scots bloke, Jock Martin, he was killed in Richmond Main later on. This fellow had just come out the first day, a new starter, down on the ground throttling him and they pulled him off of course but it was going to be murder and it turned out this bloke was a Black and Tan and Jock recognised him because Jock had been in the British Army in Ireland and one of those at mutiny that wouldn't do the dirty job and Jock recognised this bloke as a Black and Tan. That bloke never started at Richmond Main. He was driven off the pit top.

Marjorie Biggins: Even in Australia it followed him?

Jim Comerford: Yes. If that reflected religious antagonisms, which I don't think it did, but that was the nearest ever I saw to the Catholics, the Protestants, and the non-religious who got on. It would have been a breach of the friendliness and their egalitarianism in the town for anybody to discriminate on those grounds.

...

Marjorie Biggins: Did you like school?

Jim Comerford: I didn't like it in Scotland but I liked it out here because it was more relaxed. The discipline in Scotland was fierce and I'm a left-winger, left-handed, and I was forced to write with my right. You'd pick up a pencil in the class in Scotland and the teacher would give a signal to the rest of the class and they'd all jump to their feet and scream out 'cawrie-hand, cawrie-hand'. They don't do that now. If you're left-handed they leave you alone. They didn't in my day and at home the same thing. You know, did anything with your left-hand you'd be upgraded by your parents about it. Out here the teachers, my impression of the teachers in Scotland always regarded it as a social class apart from the families of the kids that they taught. Out here they drank with the blokes, they mixed with the blokes. The female teachers were friendly. You know they'd pat your head and encourage you. It wasn't like that in Scotland. I liked school very much out here. I didn't like it in the old country.

...

Marjorie Biggins: And what about discipline? How did teachers keep you disciplined?

Jim Comerford: Here?

Marjorie Biggins: Yes.

Jim Comerford: They didn't seem to have any great problem. In Scotland the strap, something like a cat-of-nine tails, kept you in line. Out here it was the cane and occasionally once or twice a day somebody would get the cuts as they called it but here was more of a camaraderie between the teachers and the pupils out here than I can remember in the old country.

...

Marjorie Biggins: I get the impression from talking to you that your family transported itself holus bolus with its values and ideas and attitudes very much intact. Were you affected very much by the Australians round you? Did it change you?

Jim Comerford: Yes, I was. Coming out on the ship there were a number of Australian children and, unfortunately, I think now I was speaking Australian when I got off the ship at Sydney. I dropped the Scots idiom and I now regard it as one of the most beautiful ways of speaking in the world. You listen to a Scot on radio, TV, they're as clear as a bell. I was affected and I tried to sloth off the accusation of being a Pommy which was firmly flung about in those days.

Jim Comerford was one of 494,733 Scots who moved beyond Europe in the 1920s, almost 100,000 of whom chose to journey to Australasia.[2] His proclamation of his Scottish identity in order to set himself apart from English migrants, presumably in the interest of social advancement, reveals that Scottishness was conceptualised in a largely positive vein by both Scots and the wider Australian public. Facilitating these expressions were the Scottish societies, as covered in the last chapter. Discussion of associational activities included substantial commentary on dancing with subsidiary reference to kilts, pipes, and the commemoration of Scottish heroes. It is these symbolic emblems of expatriate ethnicity, among other cultural aspects, that are examined in this chapter. As a commentator on associational culture has remarked, ethnic societies were established not solely for companionship but also for the expression of a collective identity, 'heightened not only by contrast to those of the native population but also by contrast to those of other newcomers'.[3]

Such public manifestations of identity can, however, be slippery and while this chapter incorporates these visible factors, it also focuses on everyday

2 Marjory Harper, *Emigration from Scotland Between the Wars: Opportunity or Exile?* (Manchester: Manchester University Press, 1998), p. 7. Between 1919 and 1938 197,325 Scots went to Canada and 178,378 chose the United States.

3 Jose C. Moya, 'Immigrants and associations: a global and historical perspective', *Journal of Ethnic and Migration Studies*, 31:5 (2005), p. 839. See also Marlou Schrover and Floris Vermeulen, 'Immigrant organisations', pp. 823–32, in the same journal.

conceptualisations of ethnic and national identity, aspects often neglected when focusing purely on festivals.[4] This is an important point, for too frequently scholars seek out visible, cultural, and group identities rather than explore the thoughts and feelings of the individuals involved in the process of migration. This chapter therefore examines issues relating to language, accent, and cultural traditions. The chapter also touches briefly on the issue of dual national attachments and considers if broad ethnic identities differed according to the divergent societies migrants found themselves in.

Language

According to Charles F. Keyes, migrants 'validate their claim to shared descent by pointing to cultural attributes which they believe they hold in common'.[5] Language is one component of this and further illuminates the importance of local connections for Scottish migrants, for in several cases Scottish migrants linked local origins with an ability to converse in Scots. Writing from the ship *Remuera*, Mary Gibson of Bannockburn, north of Falkirk, Stirlingshire, took extreme delight in puzzling her fellow passengers by speaking Scots. Indeed, the novelty of aspects of Scottish culture for other ethnicities seems to have prompted some Scots to powerfully emphasise this particular element of their national identity:

I like a talk with Mrs Connell & a Mrs McRae. They come from Glasgow & theres a Miss Murray an elderly lady from Edinburgh. So they all understand me alright. An Australian likes to torment me because he doesn't know what I say in Scotch, so I just give them all the more Scotch. The German Jew couldn't see how I knew English & yet was Scotch. I think he got mixed up because the English don't understand Scotch & yet I understand them in English.[6]

Mary also noted that one of the engineers was from Glasgow and revealed, 'I like to meet him as they get a good laugh at him & I speaking Scotch.'[7] Mary Gibson's account exposes the divides in Scottish society, in that her compatriots on board, being from districts close to her origins and familiar with the Scots she spoke, could understand her. Moreover, the transition to the New World by ship, undertaken with other ethnic groups, clearly provoked an awareness of being different. Language in Mary's account served to provoke curiosity rather than disgruntlement by others who might otherwise have felt excluded by being unable to understand her.

4 Herbert J. Gans, 'Comment: ethnic invention and acculturation, a bumpy-line approach', *Journal of American Ethnic History*, 12:1 (1992), p. 46.
5 Charles F. Keyes, 'Towards a new formulation of the concept of ethnic group', *Ethnicity*, 3:3 (1976), p. 208.
6 Shipboard journal of Mary Gibson, 1938, kindly provided by May Tapp. Extract dated 24 May 1938.
7 *Ibid.*, 30 April 1938.

Lorna Carter also discussed language in connection with other Scottish migrants whom she met in New Zealand. In April 1953 she wrote home to Oban telling how: 'I met a wee Scotsman frae Edinburgh here. He is a retired school master and is having a trip. He wouldna gi' bonny Scotland for any of this lot. Mrs McLennan was listening to him and couldn't make out half of what he was saying. He has a wee croft in Brora where he goes for the fishing and he'll be up there in June. He sails for home on the 18th.'[8] Analysis of the testimony of Scottish migrants, such as Lorna Carter, illuminates their identity in connection with language and accent.[9] Although Lorna could not speak or write Scots to any great extent, her letters contain snippets of Scots and Gaelic. Among the Scots phrases she uses are a 'rare day', a 'dreep on my nose', and 'blether'.[10] When writing of an acquaintance she 'called him a big ploch to myself' while another associate she considered a 'bit gorach on her feet'.[11] In addition, Lorna attempted some Lancashire terminology mixed in with Scots when she described a young boy as 'a reet ee ba goomer lad!! daft on fitba!'.[12] Other adults, such as Annabella Sinclair, who voyaged from Onzie-bust to Australia in 1929, displayed traces of the Scots language by utilising words such as 'bairn', while also highlighting the use of the Scots idiom in their phraseology.[13]

Most commentators, on the other hand, have focused upon the Gaelic language and customs as being a prime manifestation of a Scottish identity at home and abroad. This is surprising given that Gaelic was in sharp decline from the eighteenth century onwards.[14] The testimony unearthed for twen-tieth-century migrants, however, reveals that many identified with the Scots language. Again, this has profound implications for prior research into the Scots abroad for, as already noted, most commentators have stressed the Gaelic language as symbolising a sense of Scottish identity overseas. Only

8 Lorna Carter (Wellington) to her parents (Oban), 10 April 1953.
9 For discussion of other Scottish migrants' link to language and accent see Angela McCarthy, 'National identities and twentieth-century Scottish migrants in England', in William L. Miller (ed.), *Anglo-Scottish Relations From 1900 to Devolution and Beyond* (Oxford: Oxford University Press, 2005, Proceedings of the British Academy 128), pp. 171–82 and Angela McCarthy, 'Scottish national identities among inter-war migrants in North America and Australasia', *Journal of Imperial and Commonwealth History*, 34:2 (2006), pp. 201–22.
10 Lorna Carter (Wellington) to her parents (Oban), 25 December 1951, 23 May 1953. These phrases mean a great day, a drip, and a gossip.
11 *Ibid.*, 1 April 1953, 10 April 1953. 'Ploc' means lump in Gaelic while 'gòrach' means daft or stupid.
12 *Ibid.*, 7 April 1952. 'Fitba' is Scots for football.
13 Shipboard journal of Annabella Sinclair, 1929, in OA, D1/118.
14 See Charles W. J. Withers, *Urban Highlanders: Highland-Lowland Migration and Urban Gaelic Culture, 1700–1900* (East Linton: Tuckwell Press, 1998), especially pp. 200–7.

the testimony of Lewis migrants, however, reveals the importance of the Gaelic language for Scottish migrants. Donald 'Tulag' MacLeod recalled how when he lived in Scotland he spoke to Stornoway people in Gaelic only to be answered in English. In the United States, however, he would speak to them in English only to be answered in Gaelic. When querying this anomaly he was told, 'I never appreciated my native language till I left home!'[15]

In part, the neglect of scholars to consider the Scots language among migrants is not simply the result of a focus on Gaelic, but also a reflection of the disregard the Scots language has received in Scotland. At least four factors have contributed to this situation. First, after the 1707 Union Scots as a language was reclassified as a 'provincial dialect'. Second, from the 1840s onwards English became more widely used as a consequence of the state inspection of schools and insistence on the use of English. Third, there was no standardised Scots. This, together with the mass migration of Highland and Irish populations to the Central Belt which formed a melting pot of the Scots, Gaelic, and English languages, made the five Scots dialects vulnerable to corruption.[16] Fourth, Scots was never considered an appropriate medium for the mass media, thereby leading to the further dominance of English.[17] That Scots, like Irish Gaelic, was not a very useful means of communication in the wider world also played a part. Clearly, these factors would have far-reaching consequences for Scots-speaking migrants. By the 1920s, however, a literary resurgence led by Hugh MacDiarmid helped revitalise the use of written Scots in Scotland.

That much of the testimony emerges from Lowland Scots is intriguing given that most historians typically highlight language as a reflection of Scottish identity in connection with the Highland use of Gaelic. Such an approach, though, woefully neglects the way in which language, idiom, and brogue were ethnic identifiers for Lowlanders. This finding indicates that scholars should revisit the worlds of nineteenth-century Scottish Lowland migrants to ascertain if they emphasised the Scots language or idiom the way that Highlanders stressed Gaelic. This should be undertaken not just for Canada but for all migrant destinations. If, on the other hand, Lowland migrants only drew

15 Transcript of interview with Donald Tulag MacLeod, in Jim Wilkie, *Metagama: A Journey from Lewis to the New World* (Edinburgh: Birlinn, 1987 and 2001), p. 101.

16 The five Scots dialects are Insular (Orkney and Shetland), Northern (northeast, Caithness, Angus, and Mearns), Southern (most of the borders region), Central (Glasgow, Stirling, Perth, and Edinburgh), and Ulster (Antrim, Donegal, and Down). I am grateful to Dauvit Horsbroch for this information.

17 I am grateful to Dauvit Horsbroch for discussing this with me. See, for example, his article, 'The Scots language: an historical and political assessment', in Ignacy Ryszard Danka and Piotr Stalmaszczyk (eds), *Studia Indogermanica Lodziensia IV. Language Contact in the Celtic World* (Łódź, 2002), especially pp. 31–2.

attention to the Scottish language and idiom in the twentieth century, scholars must ascertain why this was so.

Migrants from Ireland, by contrast, did not discuss the Irish language in relation to local origins as did Scots. The relative absence of written testimony from Irish migrants and the failure of Irish interviewees to discuss whether or not they spoke Gaelic in their new homelands might imply that Gaelic meant little to them. Oral testimony, however, underscores that some migrants, even if they failed to speak Gaelic abroad, were raised in households in which both Gaelic and English were spoken. For Irish migrants, there was little to distinguish their language affiliation in the way that Scots were divided by Gaelic and the various dialects of Scots.

Michael Jordan, who grew up in Limerick city, recalled that his 'grandmother carried a lot of the Gaelic. She didn't speak the Gaelic language but she carried a lot of the Gaelic words which she used instead of English at some times but we had no problem with the English, neither, not my grandmother or my mother.' Michael's knowledge was limited as Gaelic was only taught 'one hour a day a week in our schools'.[18] Della Gleckel from Tuam, County Galway, also indicated, 'My grandparents spoke Gaelic and I can say a few words in Gaelic, I still understand a few.'[19] Catherine English also learned Gaelic at Bellavary, County Mayo, from her grandmother who 'spoke Gaelic and she spoke English but from her we learned our Gaelic. She spoke always in Gaelic not that we could answer back but we knew what she was saying. I don't know why but we knew what she was saying.'[20] Joseph Brady in Claddy, County Armagh, meanwhile, recounted saying 'my prayers in Gaelic and a little conversation but that's, that's all'. Although he claimed not to be able to conduct a conversation in Gaelic at the time of his interview, he believed he would still understand something of what was being said.[21]

Julia Carmody, on the other hand, was raised speaking Gaelic at Toormakeady, County Mayo. She asserted that when she emigrated in 1921 at 18 years of age, 'I couldn't talk English when I first come out here.' Although she claimed not to know Gaelic at the time of her interview, she did stress that she could recall 'only the dirty words [*laughs*]'.[22] Certainly there was a

18 Interview with Michael Jordan by Paul Sigrist, recorded 19 October 1993, EIOHP, EI Series 397.
19 Interview with Della Gleckel by Paul Sigrist, recorded 2 May 1995, EIOHP, EI Series 611.
20 Interview with Catherine English by Paul Sigrist, recorded 19 September 1991, EIOHP, EI Series 91.
21 Interview with Joseph Brady by Paul Sigrist recorded 25 September 1995, EIOHP, EI Series 673.
22 Interview with Julia Carmody by Paul Sigrist, recorded 18 July 1996, EIOHP, EI Series 767.

strong element of the Irish population that spoke Gaelic in earlier periods, and more work should be undertaken to assess the early to mid-twentieth-century situation.[23] Stephen Concannon of Spiddal parish in County Galway likewise spoke Gaelic, 'that's all I spoke'. He continued:

going to school at that time it was half Irish and half English, you know, but we didn't have that difficulty for example when we came like the Italians or other people. Was much harder for them that never heard a word of English that came to this country. We going to school you learned, you know, you had half English and half Irish and anyone, when anybody would go to town or Galway with selling merchandise or anything like that you'd have to speak English because in the town of Galway it's all English they could speak. It's a funny thing, for example, in my time you go back about six miles behind Galway all they spoke was Gaelic but in the town of Galway itself it was all English so you know the Irish language got pretty well eliminated. They're trying to promote it, the Government has spent millions of dollars trying to promote it.[24]

That Irish became a compulsory subject is likewise reflected in the testimony of John Lynn, who left Crossmolina, County Mayo, in 1951 at 25 years of age. He not only commented on contemporary linguistic efforts, but also on Irish being banned in earlier centuries 'because Ireland was under English rule for hundreds of years'. He indicated that his mother 'got the Gaelic from her father and then it was handed down, you know'. John Lynn also referred to Gaelic being taught at hedge schools, 'those schools that they used to out there was no roof or nothing out by a hedge you could call it a hedge row'. He joked that perhaps Gaelic was banned because 'maybe they were trying to make us all English [*laughs*]'.[25]

For Irish migrants, then, language issues were tied in to collective memories of their heritage. As with their Scottish counterparts, however, it was the oral rather than written aspects of their language which they emphasised. The reduced opportunities to converse abroad, combined with the importance of English in everyday life, presumably contributed to the declining use of Scots and Gaelic among migrants. More work, however, needs to be undertaken to support this finding. We might query too whether such usage also disappeared among the migrant and descent groups because these languages were not being written and read on a constant basis.

23 There were between 70,000 and 80,000 Irish speakers in New York in the mid to late 1800s. See Kenneth E. Nilsen, 'The Irish language in New York, 1850–1900', in Ronald H. Bayor and Timothy J. Meagher (eds), *The New York Irish* (Baltimore and London: Johns Hopkins University Press, 1996), p. 274.
24 Interview with Stephen Concannon by Janet Levine, recorded 16 September 1992, EIOHP, EI Series 212.
25 Interview with John Lynn by Janet Levine, recorded 31 July 1994, EIOHP, EI Series 510.

Accent and hostility

Apart from speaking their national languages, migrants were also distinguished by their accent and construction of the English language, aspects that are prominent in oral testimonies. Rarely, however, is accent discussed in terms of their local origins. Rather, accent is incorporated into overarching conceptualisations of Irishness or Scottishness. In some cases an accent resulted in a hostile reception. According to Kathleen Lamberti of Brackney, County Down, who arrived in New York, 'I wanted to get into the telephone company but they wouldn't take me because of my Irish accent.'[26] Harold Armstrong, who moved to New Zealand from Selkirk, in 1963, also encountered opposition due to his accent, but he met the challenge head-on:

The fact that I personally had a strong Scottish accent and my wife a liberal Northumbrian droll [*drawl*] combined with her original London accent was most confusing for the local residents many never having met overseas people until then. Like all Scots I was annoy[*ed*] to be refer[*r*]ed to as a 'Bloody Pom' and eventually discovered it was better to give the New Zealanders a dose of their own medicine and refer to them as Aussies, the more 'chucking off' one could give and take the better you were accepted.

His eldest child, however, fared less well and 'was mocked when she started school because of her slight Scottish accent'.[27] This linkage between accent, identity, and hostility is also apparent from the testimony of Scots who arrived as youngsters in the United States. Allan Gunn's discussion of his Scottish accent emerged when asked if he had encountered any prejudice. Having left Glasgow in 1925 he recalled, 'What was amazing to us, a lot of people would ask us how come you speak English so well being from Scotland, you know, and we'd kind of look at them and what are we supposed to speak, you know, and even in school they would bring that up, how come you speak English so well being over here such a short time.'[28]

The majority of recollections, however, show that the 'brogue' of young Scots marked them as different in a negative way and that the external pressure they encountered resulted in their speech being modified. Many recalled being mercilessly teased because of the way they spoke English. Their interior identity was therefore under attack from the pressures of school life which sought conformity. Mary Kendrick, for instance, a native of Auchinleck, south of Glasgow, went to the United States in 1927. Aged just seven, she later revealed that she and her brother 'spoke with a decided Scottish brogue and

26 Interview with Kathleen Lamberti by Paul Sigrist, recorded 25 February 1994, EIOHP, EI Series 439.
27 Harold Armstrong, BAIQ 007.
28 Interview with Allan Gunn by Paul Sigrist, recorded 20 June 1992, EIOHP, EI Series 179.

18 Staff and Scottish children at the Presbyterian Boys' and Girls' Home, Berhamphore, Wellington, 1940

the kids would make fun of us'.[29] Lillian Hopkins from Glasgow confirmed this predicament. She arrived in Pittsburgh at nine years of age. At school her classmates 'made fun of me because we were Scotch … wasn't very long till I got rid of that brogue so they wouldn't know'.[30] Scottish boys were susceptible to similar suffering. Patrick Peak of Glasgow was also nine years of age when he left in 1921 on the *Cameronia*. He went to a Catholic school in New Bedford and recalled the hostility he encountered: 'I had an awful school life in this country because anyone that comes over here a foreigner or with a foreign brogue, especially a Scots brogue, he gets picked on every time he turns around. I think I got into more fights over there than I ever did with the kids over in the old country.'[31]

Irish children in the dominions also encountered this hostility. Trudie Lloyd remembered hating school because she and her siblings were teased 'about our clothes and the way we spoke'. Her brother was also distinguished

29 Interview with Mary Kendrick by Paul Sigrist, recorded 7 July 1994, EIOHP, EI Series 492.
30 Interview with Lillian Hopkins by Kate Moore, recorded 18 July 1994, EIOHP, KM Series 70.
31 Interview with Patrick Peak by Nancy Dallet, recorded 15 November 1985, EIOHP, AKRF Series 84.

by wearing long pants, while the local children wore short pants.[32] In part, this adverse reception may explain the assimilation of young Irish and Scots into their host societies. Vulnerable to being audibly and visibly identified as different, they swiftly elected to embrace local speaking and dress habits.

The testimony of twentieth-century migrants, then, suggests that some Scots-speaking individuals were keen to nourish their language, at times choosing to exaggerate or powerfully assert its usage. Yet it is also apparent from migrant accounts that at times their language was suppressed or modified in public. Both approaches presumably had similar functions: to ease their integration. In other words, Irish and Scots could either emphasise their way of speaking to differentiate themselves from other ethnic groups when this would promote acceptance among the wider population (for example, for Scots to distinguish themselves from English migrants in Australia); or they could play down their language and accent so as not to be differentiated from the host society (for example, at school). Such testimony reflects the internal dynamic of language, that migrants choose to speak it when they wish. Such authenticity was a seemingly powerful mechanism for maintaining identity in the private sphere, but not in such a way that it marked Scots and Irish as outwardly different.

It is clear from some testimony, however, that accents among the descent group continued. A particularly intriguing episode in relation to the Scottish accent discussed in Lorna Carters's letters related to her encounter with a second-generation Scot. The incident is illuminating for it indicates the sense of Scottishness permeating later generations and the degree to which they were often perceived as more Scottish than the Scots-born, suggesting an urgent need to study the experiences of the multigenerational ethnic group:

I forgot to tell you the funny part of my recording. A wee old man came in with cakes for the boys' afternoon tea and just as the Road to the Isles was being cut I could see his foot going and he was thoroughly enjoying himself. He turned and asked me if any of these records were sent to England – he didn't know I'd made it – and I said what would I send them to England for – seeing as 'ow Scotland was <u>the</u> place. He turns & says 'You're not Scottish'!! He spoke with an east coast accent – and I said 'I am too' so out he comes with the priceless remark 'Whit have ye done we y're accent then!?' Well I nearly died and laughed even more when the man doing the record said that the old boy was born in Dunedin & had never been out of N.Z.!! His folks came from Fife and here he was complete with accent.[33]

32 Interview with Trudie Lloyd by Judith Fyfe, recorded 20 April 1990, in ATL OHC, Women's Division Federated Farmers of NZ (Inc) Oral History Project, OHC-0115.
33 Lorna Carter (Wellington) to her parents (Oban), 3 November 1953.

Cultural traditions and stereotypes

Exploring the identifications of the multigenerational descent group is an area of manifest neglect within studies of Irish and Scottish migration. Herbert J. Gans, however, has suggested that with a decline in the functions of ethnicity, the third generation adopts a symbolic ethnicity, defined as 'a love for and a pride in a tradition that can be felt without having to be incorporated in everyday behavior'.[34] Such symbols, Gans asserts, are visible, and for Irish and Scots kilts, tartan, pipes, shamrocks, and shillelaghs are examples of this symbolic ethnicity. Yet a symbolic ethnicity could also be a blend of both public and private expressions of ethnic identities, and was not simply the preserve of later generations. The difficulty is that in contrast with their extensive reflections on language and societies, few Scots or Irish spoke or wrote at length about the maintenance their customs abroad. Yet some glimpses can be obtained. Scottish dancing, for instance, was a major medium for expressing a sense of Scottishness. Blending stories, accent, and dancing was Agnes Schilling from Motherwell. She had emigrated in 1922 as a 15-year-old and worked as a cook for the Quigley family. When Agnes was 86 years of age she brought to mind those early years in the United States:

Michael Quigley, he liked my Scottish brogue, he loved my Scottish brogue, and once in a while he would ask me about my father and I would tell him and tell him a funny story that my father told me. When he had company and sometimes he'd have the Mayor of the town and everything, he would come in the kitchen and say, 'Agnes, would you mind coming in here and telling Mayor so-and-so the story your father told you' and I would tell him the story and they would all be laughing and I guess I had such a brogue and then I used to do the Highland fling for them and dance for them, you know, so they were very happy times.[35]

A similar proud demonstration of symbolic Scottishness is evident in testimony supplied by Mary Gibson of Bannockburn, Stirling, who sailed to New Zealand in April 1938 on board the vessel *Remuera*. During the voyage Mary kept a diary which she sent to her father John Gibson, a coal miner, upon arrival at Auckland. As she recorded in her journal, 'I was telling them they've never played a Scotch dance yet. I don't think they can play them but we will see if they can do anything like that by the time we go off. Mrs Connell & I were doing patronella, Highland Schottiche etc on our own often to let some of the Ausies & N.Zs see how we dance.'[36] By the 1950s similar displays of Scottishness, embracing external emblems, continued to

---

34 Herbert J. Gans, 'Symbolic ethnicity: the future of ethnic groups and cultures in America', *Ethnic and Racial Studies*, 2:1 (1979), p. 9.
35 Interview with Agnes Schilling by Janet Levine, recorded 16 June 1992, EIOHP, EI Series 172.
36 Shipboard diary of Mary Gibson, 1938. Extract dated 25 May 1938.

be publicly exhibited. According to Lorna Carter, 'The concert opened with 5 men & a woman playing the bagpipes – not even in kilts – the men didn't look so bad, but the female in a pink dress, and puffing and blowing into the bargain, looked decidedly odd.' Then Maori entertainers appeared: 'You'd enjoy the men doing the Haka. They jump about waggle their tongues and it's like a Highland fling gone wrong.'[37]

These institutional, social, and cultural manifestations of Scottishness were also evident elsewhere in the British World, this time Canada. Although the Younger letters indicate that Ernest maintained informal links with Tillicoultry connections in Toronto, there is no mention of his regular attendance at Scottish society events. He did, however, write of his participation in a dance organised by retired affiliates of the Black Watch, the oldest Highland regiment in Canada in 1930: 'We are supposed to be going to another dance with Jack Ross a week from Friday April 4th. It's the Black Watch dance in the Prince George Hotel. I think it is a club formed by ex-members of the Black Watch. There should be lots of Scotch dancing there'.[38] In a later letter he wrote in detail about the night: 'It was a very Scotch dance … They danced eightsome reel, quadrelles, military two step etc & the music was very good. They had five pipers there & they sure skirted. Quite a number of the men were wearing kilts & it was good to see.'[39] Ernest Younger likewise described the commemoration of Robert Burns's birthday by residents of Toronto in January 1930: '"Rabbie's" anniversary has come & gone again, the 25th is always "held" by all the Scottish Societies here.'[40] Ernest Younger also documented a public expression of Scottishness during a return trip to Scotland from Canada in 1929. Writing of a shipmate, Ernest recounted:

A lady rigged him up in one of my rugs (the cheaper one) & he had a little glengarry that someone had given him to take to a friend & with a water bottle under his arm he led the parade round the lounge. He got the prize for the most original costume. He was done up as a billie, & little whisk brush for a sporran & the water bottle was supposed to be bagpipes.[41]

On first reading, this account seems a somewhat spurious rendition of Scottishness. On closer examination, however, it shows a positive, assertive, and novel representation of Scottish identity, presumably for the benefit of other (non-Scottish) travellers. Such popular ethnic stereotypes, rather than cause divi-

---

37 Lorna Carter (Wellington) to her parents (Oban), 2 November 1952.
38 Ernest Younger (Toronto) to his parents (Tillicoultry), 24 March 1930, in NLS, Acc. 9407/3.
39 *Ibid.*, 8 April 1930, in NLS, Acc. 9407/3.
40 *Ibid.*, 27 January 1930, in NLS, Acc. 9407/3.
41 Ernest Younger (*Athenia*) to his parents (Tillicoultry), 5 October 1929, in NLS, Acc. 9407/2.

sion, served to foster friendly relations among various national groups.

Not all Scots, though, responded enthusiastically to such displays of their cultural identity. Allan Gunn, a Presbyterian who departed Glasgow in 1925 aged nine, recalled his reluctance 67 years after his migration about performing publicly:

We had to have Scottish dancing ... and we had to do the sword dance, single sword, double sword dance, Highland fling, sailors horn pipe and, of course, any time a church or some kind of function going on we were invited to dance and I hated it. And we had our kilts, of course. The only way I could get even, show my disapproval when we did the double sword dance, I would walk off the stage and let my sister pick up the swords.[42]

Allan Gunn's account is intriguing as it arose not in response to a direct question about continuities in his ethnic identity, but was rather a discussion emerging from a query as to what was the biggest influence in his life. In Allan's mind his mother was his greatest inspiration and his recollection cited above related to an incident in which he had contested her authority. Anne Quinn of Paisley was another youngster who claimed to lose an element of her Scottishness on account of teasing: 'The Highland dances, the Highland fling, that we learned in school. We used to do that but I soon forgot it because after a while I didn't do it anymore. You get teased about things like that.'[43]

In some ways dancing was an interior expression of identity, for Scots had to choose whether or not to exhibit their prowess or lack of it. Yet as migrants document, dancing was commonly conducted in public, thereby further exemplifying the blurring of interior and exterior worlds. Such a blend was also evident in celebrations of Hogmanay, which was emphasised more than Christmas. As Isabella Deeks, a Presbyterian who left Cathcart, a suburb of Glasgow, in 1923 explained, there was only one traditional aspect her family preserved:

[W]e always kept our holiday, you know, the Scottish holiday which, of course, was New Years. New Years is five hours earlier than America and so always at 7 o'clock at night we would always say happy New Year and I still do the first footing. In Scotland after the 12 o'clock you first footed. The person in your house after 12 o'clock was supposed to bring you something like bread or coal or something they had to bring you ... I still have that tradition here. Whoever comes into my house after midnight has to give me something.[44]

42 Interview with Allan Gunn by Paul Sigrist,.
43 Interview with Anne Quinn by Dennis Cloutier and Peter Kaplan, recorded 8 December 1983, EIOHP, NPS Series 146.
44 Interview with Isabella Deeks by Janet Levine, recorded 30 April 1997, EIOHP, EI Series 869.

Mary Dunn, an Episcopalian from Stirling who also left in 1923, likewise maintained a firm sense of being Scottish, which continued right up to the time of her interview in 1986. When specifically asked at the end of her interview what, if any, Scottish customs she continued, Mary responded:

Last Saturday night we went to a dinner dance honouring Robert Burns and that's his picture up there on the wall and we're going to one next Wednesday night to honour Robert Burns who is the poet, the Scottish poet, who died very young. And then we dance all the Scottish dances at these things, you know. And I have oodles of Scottish records. When I get homesick I put them on and play them. I don't really get homesick because I don't have anybody at home now.[45]

This account aptly exemplifies the way in which interior and exterior expressions of identity blended together. In this case, Robert Burns's legacy and Scottish music were celebrated both publicly and privately.

Cuisine was also occasionally portrayed in ethnic terms. Mary Dunn in the United States, for instance, admitted in stereotypical fashion, 'Oh yeah, and I make all kinds of Scottish pastry. I'm a real Scottish baker. Sorry I don't have any here today. Oh yeah, I have a little bit of shortbread.'[46] In Australia, meanwhile, in response to a query about the family's reading habits, Jim Comerford described his mother's books and periodicals which included Scottish publications: 'Mother would buy the *Strand* magazine and that still published famous cheap Scots magazine, *The People's Friend.*'[47]

Few Irish migrants proclaimed their heritage in similar ways, though Josephine Materia of Belfast also combined culinary and cultural events: 'I'm very proud of being Irish and I guess I love to hear the Irish music on St Paddy's Day. I watch the parade and have my cup of tea and I make Irish stew and soda bread.'[48] Most Irish and Scottish migrants, however, were more intrigued with the novel foods they encountered in their new destinations rather than attesting to their continuation of Irish fare. Such activities and emblems, largely invisible to external observers, unless visitors in the house, can misleadingly suggest that migrants were fully integrated into the societies in which they settled, without maintaining elements of their cultural heritage. Yet internal components of their identity were merely configured in a different way to other ethnic groups whose identities were more institutionalised.

Quite apart from discussing their involvement in societies, their use of language, and the customs they maintained, a few migrants reflected on

45 Interview with Mary Dunn by Dana Gumb, recorded 23 January 1986, EIOHP, AKRF Series 127.
46 *Ibid.*
47 Interview with Jim Comerford.
48 Interview with Josephine Materia by Janet Levine, recorded 22 June 1994, EIOHP, EI Series 482.

characteristics of their ethnicity. Most attributed negative connotations to their Scottishness. When asked if there was anything about her that was Scottish, Lillian Hopkins professed to feeling American because 'I'm not tight, I'm not frugal … I give everything away. I give money, I give everything away, not like my mother, you know, I share.' As Lillian further explained, 'Scottish people they never seemed to want anybody in their house like your neighbour to come over in case she thinks you have something better than her.'[49] Scottish identities were also internally constructed in New Zealand. Lorna Carter's letters, for instance, often self-deprecatingly linked a Scottish identity with parsimoniousness. In August 1952, for instance, Lorna notified her parents, 'The last letter I sent I typed from the last bit from the written as I wanted it to go for ⅓d also that's why I trimmed the Rugby programme. I'm still plenty Scots!!'[50] Furthermore, in preparing for a camping trip Lorna 'borrowed a haversack from Mr Boult, sox from Jean Luke, sleeping bag from Heather, ground sheet from Ron, torch from Beth and boots from Cedric – true Scot me!!'[51] The following year she claimed 'It was late night so we did the shops but being Scots didn't buy anything!!'[52] These extracts suggest that Lorna Carter was rather proud of the 'tight Scot' stereotype and that the typecast had applications for Scots both at home as well as abroad. As with a Scottish 'brogue' and Scottish dancing, then, Scottish characteristics were not always viewed positively or beneficially. Irish migrants, such as Mary Jo Lenney, on the other hand, stressed the positive elements of Irishness, in her case attributing her religion and caring nature to being a homeland trait.[53] Interviews conducted with descendants of Irish migrants in the United States also attributed traits including humour, generosity, friendliness, and caring to being Irish.[54]

Belonging at origin and destination

Mary Jo Lenney, and other migrants, also reflected on whether they felt more Irish or American. Mary Jo's testimony reveals a complex blend of linkages to her point of origin and destination, influenced by the second generation and the demise of those at home: 'You never forget your homeland. You never forget your birth land. But I'm loyal to America. I would never think of going

49 Interview with Lillian Hopkins by Kate Moore.
50 Lorna Carter (Wellington) to her parents (Oban), 3 August 1952.
51 *Ibid.*, 23 November 1952.
52 *Ibid.*, 26 April 1953.
53 Interview with Mary Jo Lenney by Paul Sigrist, recorded 21 August 1996, EIOHP, EI Series 793.
54 Reginold Byron, *Irish America* (Oxford: Clarendon Press, 1999), p. 231.

back there. My children are here. Their roots are here. My roots aren't really here. I love my homeland, I really do, but there isn't anybody there now, Paul, everybody's gone.'[55] In similar vein, Bridget Considine of County Clare mused, 'You have to love where you're born. It wouldn't be right if you didn't.'[56]

Other Irish migrants expressed a dual attachment, but frequently emphasised their allegiance to the United States in the first instance. Elizabeth Dalbey, for instance, was 98 years of age when she was interviewed. She had left Blackwater, Anfield, County Meath in the mid-1920s. When asked whether she felt Irish or American she responded, 'American'. When probed further as to what aspect of her was Irish she claimed, 'Every bit of me'. She concluded by stressing, 'I am proud to be Irish. Everybody seems to like the Irish,' while also affirming, 'I'm so proud to be an American citizen and to live in this wonderful country which is the most wonderful country in the world.'[57] John Gallogly, who arrived in the early 1950s, reiterated this complex connection: 'first I'm American but I'm still Irish and I still have the heritage and I'm happy my kids have it also.' Joseph Brady of Claddy, County Armagh, on the other hand, blended both allegiances, claiming to be an Irish–American.

Other Irish migrants were more inclined to stress their connections to the United States. John Brady of Ballyhaise, County Cavan, who emigrated in 1929 at six years of age announced, 'I think of myself as being American.' When asked gently what, if anything was Irish, he guessed, 'The name for one thing. The other thing is they say I have the map of Ireland [*laughing*] for a face.' Yet despite that qualification, John Brady reiterated, 'I consider myself an American.'[58] This assertion was replicated by John Lynn, who in 1951 left Crossmolina, County Mayo, when he was aged 25. At 66 years of age he contemplated his identity and stated, 'My allegiance is here … Oh I'm American now. American citizen … This is my country now.'[59] His wife of Cornafulla, Athlone, County Roscommon echoed the absence of an overwhelming sense of Irishness, due to living 41 years in the United States.[60] Mary McGloin offered an alternative explanation for her lack of an Irish identity: 'I'm not that much in the Irish category because I didn't live in a neighbourhood like that and you learned to live with what you have.' Instead, the 87-year-old from

55 Interview with Mary Jo Lenney.
56 Interview with Bridget Considine by Janet Levine, recorded 22 January 1996, EIOHP, EI Series 725.
57 Interview with Elizabeth Dalbey by Paul Sigrist, recorded 29 August 1995, EIOHP, EI Series 662.
58 Interview with John Brady by Paul Sigrist, recorded 22 June 1995, EIOHP, EI Series 623.
59 Interview with John Lynn.
60 Interview with Eileen Lynn by Janet Levine, recorded 31 July 1994, EIOHP, EI Series 509.

Bellavary, County Mayo, felt more inclined to stress that respect for elderly was missing.[61]

Scottish migrants, as we have seen, lengthily discussed a range of features which they considered peculiarly Scottish. Yet they too occasionally admitted to feeling a connection with their destination. Ann Nelson of Bathgate stressed this sense of dual allegiance among Scottish migrants in the United States. She had emigrated in 1923 at seven years of age and highlighted the influence of a neighbourhood community in reinforcing a sense of ethnic identity. Aged 81 she stated she was 'Very proud of my background, very. And I'm proud to be an American too, you know, but you don't forget, you know, I mean when you're surrounded by all Scotch when I was growing up, you know, at the parties, the singing the old songs and, you know, telling the old stories, it's something that just gets inside of you.'[62] Perhaps the last word for those who settled in North America, though, should go to Glaswegian Margaret Kirk. In 1994, 71 years after her arrival in New York, 92-year-old Margaret was asked at the end of her interview whether she considered herself more Scottish or American. She declared vigorously, 'I'll never be anything else but Scottish ... At heart I'll always be Scottish.'[63]

The testimonies of assisted Scottish migrants in New Zealand also include some insight into their allegiances. Their memories are of interest, for their sense of ethnicity was not a factor listed for consideration in their question-naires. Rather, the comments they made were spontaneously recorded. As with Irish migrants in the United States, they predominantly stressed their attach-ment to New Zealand. Firm conclusions cannot, however, be derived given that the majority of the sample failed to offer any observations. Among those who chose to write on this issue was Campbell Nichol of Dunfermline, who invoked a sense of kinship: 'Thanks to a unique country for adopting me.'[64] Some contemplated becoming a New Zealander, including David Gilchrist of Sandyhills, Glasgow: 'I have never had the urge to go back to Scotland and I may even become naturalised some day.'[65] Yet others declared an over-whelming sense of being a New Zealander, irrespective of obtaining citizen-ship. According to Janet Clarke, a Presbyterian from Hawick who arrived in 1956, 'I feel like a New Zealander now and have no desire to live permanently

61 Interview with Mary Margaret McGloin by Janet Levine, recorded 12 April 1994, EIOHP, EI Series 457.
62 Interview with Ann Nelson by Janet Levine, recorded 8 December 1996, EIOHP, EI Series 832.
63 Interview with Margaret Kirk by Paul Sigrist, recorded 25 February 1994, EIOHP, EI Series 440.
64 Campbell Nicol, BAIQ 193.
65 David Gilchrist, BAIQ 099.

in the U.K.'[66] In similar vein, fellow Presbyterian Harold Armstrong of Selkirk announced, 'after 30 years in Kiwiland we consider ourselves to be [*erased:* be] New Zealanders. We never obtained NZ. citizenship because we believed UK residents becoming permanent NZ's residents obtain citizenship automatically.'[67] Being and belonging, then, was increasingly complex.

Conclusion

As this chapter revealed, Irish and Scottish migrants did not solely rely on symbolical or mythical interpretations of their heritage in constructing an ethnic identity and only occasionally, in the case of language, did the responses of others play a part in their constructions. A further intriguing finding is that the self-identification of being Irish or Scottish rarely arose from an active sense of being different from each other or other national and ethnic groups. Irish and Scottish identities were not, therefore, constructed based on their positioning as 'the other' by different ethnic groups. Rather, Irish and Scottish migrants appear to have constructed their national and ethnic identities based on their own perceptions of being different. A broader methodological point should be made here: examples of national consciousness conveyed in interviews were not always formulated in response to specific questions relating to cultural continuities. Instead, they arose in connection with various themes under discussion including leisure time, education, and housing.

While both migrant groups successfully preserved an ethnic subculture, Scottish cultural identity differed from that of the Irish in several key respects. First, Scots possessed and maintained a distinctive language and a visible culture with immense popular appeal. Irish migrants, by contrast, only discussed Gaelic in connection with its use in Ireland. Those Scots who chose not to emphasise their language or accent were generally those who met with hostility as children. As seen, this could result in the abandonment of external identifiers of ethnicity which were swiftly replaced with aspects of settler culture. Ethnicity in generational terms was not seen as either a defensive or positive affirmation.

Where the testimony of Irish migrants also differed substantially from the Scots was in the absence of discussion of symbols of their ethnicity. Though other studies reveal that shamrocks and harps were symbolic of an Irish ethnicity, the testimony of Irish migrants failed to discuss such elements of Irishness. Scottish migrants, on the other hand, volubly reminisced about the visible, audible, and celebratory appeal of kilts, tartan, and pipes. These features distinguished Scots from other groups and provided them with a conspicuous

---

66 Janet Clarke, BAIQ 042.
67 Harold Armstrong, BAIQ 007.

and identifiable symbolic ethnicity that lingers to this day. That non-Scots participated in 'Scottish' events in both the twentieth and earlier centuries[68] further testifies to the ongoing attraction of visible elements of Scottishness. Clan gatherings, games, and parades were conducted in full view of a wider public. Scottishness, void of a political agenda to the degree of Irishness, transcended ethnic divisions by being non-threatening and inclusive. Irishness, on the other hand, became an ethnic militancy as the Irish increasingly pursued the nationalist cause with vigour.[69] Indeed, volatile events in Northern Ireland at the time the interviews were conducted may also have led Irish migrants to downplay their ethnic affiliation. It seems, then, that being void of a political agenda a broad sense of Scottishness could link Highlanders, Islanders and Lowlanders, Protestant and Catholic, whereas Ireland's fraught political situation prevented similar tendencies to a unifying Irishness.

A further broad finding is the dearth of institutional elements of Scottishness and Irishness, societies excepted. Presbyterianism, a central defining element of Scottishness, and Catholicism, which often implied Irishness, are conspicuously absent in many testimonies. Migrant memories, then, show little appreciation of religious affiliation being tied to an ethnic identity. As Linda Dowling Almeida found for the Irish in New York, 'one's sense of being Irish was not necessarily transmitted institutionally.'[70]

Apart from holding to various cultural aspects of their ethnicity, migrants were also conscious of jointly belonging to their new homelands. Indeed, in some cases, outright patriotism was directed to the new lands of settlement, with migrants offering little sense of being Irish or Scottish. These are the exceptions though, for as we will see in the concluding chapter, migrants maintained strong transnational ties with their points of origin, which in some cases prompted their return.

68 Rowland Berthoff, 'Under the kilt: variations on the Scottish-American ground', *Journal of American Ethnic History*, 1:2 (1982), pp. 5–34.
69 See Timothy J. Meagher, *Inventing Irish America: Generation, Class, and Ethnic Identity in a New England City, 1880–1928* (Notre Dame: University of Notre Dame, 2001), p. 361.
70 Linda Dowling Almeida, *Irish Immigrants in New York City, 1945–1995* (Bloomington and Indianapolis: Indiana University Press, 2001), p. 57.

9

'The savage loves his native shore': going home

Archibald Creen Walls was born in Nelson Street, Belfast, on 8 August 1919. A Catholic, he emigrated to the United States in 1946 on board the *Georgic*. Archibald returned to Northern Ireland in 1954, and was interviewed at Bangor in March 1998 when he was 78 years of age. Archibald's testimony considered the reasons for his return from the United States and the contrasts that he discerned upon resettling in Northern Ireland.[1]

Archibald Walls: So I came home and I got married there and I took her out to the States. She was just a little over a year in the States when we got the word about my mother so we all come home. So my father then, after my mother died, he took bad and he went into the hospital and then they found cancer in him so we brought him home and my mother-in-law she looked after him, she nursed him. She'd come up from Bangor every day and she'd stay the night time and she washed and bathed and fed and changed him and everything. He died six months after my mother. Well I had lost heart then going back to the States because my two pals were in Belfast married so Ann and I bought a wee shop in Belfast, you know, because me being an American citizen I couldn't get a job unless I had renounced my citizenship and somebody was kind enough to give me a job, you know, because they classified you as a foreigner because, like, you'd taken the American citizenship so all the locals not getting the Irish citizens, not getting so the only way I could really stay back in the country then was I bought a little shop, self employed, so that was our [*indecipherable*].

Janet Levine: What kind of a little shop was it?

Archibald Walls: It was confectionary and cigarettes and various things like that and papers. That was up the Falls Road in Belfast.

Janet Levine: And then did you keep your American citizenship?

Archibald Walls: Oh yes, I still have it. In fact my passport's out this last five years. I've never got up to renew it. I still have an American.

Janet Levine: When you were thinking of staying or leaving again was there, can you think of what was going through your mind as far as why you'd like to go back? Or,

Archibald Walls: Well, you know, I used to get, to be honest with you, I used to get homesick a lot.

---

1 Interview with Archibald Walls by Janet Levine, recorded 14 March 1998, EIOHP, EI Series 983.

Janet Levine: What would you get homesick for?

Archibald Walls: [laughs] I don't know, you know. I, you see, I just kind of never fathomed that out but that was always in the back of my mind, you know. When I'd be working about town I used to daydream, now what would we be doing this time back in Belfast? Where's my pals? What dance are we going to tonight? Or what pub are we going to to get a drink? All these silly little notions would embed themselves in my mind and could I get rid of them? No way at all … it's a hard country but you work hard, you get paid, and there's money to be made in it, if you want to make it. As I say, my time in the States was very, very happy times.

Janet Levine: Do you think you changed a little bit?

Archibald Walls: Then I started when I was out there with all the kids lying around the streets using dope and various things, you know, these things started to play on my mind. My wife was married and brought her family up out here and I'd be worrying when they come up the teenage style. Are they in these dopes or rackets or what are they doing, you know. I suppose it was a silly notion to have because life is a chance at any time whether you make a good marriage, whether you bring up a good family or not, it's a gamble but those little things niggled away, you know.

Janet Levine: Do you think you're any different as a result of living in the States for eight years compared with what your personality might be like if you never left?

Archibald Walls: Well, I don't know, it's hard to answer that question. I would say I got an education in the States to see how other people lived and how hard it was for them too to live as compared, as comparison with the times that I was coming up to live, you know. There was an unequal balance there that you had families like that in the States that we had in Ireland, you know, was getting it hard but fortunate enough I had good times there because I worked and I got well paid for it.

…

Janet Levine: How do you think about it now when you think back on those days?

Archibald Walls: I would love to go back on holiday but my wife can't travel. In fact, we are in the position we could live there for twelve months and come back here and go out but medical reasons obstructed that. I always intended go back out again but in 1982 she took this cancer because her family was up and working we could go at any time, go out and stay for six months or twelve months. We had no problem, we had no worries because their families were all at home, they were working, looking after themselves. We could be enjoying ourselves but just medical reasons come along and there's funny that notion of going back to dig up the old [*indecipherable*] again around New York and New Jersey and the Bronx and all those places.

Janet Levine: How about your religion? Did your religion stay as strong as it was when you were in the United States?

Archibald Walls: It did, because we used to, every month, we used to devote different hours [*indecipherable*] to the church. I forget what it was called then, but my brother Joe he joined it too and with it being different hours maybe from twelve to one praying in the church and meditating and various things. The next month you might be one to two [*indecipherable*] you know. My faith was still as strong in the States as it was in Ireland.

Janet Levine: And before we were talking about, you know, what it was, if you had changed in any way, if you were somehow different as a result of having lived there. Did you develop any qualities there that you might not have developed if you hadn't left here?

Archibald Walls: Well, the only thing that seems to me there is the knowledge of working on the ships … and looking at the way they worked and the way the Irish dock man worked. They were much superior in the States to what the Irish dock men were.

Janet Levine: In what way?

Archibald Walls: They were harder workers. They didn't neglect their work. They didn't drift off here they [*indecipherable*] but they were constantly at their job.

Janet Levine: Why do you think that was different?

Archibald Walls: Maybe it was because they were so hard to working. Maybe it was the money was reasonably good and maybe they were, it was their style of life for work instead of working in industry or working in the city councils or things like that, you know, that's it I looked at, you know. These men were happy doing this work and they probably wouldn't want to be working in factories or working for the city councils and various things. They're happy [*indecipherable*]. They seem to be bringing their families up well enough, can get them into universities and so forth.

Janet Levine: How 'bout the people? If you were to compare the people here in Belfast, Bangor, with the people that you, in the United States, how would they compare?

Archibald Walls: Well, I would say the people here would be a little more compassionate and considerate to just a certain amount. There is some good people in the States and there's some bad ones. But I would say there is a little more compassion here of the Irish people than the, because it is hard to define that because it's a cosmopolitan state in New York and there's so many nationalities in it. You are more or less to blend with your own Irish roots there to me. We had more freedom, more relaxing, and more safety in numbers, you know. If you were involved with any of the Italians or Germans they seem to be [*indecipherable*] to themselves. I'm not saying they were bad people. It was probably just a custom which was part of my custom when I went out there was to be affiliated with as many Irish people although I had some good friends of Germans out there and other friends, Italian friends, but I was never as much drawn to them as I was to my own Irish race and all my offsprings [*indecipherable*] of the family out there. I'm not denying those people or running them down in any way but I think that was my problem and I probably had to be born out there and reared up with these people and going to school with them with all their different nationalities of the backgrounds at the same schools and would probably just be a brother like the rest of them or a sister like the rest of them. [*Sentence indecipherable*]. But when you come from another environment, from a pure Irish environment, into a cosmopolitan country, well you have to make the best of what you got.

Return migration is an integral if often overlooked component within studies of migration, although recent explorations are counteracting this neglect.[2] Such manifest disregard in analyses of migration from Ireland and Scotland is surprising given the influence that returnees had on the economy, society, and politics of both countries. Figures for the return of Irish migrants are unknown, though presumably higher than the estimated 10 per cent who returned permanently to Ireland in the nineteenth century.[3] Scots, meanwhile, were among approximately a quarter of assisted Britons who returned to Britain from Australia after the Second World War.[4]

Irish and Scottish migrants were among many ethnic groups undertaking return movement during the twentieth century. Other migrant groups prone to such reverse mobility included Italians, one third of whom returned home between 1927 and 1943 after less than six years in Queensland, Australia. Of these, however, three-quarters went back to Australia.[5] Return migration was also considerable among many ethnic groups in the United States. Among male migrants, the British remigration rate was 19.3 per cent.[6] While twice the rate of Irish men (8.9 per cent), it fell far short of groups such as the Italians (45.6 per cent), Greeks (53.7 per cent), and Russians (65 per cent).[7]

Statistics, however, are a troubling source in analysing return migration, for they fail to incorporate those longing to return but unable to, and also because such figures are incapable of distinguishing between temporary, permanent, and multiple returns. This chapter incorporates the accounts

2 The pioneering work is Mark Wyman, *Round-Trip to America: The Immigrants Return to Europe, 1880–1930* (Ithaca and London: Cornell University Press, 1993). A recent volume containing several essays on return to Scotland in particular is Marjory Harper (ed.), *Emigrant Homecomings: The Return Movement of Emigrants, 1600–2000* (Manchester: Manchester University Press, 2005).
3 Dudley Baines, *Emigration from Europe, 1815–1930* (Basingstoke: Macmillan Education, 1991), p. 39. See also Wyman, *Round-Trip to America*, pp. 10–12.
4 A. James Hammerton and Alistair Thomson, *Ten Pound Poms: Australia's Invisible Migrants. A Life History of Postwar British Emigration to Australia* (Manchester: Manchester University Press, 2005), p. 9.
5 Geoffrey Sherington, *Australia's Immigrants, 1788–1978* (Sydney: Allen and Unwin, 1980), p. 119.
6 Thomas J. Archdeacon, *Becoming American: An Ethnic History* (New York: Free Press, 1983), p. 139.
7 *Ibid.*, p. 139.

of those who made both temporary and multiple return visits, as well as the permanent return of migrants. It assesses the impulses for return and examines the contrasts that returnees encountered between their places of origin and settlement, from the perspective of a return visit.

Longing to return

One of the most well-known episodes of return migration to Scotland in the twentieth century concerned the visits made by Scottish-Americans throughout the 1920s and early 1930s. In August 1924 the ship *California* arrived in Glasgow with more than 1,000 members of the Order of Scottish Clans in America. The *Glasgow Herald* reported that throughout the voyage 'A diversity of entertainments were held daily, including often Scottish song and Highland music and dancing.'[8] The tourists spent a month travelling round Scotland before returning to New York. Two years later approximately 1,200 members of the Order arrived in Glasgow on the *Transylvania*. At this time it was announced that such trips would continue to take place biannually. The following year, however, saw 400 members of the Lewis and Skye Societies in America journey out on the *Caledonia*, while in August the *Transylvania* brought around 800 passengers of Scottish connection back. In September many returnees were present in Edinburgh for the unveiling of a memorial to Scots killed in the First World War, 'a tribute to Scotland from men of Scottish blood and sympathies in America'. In 1928 the third trip home by the Order of Scottish Clans in America took place. Such was the interest in the event that two ships, *Caledonia* and *Transylvania*, were required to cater for around 2,000 individuals making the return trek. The publicity surrounding the trip ensured that 'thousands ... gave the returning Scots-Americans a rousing welcome.' Two years later, in 1930, the fourth annual return trip occurred, again attracting similar numbers. As the Anchor Line historian, R. S. McLellan, reported:

On this occasion nine homesick Scots had omitted to book their passages and as a result found themselves in court charged with being stowaways. Their story was that having gone down to the pier at New York to see their clansmen embark they had been so overcome with a desire to visit the homeland that they had been tempted to stow away, eight in one ship and one in the other.

The fifth biennial trip of the Order attracted just 450 returnees who voyaged on the *Caledonia* in July 1932.[9] Perhaps such numbers declined on account of the ongoing economic recession wrought by the Great Depression.

---

8 'Exile Clansmen', *The Glasgow Herald*, 4 August 1924.
9 R. S. McLellan, *Anchor Line, 1856–1956* (Glasgow: Anchor Line, 1956), pp. 74–98.

Apart from those returning from the United States, plans were also put in place to take 100 members of the Australian Scots delegation to the UK in 1928. At a dinner in London a vast display of cultural Scottishness was evident with 'heather tied with tartan ribbon; the London Scottish pipers played in the haggis; the London Gaelic choir supported the vocal music; the toast of the delegation was acclaimed with Highland honours'.[10]

Migrant testimony also reveals this propensity for return migration. Ernest Younger's correspondence dating from the 1920s is particularly acute in its depiction of multiple moves made by migrants. Describing his return voyage to Canada after a visit to Scotland, Ernest informed his parents:

Again Johnnie & I are sitting at the same table that we occupied on the homeward journey, & all our companions at table were all passengers on the trip home, just like meeting old friends. There must be at least about a dozen people we know who came over on the 'Athenia' same time as we did ... There are I think more passengers on board this trip than we had coming home but I don't think we can have a better time.[11]

The continuous flow of migrants between origin and destination prob-lematises discussion of the conceptualisation of migration as a temporary or permanent undertaking. Some migrants presumably left determined to stay but soon returned; others went with the intention of staying but elected to venture back to their homeland. Testimonies reveal these complications. Among those perceiving their venture at the outset as a temporary sojourn was Margaret Kirk, who left Glasgow in 1923 at 22 years of age. She later stated she 'had no thought of staying in America when I came'.[12] Irish migrants thought likewise. According to Kathleen Lamberti, who had moved from Brackney, County Down, in 1921 at 22 years of age: 'In the beginning of course you wanted to go back to Ireland in the worse way. Why did we leave Ireland? Why did we leave Ireland? Why did we come here? This is dreadful. Oh, in the beginning it was very bad. Many a tear you cried. The savage loves his native shore, you know.'[13] Thirty years later construction worker John Lynn left Crossmolina, County Mayo, and later shared these thoughts: 'I always thought I'd go back to Ireland. When I come here first, you know, everyone thinks that, I think.'[14]

10 *The Scotsman*, 28 July 1928.
11 Ernest Younger (*Athenia*) to his parents (Tillicoultry), 5 October 1929, in NLS, Acc. 9407/2.
12 Interview with Margaret Kirk by Paul Sigrist, recorded 25 February 1994, EIOHP, EI Series 440.
13 Interview with Kathleen Lamberti by Paul Sigrist, recorded 25 February 1994, EIOHP, EI Series 439.
14 Interview with John Lynn by Janet Levine, recorded 31 July 1994, EIOHP, EI Series 510.

Henrietta Lindsay also recalled that her widowed mother 'never ever was happy at leaving Glasgow, never'.Henrietta reported that it took her mother four to five years to accumulate enough money to take the two of them back to Scotland. Further evidence that her mother perceived the trip as merely a sojourn was cited in relation to her mother's application for a pension. Having been refused on the basis that she was out of the country at the time the pension was introduced, an appeal was lodged in which 'she told them that she had her return ticket which was fortunate because she did get the pension after that.'[15] By contrast, others, like Donald 'Tulag' MacLeod from Lewis, 'knew I was on a one-way ticket. That I'd never come back.'[16]

While there may be an assumption that those seeking a transient move were likely to choose destinations closer to home to facilitate their return, the testimony reveals that some migrants who sought distant shores were also inclined to view their migration as a sojourn. In 1951, Lorna Carter, for example, left Oban bound for Wellington, New Zealand. She declared, 'I didn't go to stay. I went to see what it was like.'[17] Such evidence is useful for the implicit insights it reveals about prospects in Scotland, for a temporary stint abroad suggests that migrants possessed a positive view of the future outlook in Scotland. This propensity to return also reflects broader analyses, for scholars have pointed out that after the First World War European migration increasingly became a temporary movement.[18] Yet in this study very few migrants elected to return permanently to Ireland or Scotland, most preferring instead to undertake brief visits home. A statistical analysis of the testimonies of Irish and Scottish migrants in the United States, excluding those individuals who returned permanently, shows that 46 per cent of Irish and 35 per cent of Scots made return visits.[19] Even more striking is the testimony of assisted Irish and Scottish migrants to New Zealand after the Second World War. Almost three quarters claimed to have visited family and friends back in Britain.[20] These findings reveal that distance was presumably less of a hindrance in the decision to

15 Interview with Henrietta Lindsay by Janet Levine, recorded 18 July 2001, EIOHP, EI Series 1211.
16 Transcript of interview with Donald 'Tulag' MacLeod in Jim Wilkie, *Metagama: A Journey from Lewis to the New World* (Edinburgh: Birlinn, 1987 and 2001), p. 102.
17 Interview with Lorna Ross by Angela McCarthy, recorded 24 February 2002.
18 Dirk Hoerder, 'Migration in the Atlantic economies: regional European origins and worldwide expansion', in Dirk Hoerder and Leslie Page Moch (eds), *European Migrants: Global and Local Perspectives* (Boston: Northeastern University Press, 1996), p. 43.
19 These percentages include those who never returned and cases where return was not mentioned.
20 BAIQ 001, 007, 013, 015, 028, 041, 042, 060, 063, 065, 066, 100, 115, 126, 135, 140, 157, 172, 173, 178, 192, 206, 208, 212, 213, 227, 230, 240, 261, 263, 264, 276, 278.

undertake return visits, than the factors facilitating such movement, including disposable income and the ability to travel by air.

For a number of migrants, contemplation of returning home took place immediately after their arrival abroad. Among a sample of assisted Irish and Scottish migrants in New Zealand, 43 per cent considered returning home in the initial years after settlement.[21] This was slightly higher than the combined British/Irish assisted group, of whom 31 per cent pondered such a move.[22] While the reasons for this deliberation are unknown, evidence from the testimonies of migrants who moved to the United States provides some insight. A number of migrants, for instance, stated that shortly after their arrival they found themselves passionately longing for home. In 1927 nine-year-old Thomas Allan found himself yearning 'to go back to bonny Scotland'.[23] Maisie Pedersen of Greenock, an 18-year-old in 1924, also professed, 'I missed my family very much. And many a time I wanted to go back but I says no, I'm not going back. I'll stick it out. I did.'[24] Mary Harney, daughter of a farmer in County Roscommon who left in 1925, expressed a similar emotion: 'I missed Ireland so much', especially her parents. 'I always wanted to go on a trip, take a trip to the old country but I never did go over there after coming here,' she wistfully imparted.[25] Fellow Roscommon migrant Mary Kelly similarly recalled, 'many nights I went to bed and cried myself sick.'[26] So acute was the longing to go back that many migrants tried to obtain financial assistance from home to facilitate a return. Anne O'Connor of Ballyhack, County Mayo, arrived as a 20-year-old in 1923. She testified, 'Oh I wrote to my father to send the fare to me to come back to you. I sure did. I wasn't happy at all here for a long time.'[27] Eighteen-year-old Julia Carmody from Toormakeady, County Mayo, was similarly unimpressed in 1921: 'if I had the money I would have went right back. I hated Perth Amboy' [New Jersey].[28] Sixteen-year-old Mary

21 BAIQ 013, 028, 041, 042, 063, 100, 135, 157, 160, 165, 172, 191, 192, 193, 194, 206, 213, 230, 240, 261.
22 Megan Hutching, *Long Journey for Sevenpence: Assisted Immigration to New Zealand from the United Kingdom, 1947–1975* (Wellington: Victoria University Press, 1999), p. 168.
23 Interview with Thomas Allan by Jean Kolva, recorded 16 July 1984, EIOHP, NPS Series 149.
24 Interview with Maisie Pedersen by Paul Sigrist, recorded 26 February 1994, EI Series 442.
25 Interview with Mary Harney by Paul Sigrist, recorded 11 October 1991, EIOHP, EI Series 107.
26 Interview with Mary Kelly by Paul Sigrist, recorded 2 May 1995, EIOHP, EI Series 613.
27 Interview with Anne O'Connor by Janet Levine, recorded 26 October 1994, EIOHP, EI Series 559.
28 Interview with Julia Carmody by Paul Sigrist, recorded 18 July 1996, EIOHP, EI Series 767.

Kelly from Toberclare, County Westmeath, found herself in a similar predicament, stating that she wrote to her father and asked him to send the money for her to return.[29] Such testimony is, by contrast, relatively absent in the memories of assisted Irish and Scottish migrants in New Zealand, although Georgina Prentice from Glasgow confessed, 'I was dreadfully homesick and even after 37 years I still miss the U.K. and often think if I had to do it all again I dont think I would emigrate ... Sunshine & good food are not everything!!'[30]

This ache to return home predominantly suffused the memories of female migrants. While not discussed in their testimonies, that these migrants remained in their new homelands indicates that those at home were either unable or unwilling to facilitate such return passages. Or perhaps migrants eventually changed their mind as they came to engage more fully with everyday life in their new homelands.

Reasons for moving back

Claims of missing home are suggestive that some migrants suffered severe homesickness during the initial years of settlement overseas. The issue of homesickness is clearly an interesting one, as few migrants who did return permanently attested to having been motivated by a pining for home, though Archibald Walls's recollection is interesting in this regard, given that most admissions of homesickness generally emerge from women.[31] Most accounts of a hunger for home emerge from Highland migrants, though the surviving testimony is conflicting. According to Lewis migrant Dòmhnall Chrut, 'Everyone who left from here had "cianalas" for the first month or two. Everyone was young though and after the first year or two that wore off.'[32] By contrast, Norman Smith, also of Lewis asserted, 'I was never homesick. I was more homesick when I returned home than I had ever been when I left. I've no idea why I returned. I only came to visit and I got married and she kept me at home.'[33]

That few migrants claimed to have been homesick may be the result of the extensive networks of family and friends abroad that they were incorporated into, and may explain the difference with post-war migrants moving to Australia. Or it may simply be that such times were no longer brought to

29 Interview with Mary Kelly by Paul Sigrist, recorded 10 September 1997, EIOHP, EI Series 936.
30 Georgina Prentice, BAIQ 213.
31 Assisted postwar British women in Australia recalled being homesick six times more than men. See Hammerton and Thomson, *Ten Pound Poms*, p. 289.
32 Interview with Dòmhnall Chrut in CEN, Emigration folder. 'Cianalas' means a deep form of homesickness.
33 Interview with Norman Smith in CEN, Emigration folder.

mind or were still too painful to recall. The ambiguity of such recollections is evident in the story of Lorna Carter, who was adamant that a longing for home did not prompt her return. Instead, Lorna resolutely insisted in her interview that she had no sense of melancholy: 'I didn't miss anything. I really didn't miss anything. I had no homesickness. It was all so interesting.' In part she attributed this lack of homesickness not only to being an only child, but also to her previous extended absences from home: 'I think it was because I was an only child and you see I'd been in the Wrens and there's no use, if you can't get home you can't get home. I was never homesick ever in my life.'[34] Lorna's contemporary letters, however, cast a slight doubt on her memory. In May 1952, when discussing an acquaintance's melancholy, Lorna inadvertently pointed to the isolation she had experienced. Her acquaintance, Lorna noted, was 'pretty homesick *homesick* at the moment, looking for letters every post, like I was myself'.[35] More overtly, Lorna wrote in July 1953, 'I got a film on the Highlands, an old one (by the fashions) in colour and I saw Oban the prom, the war memorial and Kerrera. It was lovely. I saw the Oban Pipe Band at a Games somewhere, so I was fair homesick.'[36] This nostalgia for her immediate neighbourhood in Scotland was also conveyed in a more regional sense a month earlier, when Lorna described attending a technicolour film in which 'we saw some lovely scenes of the Hielans and the heather, also of the Braemar Games – and my handsome friend Jack Hunter was seen throwing the hammer – I felt like standing up and saying "See how we grow 'em in Scotland"!! We had plenty of bagpipes, to bring a tear to my eye. There isn't much can beat them, for making you want to up and march along, to a Scot anyway'.[37]

This extract reveals the discrepancies that can exist in relation to memory in oral accounts and the ways interviewees recast their earlier experiences in life. It seemingly reflects Lorna's desire to portray her time abroad in the most favourable light, choosing to forget the occasional melancholy that her letters fleetingly reveal. Or it may simply be that in later years other events generated more emotional feelings that superseded Lorna's memories of being homesick abroad. As Richard White has mused in a memoir about his Irish mother's stories, 'What happened afterward would always lie in the shadow of these years and be measured against them. Later experiences never equaled those in the past.'[38] Although the excitement evident in Lorna's letters during her time abroad may never have been surpassed, it is unlikely that she never

34 Interview with Lorna Ross.
35 Lorna Carter (New Zealand) to her parents (Oban), 14 May 1952. The Carter letters were kindly provided by Lorna Ross.
36 *Ibid.*, 4 July 1953.
37 *Ibid.*, 13 June 1953.
38 Richard White, *Remembering Ahanagran: Storytelling in a Family's Past* (New York: Hill and Wang, 1998), p. 298.

experienced emotions that exceeded the occasional lonely day encountered in New Zealand.

Irrespective of feelings of homesickness, the majority of migrants elected to remain in their destination of choice. For those who returned, such a move was not necessarily the result of failure abroad, as scholars have sometimes assumed. In their study of return migrants from Australia to Britain after the Second World War, Hammerton and Thomson indicate that few returned because of deficiencies in their character. Rather, their valuable compilation of explanations enables insight into the various motives governing return journeys. While one quarter returned for economic reasons and a third because of homesickness, half of Hammerton and Thomson's sample returned to Britain because of family relationships.[39] A study of migrants who left Ireland in the 1980s only to return the following decade has attributed their return to the desire for a better and slower quality of life, sociability, and more time.[40] Although few migrants in this study returned permanently and cannot be considered representative, their explanations give a fleeting insight into the various factors stimulating permanent return.

Among the most common factors sparking the return migration of Irish and Scots were illness and death. Ann Conway, for instance, left Esker, County Tyrone, at 22 years of age in 1929. Notification of her mother's illness some years later prompted her back to the family farm. Ann's mother eventually died and although Ann contemplated returning to the United States, she chose instead to spend some time in England before settling in County Tyrone. According to Ann, her brother's sudden death eighteen months after her mother's demise was a major factor in her decision to remain permanently in Northern Ireland: 'They tell me too that if I hadn't have stayed there'd be no home here for them.'[41] Catherine English and her sister were also propelled home to County Mayo on account of their mother's ill health. Unlike Ann Conway, however, Catherine and her sister returned to the United States after their mother's death from cancer of the jawbone.[42] Marion Kerr's family, on the other hand, were directed back to Scotland because of her mother's arthritis: 'They were advised by a doctor there either to come back home or go to California.' Deciding that her mother might not recuperate in California, the family returned to Paisley in the late 1920s, about five years after

---

39 Hammerton and Thomson, *Ten Pound Poms*, pp. 276, 278.
40 Mary P. Corcoran, 'The process of migration and the reinvention of self: the experiences of returning Irish emigrants', *Éire-Ireland*, 37:1 (2002), p. 190.
41 Interview with Ann Conway by Janet Levine, recorded 11 March 1998, EIOHP, EI Series 981.
42 Interview with Catherine English by Paul Sigrist, recorded 19 September 1991, EIOHP, EI Series 91.

their arrival in the United States.[43] The factors bringing these women home clearly differed from those motivating their nineteenth-century counterparts, who frequently returned in search of a husband.[44]

Collective obligations towards those at home not only propelled some migrants back to their places of origin, but also directed those who moved within family groups. This was particularly the case for women and children, who could be subject to the whims of male family members. The Vaughn family moved to the United States in 1952 and by 1955 had returned to Glasgow. As Maureen Vaughn plainly put it, 'My father didn't settle'. Elaborating further, she speculated as to his mindset: 'I think the grass was always greener especially on the other side of the Atlantic so I mean when he was over there Scotland was wonderful'. The decision to return clearly caused a degree of tension between Maureen's parents: 'I don't think we'd been there a fortnight and my mother said to him, "we need to see about getting a house of our own, we can't stay with Nancy for too long because it's too much of an imposition". He says, "Why not, we're going home". And she said, "Do you mean to say you have dragged me with four children under ten and your mother across the Atlantic just to tell me we're going home?"'[45] Both gender and generation in this case were subject to a paternal decision and the family returned permanently to Scotland.

Occasionally, migrants were propelled home by circumstances seemingly out of their control. Catherine Aitchison, for instance, left Glasgow in 1958. She returned a year later before travelling once again to the United States eighteen months later. During the next eight years Catherine developed seizures after being 'belted on the head with the baseball' in Central Park, New York. Although finding it difficult to control her convulsions and obtain a job, other factors played just as substantial a part. As Catherine explained: 'Well, I had a baby to an Italian fella I met in the bank where I worked. And my brother phoned me one day and said, "if you don't come home, I'm comin over tae get ye." So I came home and I had the baby.' The role of her family in this episode is even clearer, for it was Catherine's sister who had observed her pregnancy during a visit to the United States and subsequently informed their parents.[46] Again, generational and gender factors played a considerable role in the process.

43 Interview with Marion Kerr by Janet Levine, recorded 17 July 2001, EIOHP, EI Series 1029.
44 Arnold Schrier, *Ireland and the American Emigration, 1850–1900* (Chester Springs: Dufour Editions, 1997; 1st pub. 1958), p. 130.
45 Interview with Maureen Vaughn by Janet Levine, recorded 24 July 2001, EIOHP, EI Series 1217.
46 Interview with Catherine Aitchison by Janet Levine, recorded 19 July 2001, EIOHP, EI Series 1214.

For others, their return was simply derived from a desire to be home. Kathleen Lamberti went briefly back to Brackney, County Down, in 1929, eight years after her departure. 'I felt that that was just home. Why is it we always say back home? It's not my home anymore. This is my home.'[47]

Migrants in their homelands

The effect of return migrants on the hearts and minds of those contemplating migration was explored earlier in this book. But what of the thoughts and feelings of those who made the return journey? How were they received and what impressions did they have of the societies they had left? Were they welcomed with open arms or derided, and did their return generate relief that they had emigrated or sadness for all that had been left behind? Were they a stranger among strangers as Alfred Schuetz has stated?[48]

Regrettably, migrants rarely commented on the receptions they received when returning to Ireland and Scotland. Yet the testimony of some reveals how they proved to be a source of information about their destination. According to Ena Hughes, who returned from Sydney, 'People thought the kangaroos were eating out of your the hand at the kitchen door I think because when we went back that was one of the first things people said to me, "Oh tell us about kangaroos."'[49] Information provided by return migrants, as portrayed in Chapter 2, could be erroneous and here again is an example of stereotyped images of the destinations to which migrants gravitated.

In the nineteenth century those returning from the United States to Ireland were noted for their visual impact on home communities. They returned resplendent in fine clothes and equipped with impeccable manners and self-confidence. Their alleged cleanliness and industry also provoked comment, as did their accent.[50] In 1928 Marion Kerr, still a youngster, returned to Scotland. The experience, as she remembered it, was far from pleasant: 'It wasn't very good because there was one teacher when I started who made a dreadful fool of me with my American accent because it was quite, I mean, you would have thought I'd been brought up in Brooklyn or something, you know, but she thought it was funny.'[51] Other reactions, likewise, expose the antagonism that could be directed towards returnees. John Lynn of Crossmolina, County Mayo, frankly asserted, 'People there they don't like to see you come

47 Interview with Kathleen Lamberti by Paul Sigrist.
48 Alfred Schuetz, 'The homecomer', *American Journal of Sociology*, 50:5 (1945), pp. 369–76.
49 Interview with Ena Hughes by Bronwyn Hughes, recorded 1987, in OHC NLA, NSW Bicentennial Oral History Project, Oral TRC 2279/8.
50 Schrier, *Ireland and the American Emigration*, p. 133–6.
51 Interview with Marion Kerr.

home with a load of money and buy a big house.'[52] His comment echoes the lukewarm receptions afforded to those returned migrants from the United States to Ireland in the nineteenth century who deviated from others in their communities.[53]

Other migrants were subjected to the gossip and remonstrations of those at home. Returning to Scotland during the late 1920s, Margaret Kirk enjoyed the experience so much that she extended her trip. Yet this created numerous rumblings about the effect the separation would have on Margaret's marriage: 'People were thinking your husband's all alone. I'd say, "Oh to hell with him. He can have a good time with all those girls he wants to while I'm away, I don't care … As long as he doesn't come home to me with a dose of venereal disease, I don't care where he goes."'[54] Margaret's retort was presumably less a result of conditions in the 1920s but rather influenced by the increased independence of women by the 1990s. Nevertheless, her comment fits with the remainder of her testimony, which reveals her to be a plucky, forthright individual.

Apart from discussing aspects of the receptions they made during return visits to Ireland and Scotland, a number of migrants also provided scintillating impressions of the differences they discerned between home and abroad after their return. In such cases the homelands were assessed from the point of reference of the new lands. Three aspects are prominent in these reflections: characteristics of the population, a depressing climate, and poor economic conditions. Similar disgruntlement was conveyed by those returning to Ireland in the 1970s, who complained of 'the poor economic situation, the attitudes and gossip of locals, inefficiency, and the slow pace of life'.[55]

John Lynn of Crossmolina, County Mayo, had left in 1951 and was cutting in his impressions. Of the Irish he judged, 'They're not as openminded as the Americans,' considering them 'afraid to say anything, you know'.[56] Ann Conway's account was more contradictory. In Ireland, she supposed the 'people here are more rougher, you know, rougher out in the country working land and everything'. As for those in the United States, 'The men drink a lot, you know, and booze a lot and I would think they have a very hard life the women. I wouldn't like that.'[57] Desmond Black also left home in 1929 for the United States and like Ann Conway returned in 1936. This enabled him to provide comparisons between life in the United States with Omagh, County Tyrone:

52 Interview with John Lynn.
53 Schrier, *Ireland and the American Emigration*, p. 139.
54 Interview with Margaret Kirk by Paul Sigrist.
55 Corcoran, 'The process of migration and the reinvention of self', p. 178, summarising Fiona McGrath's study.
56 Interview with John Lynn.
57 Interview with Ann Conway.

it's very confining, you know, and very conventional and so on … I'm not suggesting that my people were bigoted in any way because they were not, they were broadminded really, I must say that. We always were what. You're restricted in your views, you know. I think you change really when you meet other people from different parts, different customs, and different ways of life. It opens up more or less a new line of thought for you. You see things in a completely different light, I think.[58]

The same old environment, meanwhile, prompted the criticism of some. Henrietta Lindsay returned to Glasgow in the late 1920s as a teenager and she noticed 'coming back here and thinking how dull all the buildings were after the lovely red buildings out there'.[59] The transformation of the landscape captured the imagination of others, including Eileen Lynn from Cornafulla, near Athlone, County Roscommon. Having left in 1953 Eileen discovered during a return visit during the 1980s, 'It's getting much like here. Very busy now, lot of cars, and they have the supermarkets like here.'[60]

The more common outcome, however, was that a return visit provoked comparisons that clearly favoured life abroad, reinforcing for migrants the decision to remain overseas. Having visited Scotland, Mary MacIver of Toronto remarked, 'Lewis wasn't very prosperous when we went back, and we were glad to get back here. Maybe it was the weather – I don't know – but we thought it was a better place to live.'[61] Other migrants specifically targeted the weather in their decision to remain abroad. Comparing Ireland and the United States, Eileen Lynn concluded: 'It's cooler back there. Now I wouldn't stay in that climate back there. It rains a lot and very damp. They don't get much summers. But it's peaceful though there but you're used to the rat race here. In the country it's very lonely when you go back'.[62] According to the Crutchleys, who returned to Belfast in 1966 but went back to New Zealand the following year, they were 'used to a nice climate here [*New Zealand*] and the climate over there [*Northern Ireland*] we had forgotten almost what it was like but it was pretty horrible'.[63] Other migrants merged accounts of the climate with Ireland's poor economic situation. Johanna Flaherty from Castlewest, County Limerick, explained:

58 Interview with Desmond Black by Janet Levine, recorded 12 March 1998, EIOHP, EI Series 982.
59 Interview with Henrietta Lindsay.
60 Interview with Eileen Lynn by Janet Levine, recorded 31 July 1994, EIOHP, EI Series 509.
61 Transcript of interview with Mary MacIver in Wilkie, *Metagama*, p. 129.
62 Interview with Eileen Lynn.
63 Interview with Annie and Bob Crutchley by Megan Hutching, recorded 27 February 1998, in ATL OHC, 1998 New Zealand Citizenship Oral History Project, OHC-0421.

I never was once sorry that I left Ireland. I would love to live in Ireland and I still would love to live in Ireland but you haven't got the conveniences there. The jobs aren't there. There's no jobs there for the younger people and now that they've stopped immigration it's very hard on the Irish people because they can't come out here like they used to but I love to go back to visit. I go back every year. ... And then I think the winters over there are very cold. ... It's a damp, very damp, it's raining most of the time. Now we were over there last summer and it rained practically every day we were there.[64]

The economy and technology found expression in the observations of others. Mary Jo Lenney returned to Ballina, County Mayo, just after the Second World War. After a week in England she arrived in independent Ireland:

The devastation was terrible. There was so much poverty. I had a suit, I had some clothes in my suitcase, Paul, that I would not take out because there was so much they didn't have anything. Even though they weren't involved in the war they didn't have any. To have light in the house they couldn't get kerosene, everything was so scarce. My father grew sugar beet which they didn't have the proper refining system for and they didn't have, they had very little flour.[65]

Others who had made a decision to return permanently simply felt they were making little progress at home. Edward Dowling returned to Kilkenny in 1962, but later that year developed itchy feet.

I had no passage booked back but one day I was sitting in a pub in Kilkenny and I thought there's no future in this. It had been nice summer days and all that but I thought I'm not going to get anywhere by just sitting and drinking, drinking Guinness. So there was a travel agent up the road a couple of doors up the road from the pub and I just decided on spec I would go in and see and say, I want to get back to New Zealand, can you book me a passage?' And he said, 'I'll see what I can do for you' and a week later he sent me word, 'I've got you a passage on the *Northern Star*.' He said, 'It's a brand new liner, on its maiden voyage, it'll be leaving Southampton on such and such a date, I've booked your passage on it.' I said, 'Fair enough, I'm down to the bank and I'll pay you straight away.'

The decision was apparently troubling, for Dowling acknowledged, 'I didn't want to tell my brother in Ireland that that would be it. I thought it's too cruel, you know, so I said to him, "I'm just going to pop over to England and see the people over there again."'[66] Dowling never returned to Ireland, but arrived back in New Zealand in September 1962.

64 Interview with Johanna Flaherty by Debra Allee, recorded 29 May 1986, EIOHP, AKRF Series, 182.
65 Interview with Mary Jo Lenney recorded by Paul Sigrist, 21 August 1996, EIOHP, EI Series 793.
66 Interview with Ted Dowling by Ian Robertson, recorded 4 August and 27 September 1995, in ATL OHC, Wellington City Transport European Immigrants Oral History Project, OHC-0012.

Despite these impressions, which posited the point of origin as negative in such contrasts, some migrants felt that life in Ireland and Scotland was better than settlement abroad, particularly for the aged. 'Lewis is a better place for elderly people to live in. I visited the three homes in Stornoway and I never saw people getting the same attention [in Canada]', indicated Mary MacIver of Toronto.[67] Dòmhnall Chrut also maintained, 'If Lewis then had been like Lewis now nobody would have left. It is just as good now as any place in either Canada or America. Although the towns aren't as large, you are just as well off as you would be in Canada. But 57 years ago there was nothing here.'[68] Anne Craven made a similar assessment: 'Today they're living way better. The people, the older people in Ireland are way better than they are in this country very comfortable and very nice'.[69]

Counterfactual reflections

In a venture in counterfactual history, several migrants were asked to imagine how their lives might have differed had they remained in Ireland or Scotland instead of choosing to live abroad. Such a provocative suggestion was another way in which migrants could reflect comparatively. A number of different alternatives emerge from such musings, encompassing economic prospects, educational potential, character, and lifespan.

A number of migrants simply felt that the spirit of their homeland and the potential for economic progress was poor. Paul O'Dwyer of Bohar, County Mayo, reckoned grimly that had he not left in 1925, 'I think it would be quite different. I had thought of going back ... whereas if you were in Ireland there were hard times in the first place under British authority it would be unthinkable and even under the Irish authority the spirit period of time under slavery is such enough to dampen the spirit I don't think I could ever have enjoyed it.'[70] Glaswegian Joseph Delaney who left in 1922 aged 18 made a similar gloomy observation: 'It would have been a rough life, poor, poor way, very poor way of making a living.'[71] These verdicts were replicated by some assisted Scottish migrants in New Zealand who felt economic opportunities in New Zealand were far superior. As George Smith, originally from Dumbarton, wrote approvingly, 'After nearly 30 years here I have no regrets. I would never

67 Transcript of interview with Mary MacIver in Wilkie, *Metagama*, p. 130.
68 Interview with Dòmhnall Chrut in CEN, Emigration folder.
69 Interview with Anne Craven by Paul Sigrist, recorded 2 October 1991, EIOHP, EI Series 102.
70 Interview with Paul O'Dwyer by Paul Sigrist, recorded 17 July 1993, EIOHP, EI Series 362.
71 Interview with Joseph Delaney by Dana Gumb, recorded 5 September 1985, EIOHP, AKRF Series 23.

have had in Scotland what I have here.'[72] This was shared by Moray Wilson of Midlothian: 'I could never have been so "well off" in UK ... I have never regretted settling in the greatest little country in the world. (Sounds like a true kiwi!!).'[73] Such conclusions are intriguing as they were penned on question-naires without any form of prompting.

Yet others strongly believed that emigration had failed to make a differ-ence to their financial prospects, as they considered they would have achieved success had they never migrated. This conclusion was usually reached by comparing their lives with those of their compatriots who had remained at home. According to Anne Craven of County Offaly, who had left in 1925: 'Well I really don't know. Anybody that I go see there now that's in my age bracket, not too many left, but they're all very well off and very comfortable so I don't think we did any better than we would have done had we stayed in our own country. I think anybody who makes it in their own country should stay there.'[74] Joseph Brady likewise reflected thoughtfully on how his life might have transpired had he remained in 1925 at Claddy, County Armagh, drawing comparisons with the achievements of his brother: 'He made out very well and wound up with a nice pension and also had a social security or whatever they call it over there, and he had a car and a nice house and all so he did all right ... I might have made out pretty good but it's that's difficult to say.'[75] In similar vein, Dublin Jew Manny Steen met up with an old friend when he returned to his home city in the 1950s, some three decades after his departure, and was suitably impressed:

I saw Sam who had been a very poor boy like I did when I left now living in a beautiful home ... I said, 'Sam where did this come from?' He says, 'Manny, if you had stayed here you too could have had this.' From a poor boy he now had this he had a five-storey building and two factories and he had his home and everything. I was delighted for his sake. I said, 'Well I haven't done so bad either, you know,' but he had done well.[76]

Other migrants reflecting on their alternative life histories supposed that they might have pursued more rigorously an academic education. In such speculations they frequently emphasised their own character and also the fact that life turned out well in any case. Among them was Mary Kendrick, who wondered often how her life might have turned out had she not left Auchin-leck in 1927 as a 7-year-old. She summarised, 'Maybe I would have gone on

72 George Smith, BAIQ 230.
73 Moray Wilson, BAIQ 271.
74 Interview with Anne Craven.
75 Interview with Joseph Brady by Paul Sigrist recorded 25 September 1995, EIOHP, EI Series 673.
76 Interview with Manny Steen by Paul Sigrist, recorded 22 March 1991, EIOHP, EI Series 33.

for more education than what was offered at that time, I don't know. I've always been a very curious kind of a pushy [*laughs*] kind of person so you know I may have had had some good opportunities there too like I did here. Even without a college education I did all right for myself.'[77] Those leaving in later decades felt much the same way as Maureen Vaughn, who returned permanently after three years in the United States in the early 1950s: 'It certainly altered my life. I think if I'd stayed in this country I would have gone straight through as an A student and gone to university. My mother would have managed it somehow. But with breaks in education it, that didn't happen. But on the other hand I certainly broadened my outlook.'[78]

Indeed, the most extensive reflections among migrants concerned the state of their mindset had they remained in their homelands. Many felt that emigration had extended their viewpoints rather than leaving them stifled. This was acutely noted by Stephen Concannon from the Spiddal parish, County Galway, who left in 1921: 'I had opportunities to, to read and to broaden my mind and see different things that if I would have stayed on the farm over there I would be absolutely cut off from a lot of things I got to know here.'[79] Scottish women shared his perception even when they had departed as children. Marion Kerr, who left Paisley as a child in the early 1920s and spent about five years in the United States, believed she would have had a different attitude to what she developed in Scotland had she not spent time overseas.[80] This was echoed profoundly by Isabella Deeks, who was just ten years old when she left Cathcart in 1923. According to Isabella, migration to the United States:

made me, I think, a better person, a more outgoing person because I learned to live with all kinds of people that maybe in Scotland I would have been a little more prejudiced because we would've lived in the same community, you know, and gone to the same churches and all that sort of thing and a lot of people just stick together. You even find that today with immigrants ... I think it gave me a broader outlook on life and I think that is why in today's world everybody is the same as far as I'm concerned. I don't care what religion, what race you are or anything. You are my friend until you show me that you're not.[81]

77 Interview with Mary Kendrick by Paul Sigrist, recorded 7 July 1994, EIOHP, EI Series 492.
78 Interview with Maureen Vaughn.
79 Interview with Stephen Concannon by Janet Levine, recorded 16 September 1992, EIOHP, EI Series 212.
80 Interview with Marion Kerr.
81 Interview with Isabella Deeks by Janet Levine, recorded 30 April 1997, EIOHP, EI Series 869.

Perhaps the biggest change was the self-confidence that migrant seemingly developed during their time overseas.[82] Maureen Vaughn was quite young when the family left Glasgow in 1952, and even though they spent just three years abroad Maureen attributes this aspect of her life to her current mindset:

I think it probably gave me more self-confidence, confidence to speak out. Before I tended to be quiet but because you were noticed anyway in class in the States because you were different. When you come back here you tended to miss that a bit. You weren't unique, you weren't the only Scot, you know. You were all Scots and when we first came back I rushed my mother out to buy me a complete school uniform … because I wanted to be the same as everyone else, I was tired of being different. But then I realised I was, I still was different. I'd had this experience that the rest hadn't had … It certainly built up my self-confidence. It gave me a broader outlook. I mean in this country in those days you very rarely saw a coloured person in the 1950s and I wasn't sure, you know, and my mother said that everybody is, is made equal and that's the American thing but when I got there it wasn't, you know. There was discrimination and I was there from the first black pupil came into the school and, of course, people talking about oh not riding in the school bus and my mother had said, 'Everyone's equal and you will ride in that school bus' and … it made me more interested in politics. When I was over there I was very much SNP, liberate Scotland, you know, from the cursed English … and so then I came back and discovered that people didn't really care that much, so long as things go on and they're not really disturbed.[83]

The other counterfactual observation that migrants made concerned their lifespan, with some speculating that their lives might have ended had they remained in Scotland, particularly given the effects of the Second World War. Allan Gunn left in 1925 as a nine-year-old from Glasgow and gratefully recognised: 'I'd have been in the service over there for one thing and it wouldn't have been near as good as what it was here. … Good chance I wouldn't be here now.'[84] Anne Quinn of Paisley similarly felt, 'I imagine it would have been altogether different although today they have a better standard of living than we did when we lived there.' Describing the devastation caused by the war, including 'there was one night the bombing was so bad, so bad in that particular town that there was 400 people killed in the town', Anne mused, 'I may not even be here today if I had lived in Scotland.'[85] By contrast with these

82 Self-confidence and self-assurance also distinguished returnees to Ireland in the 1990s from their non-migrant counterparts. See Corcoran, 'The process of migration and the reinvention of self', p. 185.
83 Interview with Maureen Vaughn.
84 Interview with Allan Gunn by Paul Sigrist, recorded 20 June 1992, EIOHP, EI Series 179.
85 Interview with Anne Quinn by Dennis Cloutier and Peter Kaplan, recorded 8 December 1983, EIOHP, NPS Series 146.

sombre meditations, some migrants commented more glibly on their possible alternative life. As Mary Dunn of Stirling joked good-naturedly, 'Well I had a boyfriend in Scotland. I might have married him [*laughs*] but other than that I don't know.'[86]

Conclusion

Clearly more research is required into the experience of return migration with an agenda combining quantitative and qualitative approaches. We need to know how many migrants returned home and from where, when they returned, why they returned, and whether they then moved on again. Their experiences at home as either temporary visitors or permanent returnees needs further investigation, along with the practical, social, economic, and political effects that returnees had on the homelands.

Meantime, this chapter has offered some initial gleanings. It reveals, for instance, that despite intentions for temporary or permanent migration at the outset, such initial conceptualisations were not set in stone. Migrants could and did return, while others despite longing to return remained abroad. This chapter has also explored some reasons for return migration and assessed the responses to migrants together with their own impressions of their homelands. The testimony shows that there was very little difference between Irish and Scots in this regard. The chapter also ended with a relatively novel exercise in counterfactual history by exploring the ways in which migrants felt their lives might have differed had they never undertaken to leave home.

The absence, to date, of many emigrant letters for this period of migration militates against a number of other critical issues worth exploring. What positive images, for instance, did home readers offer in order to entice migrants home? Did they emphasise use of the word 'home' in their communications, as did their nineteenth-century counterparts?[87] Perhaps most importantly, given the prevalence of the desire to return, why did so few fulfil this objective? Were they simply content abroad or did they merely not have access to financial resources?

Irrespective of such questions, it is evident from this book that migrants maintained transnational lives. This is demonstrated in the advice that intending migrants sought from those already settled and in the assistance that newcomers received after arrival. Their ongoing ties to home also encouraged

---

86 Interview with Mary Dunn by Dana Gumb, recorded 23 January 1986, EIOHP, AKRF Series 127.
87 See David Fitzpatrick, *Oceans of Consolation: Personal Accounts of Irish Migration to Australia* (Cork: Cork University Press, 1995); Angela McCarthy, *Irish Migrants in New Zealand, 1840–1937: 'The Desired Haven'* (Woodbridge: Boydell Press: 2005).

the departure of other migrants while robust bonds also facilitated return. In many ways these migrants were still betwixt and between two worlds and embraced the best of both.

Conclusion

This study has focused upon two groups of migrants, the Irish and the Scots, concentrating upon the important period 1921 to 1965, an era illuminated in rich detail by the types of sources utilised, particularly interviews. The book has tried also to engage with migration streams across the diversity of the Anglophone world, drawing upon the experiences of both Scottish and Irish migrants who went to the United States, Canada, New Zealand, and Australia. The study has revealed that a close reading of personal testimonies can expose assorted similarities and differences between Irish and Scots. As highlighted in the main themes of this book, subtle differences rather than yawning cultural gaps are apparent; similarities in attitude and expectation are more common than divergent or unique experiences. The key revelation of the work is that, despite a number of peculiarities characterising their individual and collective experiences of migration, both the Irish and Scots were relatively successful migrants in the period under consideration. In other words, similarities tied them together, rather than differences setting them apart.

This finding may partly be due to the nature of the surviving evidence, in which only those who had achieved a measure of success and satisfaction as emigrants were seemingly willing and able to reflect on their past. But this broad finding is also connected to issues of transnationalism and the character of the nations in which Irish and Scots settled. Transnational ties gave intending migrants vital knowledge about potential destinations and their eventual settlement abroad was eased substantially by the established migration patterns to the United States and British World. The comparative agenda adopted in the book has facilitated exploration of these aspects and also enabled analysis of a selection of major themes that were systematically examined to unearth particular and general experiences of migration.

The book has two methodological contributions. First, it utilised a variety of personal testimonies including private correspondence, interviews, questionnaires, and shipboard journals, together with more traditional documentary sources such as immigration files and maritime records. In recent years, the use of such sources has increased. Yet until now, comparative work has not been undertaken to see if life-ways, expectations, and experiences differed between groups and across places, as revealed in the migrants' own words. In this respect the second systematic contribution is in the comparative examination of these sources between two migrant groups and the destinations in which they settled. The inclusion of so many diverse and penetrating materials sourced from several avenues reduces any overarching bias in a study focused on one source. The study makes a particular contribution, however, in its inclusion of interviews, both spoken and written, and grapples with issues of why and how versions of the past are represented and what they mean. Using reminiscences also means considering the interface between individual and collective memory and the book has sought to analyse a number of testimonies in relation to one another to expose general and particular elements of the process of migration. In doing so it has engaged with a central challenge connected to the use of personal testimonies as historical evidence: their uniqueness and typicality. Furthermore, in using personal narratives the book portrays individual migration experiences which are often hidden in studies based on statistical analysis. Only by retrieving such sources can we get to the heart of what those involved in such a life-changing event thought and felt and witnessed.

A threefold comparative methodology devised by Nancy Green has facilitated the overall endeavour. It has illuminated, for instance, a number of similarities and differences between Irish and Scots in the ways they sensitively perceived their experiences of migration. Comparison has also shown that a number of contrasts emerge in the testimonies according to the destinations in which migrants settled. By gravitating to Canada and Australasia in the British World and also to the United States, all English-speaking destinations, Scottish and Irish migrants, together with their British counterparts, were at an obvious advantage compared with migrants from continental Europe and Asia. They spoke English and entered culturally similar societies. The transnational and comparative approaches are also significant for distinguishing a number of themes which guide the book, including multiple motives for migration and return, the anxious transition to and initial reception in new societies, the keen attachments to social networks and ethnic societies, and the energetic retention of cultural identities. Each of these will now be considered in turn.

Migrant testimonies capture vividly and emotionally the range of multiple motives propelling Irish and Scots on to distant shores. Economic, social, political, and demographic factors combined, revealing that migration arose out of wide-ranging and complex circumstances. These decisive elements, however, varied over time, with the quest for adventure becoming an increasingly dominant trope as the century advanced. Irish migrants were also more inclined to incorporate accounts of an edgy political environment in their decision to emigrate, though such explanations were more prominent among the Irish in the United States. Overall, however, Scots and Irish offered

similar justifications for their departures. Seductive images of potential destinations and the captivating stories of triumphant returned migrants, emphasising monetary gain in the United States and lifestyle factors in the British
World, proved particularly influential among migrants from both countries
deciding to move overseas. The complexities associated with the process of
migration have also been reconstructed, including consideration of alternative competing and alluring destinations.

The guidance and presence of a range of networks of family and friends
already settled abroad similarly enticed intending migrants. These intimate
connections offered critical practical assistance in the form of lodging and
housing, as well as emotional succour, as apprehensive, wide-eyed newcomers
confronted disorienting elements of their new homes. Likewise, these durable
transnational ties lured migrants home, sometimes permanently, more often
temporarily. They also provided vital financial support, with migrants moving
to the United States more inclined to make use of such assistance, while
migrants selecting the British World claimed government subsidies. Scots,
however, qualified for assisted passages to a greater degree than their Irish
counterparts, and tended to travel in family groups rather than as single adults
as the Irish did. Scottish access to subsidised passages furthermore ensured
that the British World continued to attract more Scots than Irish, while Irish
migration to the United States maintained its impetus until the 1950s. Complex
individual decisions to move therefore operated within broader contexts
involving collective family interests, the influence of emigration agents, and
the provision of financial subsidies, at both official and private levels.

The giddy transition to new lands was a liminal phase in which migrants
were caught betwixt and between two worlds. This evolution began at home
with frenzied preparations for departure and harrowing separations from loved
ones, the latter a particularly potent aspect of leaving Ireland. At sea, migrants
enthusiastically and wanly embraced novel sights, sounds, and smells, especially
pertinent for those making the longer voyage to the Antipodes, while the rapid
ocean passage to the United States made redundant the provision of extensive
entertainment pursuits at sea. This deeply transformative phase continued
after arrival. The overwhelming first impressions held by Irish and Scots in
the United States and British World show that both were captivated by similar
novelties particularly in relation to technological contrasts between home and
abroad, and in differences of food and climate, with little discrepancies distinguishable according to time of arrival. Migrants in all destinations similarly
situated these abundant contrasts within contemporary unease surrounding
the lenient treatment afforded to new arrivals and current disquieting conditions in the New World. Yet significant differences existed between their
varied experiences in their respective destinations. Irish and Scots entering

the United States through Ellis Island, for instance, underwent distressing events that remained with them. The United States was also the dominant receptor of a vast array of migrants from Europe and elsewhere, whereas New Zealand, Australia, and Canada continued to predominantly receive British and Irish migrants. The long history of Irish and Scottish migration to these British World destinations seemingly facilitated their relatively comfortable settlement throughout the twentieth century.

Despite the frequently disruptive character of their voyage and arrival, migrants energetically maintained compelling elements of their cultural identities. The testimonies reveal that ethnic societies and associational culture, especially for Scots in North America, were particularly prevalent in the memories of migrants. Moreover, by blending exterior/institutional and interior/personal worlds, the self-profession of tight local connections has been emphasised. Specific places were central to identity among these migrants, but so too was an overarching sense of their ethnic national identity. Scots were particularly voluble in this regard, with their confident narratives highlighting a striking demonstration of symbolic ethnicity, compared with the Irish. Scots reminisced extensively about the visible, audible, and celebratory appeal of kilts, tartans, and pipes, features that provided them with a conspicuous and identifiable symbolic ethnicity lingering to this day. Irish migrants, on the other hand, failed to vociferously assert a symbolic ethnicity, perhaps due to political tensions in Northern Ireland at the time their interviews were conducted. Similarly, the Irish, though alert to elements of a Gaelic-speaking upbringing, appear only to have used English in the New World, perhaps as a defensive measure due to social prejudice, but more probably to obtain social and economic advancement. Scots, on the other hand, took pride in emphasising their distinctive language and dialects, in part to distinguish themselves from their English counterparts. Migrants from both groups, however, were similarly conscious of jointly belonging to their new homelands.

What, then, are the implications of these findings for future research? First, the study has demonstrated that personal testimonies offer unparalleled insights into experiences of migration. By focusing on real people who felt pain, sadness, and fear, as well as excitement, happiness, and hope, we have gained intimate entry into their mindsets. What, though, are the experiences of other migrant groups across a range of destinations? Can similar elements be found in an overarching conception of migration? Second, the study has also incorporated the emotions and memories of child migrants, but future work urgently needs to engage with the entire multigenerational group. Did they similarly and relentlessly emphasise a robust ethnic heritage, and if so why and how? How did their experiences differ from the migrant generation? Third, we need to know more about the period after 1965, a phase of migration differing in many critical respects with what went before. Immigration policies altered, migration streams diversified, undocumented migration flourished, and transnational characteristics differed. Comparative research on the period after 1965 promises further critical insight as immigration and the hotly contested issues of assimilation, acculturation, and multiculturalism continue to generate widespread public debate and controversy across the globe.

Appendices

Appendix 1: emigration from Scotland and Ireland to the United States, Canada, and Australasia, 1921–38

	Overall total		US		Canada		Australasia	
	Ireland	*Scotland*	*Ireland*	*Scotland*	*Ireland*	*Scotland*	*Ireland*	*Scotland*
1921	24,828	35,390	19,234	12,990	3,394	15,453	2,200	6,947
1922	20,222	35,813	15,076	13,791	3,212	12,278	1,934	9,744
1923	32,827	84,572	23,815	46,343	7,323	29,070	1,689	9,159
1924	26,480	35,110	13,503	6,465	10,278	19,136	2,699	9,509
1925	38,071	33,800	29,285	12,952	5,203	11,040	3,583	9,808
1926	42,044	44,278	28,964	13,978	8,336	14,735	4,744	15,565
1927	38,356	39,427	26,951	12,258	7,941	15,473	3,464	11,696
1928	34,143	34,134	24,192	11,541	7,609	15,434	2,342	7,159
1929	32,687	39,231	22,031	14,736	9,080	20,090	1,576	4,405
1930	24,616	22,969	19,270	12,320	4,421	8,878	925	1,771
1931	2,028	3,586	931	949	755	1,931	342	706
1932	943	1,433	378	273	288	706	277	454
1933	1,062	1,360	502	387	237	508	323	465
1934	1,273	1,568	640	566	347	474	286	528
1935	1,147	1,380	553	342	254	508	340	530
1936	1,212	1,345	590	280	191	517	431	548
1937	596	1,596	217	462	187	557	192	577
1938	486	1,504	143	247	172	594	171	663
Totals	323,021	418,496	226,275	160,880	69,228	167,382	27,518	90,234

Source: Extracted from N. H. Carrier and J. R. Jeffery, *External Migration: A Study of the Available Statistics, 1815-1950* (London, 1953), Table D/F/G (1), p. 96.

Appendix 2: numbers and percentage (of total population and non-United States born population) of natives of Scotland and Ireland in United States, 1920–50

Census year	Scottish-born			Irish-born (including Northern Ireland)		
	Number	*% total pop*	*% foreign-born*	*Number*	*% total pop*	*% foreign-born*
1920	254,570	0.24	1.83	1,037,234	0.98	7.45
1930	354,323	0.29	2.49	923,642	0.75	6.50
1940	279,321	0.21	2.45	679,347	0.52	5.95
1950	244,200	0.16	2.40	520,359	0.35	5.12

Source: Figures calculated from *Sixteenth Census of the U.S. (1940)*, II, 43: 1950 figures from U.S. Bureau of the Census. Extracted from Rowland Tappan Berthoff, *British Immigrants in Industrial America, 1790-1950* (Cambridge: Harvard University Press, 1953), Table 2, p. 7.

Appendix 3: numbers and percentage (of total population and non-Canadian born population) of natives of Scotland and Ireland in Canada, 1921–61

Census Year	Scottish-born			Irish-born (including Northern Ireland)		
	Number	*% total pop*	*% foreign-born*	*Number*	*% total pop*	*% foreign-born*
1921	226,481	2.58	11.58	93,301	1.06	4.77
1931	279,765	2.70	12.12	107,544	1.04	3.73
1941	234,824	2.04	11.64	86,126	0.75	4.27
1951	226,343	1.62	10.99	80,795	0.58	3.92
1961	244,052	1.34	8.58	92,477	0.51	3.25

Source: Figures calculated from *Statistics Canada: Historical Statistics of Canada* on line at http://www.statcan.ca/english/freepub/11-516-XIE/sectiona/sectiona.htm.

Appendix 4: Scots and Irish in New Zealand as percentage of total population and non-New Zealand born population, 1921–71

Census year	Scottish-born			Irish-born (including Northern Ireland)		
	Number	% total pop	% non-NZ	Number	% total pop	% non-NZ
1921	51,654	4.2	16.5	34,419	2.8	11.0
1936	54,188	3.7	18.4	25,865	1.6	8.8
1945	43,818	2.8	17.5	18,615	1.1	14.3
1951	44,049	2.3	16.5	17,172	0.9	6.4
1956	46,399	2.1	14.9	17,508	0.8	5.6
1961	47,078	1.9	16.9	17,793	0.8	6.4
1966	49,937	1.9	15.3	17,603	0.7	5.4
1971	47,508	1.7	11.4	16,165	0.6	3.9

Source: Figures calculated from *New Zealand Population Census* (Wellington, 1923, 1945, 1952, 1959, 1964, 1969, 1975).

Appendix 5: Scots and Irish in Australia as percentage of total population and non-Australian born population, 1921–70

Census year	Scottish-born			Irish-born (including Northern Ireland)		
	Number	% total pop	% non-Aust	Number	% total pop	% non-Aust
1921	108,756	2.0	12.7	105,033	1.9	12.3
1933	132,489	2.0	14.7	78,652	1.2	8.7
1947	102,998	1.4	13.8	44,813	0.6	6.0
1954	123,634	1.4	9.6	47,673	0.5	3.7
1961	132,811	1.3	7.5	50,215	0.5	2.8
1966	152,275	1.3	7.1	55,176	0.5	2.6
1971	159,292	1.2	6.2	63,790	0.5	2.5

Source: Figures calculated from *Australian Immigration: Consolidated Statistics*, No. 4 (Canberra, 1970), pp. 12-13, and *Australian Immigration: Consolidated Statistics*, No. 13 (Canberra, 1983), pp. 12-13. I am grateful to Professor Eric Richards for providing me with copies of this information.

Appendix 6: migrants from Ireland in Australia, 1947–71

Census Year	Ireland Republic	Ireland undefined	Northern Ireland	Total
1947	4,664	34,610	5,539	44,813
1954	5,992	32,178	9,503	47,673
1961	7,628	29,429	13,158	50,215
1966	8,340	29,776	17,060	55,176
1971	8,308	33,546	21,936	63,790

Source: Figures calculated from *Australian Immigration: Consolidated Statistics*, No. 4 (Canberra, 1970), pp. 12-13, and *Australian Immigration: Consolidated Statistics*, No. 13 (Canberra, 1983), pp. 12-13. I am grateful to Professor Eric Richards for providing me with copies of this information.

Appendix 7: migrants from Ireland in New Zealand, 1936–71

Census Year	Ireland Republic	Ireland undefined	Northern Ireland	Total
1936	24,077*		1,788	25,865
1945	9,591*		9,024	18,615
1951	6,423	1,932	8,817	17,172
1956	6,566	1,857	9,085	17,508
1961	6,784	2,026	8,983	17,793
1966	6,539	1,909	9,155	17,603
1971	5,922	1,534	8,709	16,165

Source: Figures calculated from *New Zealand Population Census* (Wellington, 1945, 1952, 1959, 1964, 1969, 1975).
* = includes Ireland undefined.

Appendix 8: top ten foreign-born migrant groups in Australia, 1921, 1933, 1947

1921		1933		1947	
England	446,124	England	486,831	England	381,592
Scotland	108,756	Scotland	132,489	Scotland	102,998
Ireland	105,033	Ireland	78,652	Ireland	34,610
Germany	22,396	Italy	26,756	Italy	33,632
China	15,224	Germany	16,842	Germany	14,567
Wales	13,490	Wales	14,486	Greece	12,291
Italy	8,135	China	8,579	Wales	11,864
India	6,918	Greece	8,337	India	8,160
USA	6,604	India	6,774	Poland	6,573
Denmark	6,002	South Africa	6,199	Yugoslavia	5,866

Source: Figures extracted from *Australian Immigration: Consolidated Statistics*, No. 4 (Canberra, 1970), pp. 12-13. I am grateful to Professor Eric Richards for providing me with copies of this information.

Appendix 9: top ten foreign-born migrant groups in Australia, 1954, 1961, 1966

1954		1961		1966	
England	478,411	England	556,478	England	681,526
Scotland	123,634	Italy	228,296	Italy	267,325
Italy	119,897	Scotland	132,811	Scotland	152,275
Germany	65,422	Germany	109,315	Greece	140,089
Poland	56,594	Netherlands	102,083	Germany	108,708
Netherlands	52,035	Greece	77,333	Netherlands	99,549
Ireland	32,178	Poland	60,049	Yugoslavia	71,277
Greece	25,862	Yugoslavia	49,776	Poland	61,641
Yugoslavia	22,856	Malta	39,337	Malta	55,104
Malta	19,988	Hungary	30,553	Ireland	29,776

Source: Figures extracted from *Australian Immigration: Consolidated Statistics*, No. 4 (Canberra, 1970), pp. 12-13. I am grateful to Professor Eric Richards for providing me with copies of this information.

Bibliography

1. Personal testimonies

Alexander Turnbull Library, Wellington

Letters of Lorna Carter, August–October 1951, MS-Papers-7377.

Alexander Turnbull Library, Wellington – Oral History Centre

Interview with John Bell Brotherston by Judith Fyfe, recorded 1 June 1989, New Zealand Society for the Intellectually Handicapped (Inc) Oral History Project, OHC-0080.

Interview with Annie and Bob Crutchley by Megan Hutching, recorded 27 February 1998, 1998 New Zealand Citizenship Oral History Project, OHC-0421.

Interview with Ted Dowling by Ian Robertson, recorded 4 August and 27 September 1995, Wellington City Transport European Immigrants Oral History Project, OHC-0012.

Interview with John Gallagher by Robert Paton, recorded 1 September 1993, Labour Movement Oral History Project – Part II, OHC-0059.

Interview with George Gunn by Julian McCarthy, recorded 4 December 1996, Conscientious Objectors of World War II, OHC-0426.

Interview with Jock Hunter by Cath Kelly, recorded 27 September 1988, Trade Union Oral History Project, OHC-0112.

Interview with James Killeen by Madeline McGilvray, recorded 13 April 1999, Southland Oral History Project, OHC-0464.

Interview with Trudie Lloyd by Judith Fyfe, recorded 20 April 1990, Women's Division Federated Farmers of NZ (Inc) Oral History Project, OHC-0115.

Interview with David Mackie by Jamie MacKay, recorded 25 February 1992, Huntly Coalfields Oral History Project, OHC-0020.

Interview with Sister Mary Catherine Laboure McAleese by Jacqueline Gallagher, recorded 19–26 October 1993, Reading, Writing and Rosaries: Life Stories of Seven Dominican Nuns, OHC-0554.

Interview with Robert Paton by Joyce Paton, recorded 1982–84, Hawkes Bay Oral History Project, OHC-0438.

Interview with Andrew Rae by Robert Paton, recorded 9 December 1991, Labour Movement Oral History Project, OHC-0056.

Interview with Walter and Isabella Solly by Rosie Little, recorded 16–20 August 1985, Nelson and Golden Bay Oral History Project, OHC-0053.

Auckland City Libraries – Special Collections

Interview with Sydney Samuels by Sarah Dalton, recorded 13 February 1990, Glen Innes Oral History Project, Special Collections, 90-OH-012/1–2.

Comann Eachraidh Nis – Emigration folder

Interview with Dòmhnall Chrut.
Interview with Muchardh Domhnallach.
Interview with Seonaidh Shiurra.
Interview with Norman Smith.

Ellis Island Oral History Project, New York Statue of Liberty/Ellis Island National Monument

Interview with Catherine Aitchison by Janet Levine, recorded 19 July 2001, EI Series 1214.
Interview with Thomas Allan by Jean Kolva, recorded 16 July 1984, NPS Series 149.
Interview with Desmond Black by Janet Levine, recorded 12 March 1998, EI Series 982.
Interview with John Brady by Paul Sigrist, recorded 22 June 1995, EI Series 623.
Interview with Joseph Brady by Paul Sigrist recorded 25 September 1995, EI Series 673.
Interview with Julia Carmody by Paul Sigrist, recorded 18 July 1996, EI Series 767.
Interview with Jack Whitecross Carnegie by Janet Levine, recorded 15 February 1996, EI Series 729.
Interview with Stephen Concannon by Janet Levine, recorded 16 September 1992, EI Series 212.
Interview with Bridget Considine by Janet Levine, recorded 22 January 1996, EI Series 725.
Interview with Ann Conway by Janet Levine, recorded 11 March 1998, EI Series 981.
Interview with Anne Craven by Paul Sigrist, recorded 2 October 1991, EI Series 102.
Interview with Elizabeth Dalbey by Paul Sigrist, recorded 29 August 1995, EI Series 662.
Interview with John Patrick Daly by Elysa Matsen, recorded 16 September 1994, EI Series 558.
Interview with Isabella Deeks by Janet Levine, recorded 30 April 1997, EI Series 869.
Interview with Joseph Delaney by Dana Gumb, recorded 5 September 1985, AKRF Series 23.
Interview with Mary Dunn by Dana Gumb, recorded 23 January 1986, AKRF Series 127.
Interview with Catherine English by Paul Sigrist, recorded 19 September 1991, EI Series 91.
Interview with Johanna Flaherty by Debra Allee, recorded 29 May 1986, AKRF Series, 182.
Interview with John Joe Gallogly by Janet Levine, recorded 6 March 2001, EI Series 1194.
Interview with Della Gleckel by Paul Sigrist, recorded 2 May 1995, EI Series 611.
Interview with James Gleeson by Janet Levine, recorded 15 April 1993, EI Series 277.
Interview with Elizabeth Griffin by Andrew Phillips, recorded 26 May 1989, DP Series 38.
Interview with Allan Gunn by Paul Sigrist, recorded 20 June 1992, EI Series 179.
Interview with Helen Hansen by Andrew Phillips, recorded 30 August 1989, DP Series 46.
Interview with Mary Harney by Paul Sigrist, recorded 11 October 1991, EI Series 107.
Interview with Patrick Henderson by Paul Sigrist, recorded 7 August 1994, EI Series 524.
Interview with Frances Hoffman by Janet Levine, recorded 20 February 1997, EI Series 853.
Interview with Lillian Hopkins by Kate Moore, recorded 18 July 1994, KM Series 70.
Interview with Bridget Jones by Margo Nash, recorded 15 November 1974, NPS Series 78.

Interview with Michael Jordan by Paul Sigrist, recorded 19 October 1993, EI Series 397.

Interview with Mary Kelly by Paul Sigrist, recorded 2 May 1995, EI Series 613.

Interview with Mary Kelly by Paul Sigrist, recorded 10 September 1997, EI Series 936.

Interview with Mary Kendrick by Paul Sigrist, recorded 7 July 1994, EI Series 492.

Interview with Marion Kerr by Janet Levine, recorded 17 July 2001, EI Series 1029.

Interview with Margaret Kirk by Paul Sigrist, recorded 25 February 1994, EI Series 440.

Interview with Kathleen Lamberti by Paul Sigrist, recorded 25 February 1994, EI Series 439.

Interview with Mary Jo Lenney by Paul Sigrist, recorded 21 August 1996, EI Series 793.

Interview with Henrietta Lindsay by Janet Levine, recorded 18 July 2001, EI Series 1211.

Interview with Rose Loughlin by Janet Levine, recorded 30 April 1995, EI Series 607.

Interview with Eileen Lynn by Janet Levine, recorded 31 July 1994, EI Series 509.

Interview with John Lynn by Janet Levine, recorded 31 July 1994, EI Series 510.

Interview with Dannie Madden by Janet Levine, recorded 25 October 1993, EI Series 402.

Interview with Josephine Materia by Janet Levine, recorded 22 June 1994, EI Series 482.

Interview with Malachy McCourt by Margo Nash, recorded 20 March 1975, NPS Series 89.

Interview with Mary Margaret McGloin by Janet Levine, recorded 12 April 1994, EI Series 457.

Interview with William McGuire by Kate Moore, recorded 30 July 1994, KM Series 77.

Interview with Sr Helen McNally by Paul Sigrist, recorded 28 April 1995, EI Series 606.

Interview with Brigid McNulty by Janet Levine, recorded 24 November 1998, EI Series 1029.

Interview with Sarah McQuinn by Janet Levine, recorded 12 June 1996, EI Series 755.

Interview with Margaret McSween by Janet Levine, recorded 7 April 2000, EI Series 1144.

Interview with Ann Nelson by Janet Levine, recorded 8 December 1996, EI Series 832.

Interview with Anne O'Connor by Janet Levine, recorded 26 October 1994, EI Series 559.

Interview with Paul O'Dwyer by Paul Sigrist, recorded 17 July 1993, EI Series 362.

Interview with Sr Rose O'Neill by Paul Sigrist, recorded 3 June 1998, EI Series 1003.

Interview with Patrick Peak by Nancy Dallett, recorded 15 November 1985, AKRF series 84.

Interview with Maisie Pedersen by Paul Sigrist, recorded 26 February 1994, EI Series 442.

Interview with Anne Quinn by Dennis Cloutier and Peter Kaplan, recorded 8 December 1983, NPS Series 146.

Interview with David Saltman by Janet Levine, recorded 26 September 1991, EI Series 97.

Interview with Agnes Schilling by Janet Levine, recorded 16 June 1992, EI Series 172.

Interview with Elizabeth Schmid by Janet Levine, recorded 20 June 1992, EI Series 177.

Interview with Patrick Shea by Harvey Dixon, recorded 7 May 1980, NPS Series 120.

Interview with Christina Spratt by Janet Levine, recorded 15 March 1999, EI Series 1049.

Interview with Edward Stack by Paul Sigrist, recorded 23 July 1993, EI Series 356.

Interview with Mannie Steen by Paul Sigrist, recorded 22 March 1991, EI Series 33.

Interview with Maureen Vaughn by Janet Levine, recorded 24 July 2001, EI Series 1217.

Interview with Archibald Walls by Janet Levine, recorded 14 March 1998, EI Series 983.

Interview with James Joseph Walls by Janet Levine, recorded 20 July 1996, EI Series 771.

Interview with Anne Walsh by Nancy Dallett, recorded 26 June 1986, AKRF Series 200.

Interview with John Waters by Margo Nash, recorded 15 February 1974, NPS Series 49.

Interview with Archibald Wilkinson by Paul Sigrist, recorded 25 April 1995, EI Series 599.

Interview with John Will by Elysa Matsen, recorded 16 September 1994, EI Series 547.

Interview with Cecilia Zeilan by Janet Levine, recorded 2 August 1994, EI Series 514.

Hamilton City Libraries

Interview with Doreen Wilkinson by Sarah Smith, recorded 1995, OH0253.

Ministry of Culture and Heritage, New Zealand – British Assisted Immigrants Questionnaire

Anne Denham Craigmyle Anderson, 001.
Harold Fraser Armstrong, 007.
Dorothy Batcheler, 013.
Anne Jean Bays, 015.
Thomas Brown, 028.
Bruce Currie Clarke, 041.
Janet Inglis McVittie Clarke, 042.
Margaret Duchart Dodd, 060.
Evelyn Jean Duncan, 063.
Joan Frances Dunn, 065.
Stanley Edward Dunn, 066.
William Robert Ewart, 075.
David McPhun Gilchrist, 099.
Catherine Kinnear Graham, 100.
Elizabeth F. Harris, 107.
Elizabeth Ann Hicks, 115.
Thomas Johnstone Howatson, 126.
Alexander Campbell Johnstone, 135.
Frances Connor Jones, 137.
Thomas Francis Keane, 140.
Christina Watson Lovatt, 157.
James Macfarlane, 160.
David Robertson MacLeod, 165.
James Findlay McLachlan, 172.
James Alexander McMeekin, 173.
Elizabeth Jane Jolly Meyer, 177.
George Michie, 178.
Caroline Miller, 179.
George Nicholson, 191.
Sylvia Gibson Nicholson, 192.
Campbell Nicol, 193.
Flora Noke, 194.
Robert Paton, 206.
Jack Antony Pepper, 208.
Archibald Campbell Prentice, 212.
Georgina Prentice, 213.
David Reid, 219.
James Andrews Simms, 227.

George Kenneth Smith, 230.
Patrick Joseph Sweeney, 240.
Kenneth Ward, 261.
Kathleen Watters, 263.
William Smith Watters, 264.
Moray Dugald Stuart Wilson, 271.
James Wood, 275.
George James Alexander Wright, 276.
Isobel Christie Ness Yerbury, 278.

Oral History Collection, National Library of Australia, Sydney

Interview with Jim Comerford by Marjorie Biggins, recorded 15 May 1987, NSW Bicentennial Oral History Project, Oral TRC 2301/54.
Interview with Ena Hughes by Bronwyn Hughes, recorded 1987, NSW Bicentennial Oral History Project, Oral TRC 2279/8.
Interview with Angus Macdonald by Paula Hamilton, recorded 1 September 1987, NSW Bicentennial Oral History Project, Oral TRC 2301/137.
Interview with Hugh S. Roberton by Mel Pratt, recorded 8 July 1974, Mel Pratt Collection, Oral History Section, Oral TRC 121/53.

National Library of Scotland, Edinburgh

Letters of Ernest Younger, 1924–36, Acc. 9407/1–4.

Orkney Archives, Orkney

Shipboard journal of Annabella Sinclair, 1929, D1/118.

Private Possession

Lorna Carter's correspondence, 1951–54, kindly supplied by Lorna Ross.
Brigid Dawson's letter to her sister Ellen Quinn, 30 July 1924, kindly supplied by Joan Leonard.
Mary Gibson's shipboard journal, 1938, kindly supplied by May Tapp.
Robertson family information, kindly provided by Melanie King.

Wilkie Transcripts

Transcript of interview with Angus MacDonald.
Transcript of interview with Mary Ann MacDonald.
Transcript of interview with Mary MacIver.
Transcript of interview with Murdo M. MacLean.
Transcript of interview with Donald 'Tulag' MacLeod.
Transcript of interview with Norman 'Broxy' MacKenzie.

2. Unpublished manuscript sources

Archives New Zealand/Te Whare Tohu Tuhituhinga O Aotearoa, Head Office, Wellington

Labour Department – L – Vol. 1 Series 1, Subseries 22

L1 22/1/1	Secretary of State for Dominion Affairs, London Agreements (1936–46).
L1 22/1/3	Suggestions for state-aided migration, pts 1–2 (1936–46).
L1 22/1/4	Dominion Settlement Association – Immigration and Settlement in New Zealand (1936–55).
L1 22/1/5	Post-war Migration to New Zealand, pts 1–2 (1941–54).
L1 22/1/7	Salvation Army Training Scheme (1944–53).
L1 22/1/8	Australia – Policy, pts 1–4 (1930–58).
L1 22/1/9	Child Migration, pt 1 (1945–48).
L1 22/1/10	Populations and Migration. Figures and Trends.
L1 22/1/18	Transport and shipping to NZ, pt 1 (1946–50).
L 1 22/1/28	Suggestions and Criticisms, pts 1–2 (1947–57).
L 1 22/1/37	Reports from High Commissioner London, pts 1–3 (1947–57).
L 1 22/1/42	Fairbridge Farm Schools (1947–55).
L1 22/1/43	British Boys for British Farms YMCA Scheme (1947–48).
L 1 22/1/49	Newsletter and New Settler magazine (1948–59).
L 1 22/1/138	Canada – Policy and General (1947–61).
L 1 22/1/168	Spinster Shortage in New Zealand (1958).
L 1 22/1/181	New Settlers Committee – Presbyterian Church (1955–56).
L 1 22/2/1	New Zealand Prospects of Settlement, pts 4–5.
L1 22/2/2	Nursing and hospital employment, pt 1 (1952–54).
L 1 22/2/14	Advertising and Publicity.
L 1 22/2/19	General information supplied overseas.
L1 22/6	UK Immigration.

National Maritime Museum, Greenwich

White Star Line Ephemera.
Cunard Ephemera.
Canadian Pacific Ephemera.
Cook's Ocean Sailing List with Hints to Intending Travellers by Sea, May 1928.
P&O Ephemera.
P&O Menu card samples, P&O/74/5–6.
P&O Company Records: P&O Ships' Movements, P&O/42/23.
P&O Handbook of Information (January 1929).
P&O Handbook of Information (January 1938).
Royal Mail Line Limited Regulations 1950, RMS/67/1.
White Star Line Ephemera, E/WS/3.
Shaw Savill Ephemera.
Shaw Savill & Albion Co. Ltd Passenger Office Records: Outward Passage Money Sheets, SSS/2/31.
Voyage from New Zealand to London, 1930, MSS/82/079.1.

New Zealand Maritime Museum, Auckland

Rangitata Jockey Club Programme, 1 June 1959.

3. Internet sources

Scotsman Digital Archive: http://archive.scotsman.com

4. Secondary sources

Books

Akenson, Donald Harman, *The Irish Diaspora: A Primer* (Toronto and Belfast: P. D. Meany Company, Inc. and The Institute of Irish Studies, Queen's University of Belfast, 1996).

Almeida, Linda Dowling, *Irish Immigrants in New York City, 1945–1995* (Bloomington and Indianapolis: Indiana University Press, 2001).

Appleyard, R. T., *British Emigration to Australia* (London and Canberra: Australian National University, 1964).

Appleyard, Reg, with Alison Ray and Allan Segal, *The Ten Pound Immigrants* (London: Boxtree, 1988).

Archdeacon, Thomas J., *Becoming American: An Ethnic History* (New York: Free Press, 1983).

Baines, Dudley, *Emigration from Europe, 1815–1930* (Basingstoke: Macmillan Education, 1991).

Bayor, Ronald H., *Neighbors in Conflict: The Irish, Germans, Jews, and Italians of New York City, 1929–1941* (Urbana and Chicago: University of Illinois Press, 1988, 2nd edn).

Belich, James, *Paradise Reforged: A History of the New Zealanders from the 1880s to the Year 2000* (Auckland: Penguin, 2001).

Berthoff, Rowland Tappan, *British Immigrants in Industrial America, 1790–1950* (Cambridge: Harvard University Press, 1953).

Bönisch-Brednich, Brigitte, *Keeping a Low Profile: An Oral History of German Immigration to New Zealand* (Wellington: Victoria University Press, 2002).

Brettell, Caroline, *Anthropology and Migration: Essays on Transnationalism, Ethnicity, and Identity* (Walnut Creek: Altamira Press, 2003).

Brettell, Caroline B. and James F. Hollifield (eds), *Migration Theory: Talking Across Disciplines* (New York: Routledge, 2000).

Broun, Dauvit, Richard J. Finlay, and Michael Lynch (eds), *Image and Identity: The Making and Re-making of Scotland Through the Ages* (Edinburgh: John Donald Publishers, 1998).

Byron, Reginald, *Irish America* (Oxford: Clarendon Press, 1999).

Cohen, Robin, *Global Diasporas: An Introduction* (London: UCL Press, 1997).

Colley, Linda, *Britons: Forging the Nation, 1707–1837* (London: Vintage, 1996; 1st edn 1992).

Connolly, S. J., Rab Houston, and R. J. Morris (eds), *Conflict, Identity and Economic Development: Ireland and Scotland, 1600–1939* (Preston: Carnegie Publishing, 1995).

Constantine, Stephen, (ed.), *Emigrants and Empire: British Settlement in the Dominions Between the Wars* (Manchester: Manchester University Press, 1990).

Cullen, L. M. and T. C. Smout (eds), *Comparative Aspects of Irish and Scottish Economic and Social History, 1600–1900* (Edinburgh: John Donald, 1977).

Daniels, Roger, *Guarding the Golden Door: American Immigration Policy and Immigration Since 1882* (New York: Hill and Wang, 2004).

Delaney, Enda, *Demography, State and Society: Irish Migration to Britain, 1921–1971* (Liverpool: Liverpool University Press, 2000).

Delaney, Enda, *Irish Emigration Since 1921* (Dublin: The Economic and Social History Society of Ireland, 2002).

Devine, T. M., *Scotland's Empire, 1600–1815* (London: Allen Lane, 2003).

Devine, T. M., *The Scottish Nation, 1700–2000* (London: Penguin, 1999).

Devine, T. M. (ed.), *Scotland's Shame: Bigotry and Sectarianism in Modern Scotland* (Edinburgh and London: Mainstream Publishing, 2000).

Devine, T. M. and David Dickson (eds), *Ireland and Scotland, 1600–1850: Parallels and Contrasts in Economic and Social Development* (Edinburgh: John Donald, 1983).

Devine, T. M. and R. J. Finlay (eds), *Scotland in the Twentieth Century* (Edinburgh: Edinburgh University Press, 1996).

Devine, Tom and Paddy Logue (eds), *Being Scottish: Personal Reflections on Scottish Identity Today* (Edinburgh: Polygon, 2002).

Donaldson, William, *Popular Literature in Victorian Scotland: Language, Fiction, and the Press* (Aberdeen: Aberdeen University Press, 1986).

Ellis, David M., James A. Frost, Harold C. Syrett, and Harry J. Carman, *A History of New York State* (Ithaca, NY: Cornell University Press, 1967, revised edn, 1st pub. 1957).

Farry, Michael, *The Aftermath of Revolution: Sligo, 1921–23* (Dublin: University College Dublin Press, 2000).

Ferriter, Diarmaid, *The Transformation of Ireland, 1900–2000* (London: Profile Books, 2004).

Finlay, Richard J., *Modern Scotland, 1914–2000* (London: Profile Books, 2004).

Fitzpatrick, David, *Irish Emigration, 1801–1921* (Dublin: The Economic and Social History Society of Ireland, 1984).

Fitzpatrick, David, *Oceans of Consolation: Personal Accounts of Irish Migration to Australia* (Cork: Cork University Press, 1995).

Flinn, Michael (ed.), *Scottish Population History from the 17th Century to the 1930s* (Cambridge: Cambridge University Press, 1977).

Fry, Michael, *The Scottish Empire* (East Linton: Tuckwell Press, 2001).

Gabaccia, Donna R., *Italy's Many Diasporas* (Seattle: University of Washington Press, 2000).

Gallman, J. Matthew, *Receiving Erin's Children: Philadephia, Liverpool, and the Irish Famine Migration, 1845–1855* (Chapel Hill: University of North Carolina Press, 2000).

Genepp, Arnold van, *Rites of Passage*, translated by Monika B. Vizedom and Gabrielle L. Caffee, with an introduction by Solon T. Kimball (London: Routledge and Kegan Paul, 1960).

Gjerde, Jon, *The Minds of the West: Ethnocultural Evolution in the Rural Middle West, 1830–1917* (Chapel Hill and London: University of North Carolina Press, 1997).

Gray, Breda, *Women and the Irish Diaspora* (London and New York: Routledge, 2003).

Hammerton, A. James and Alistair Thomson, *Ten Pound Poms: Australia's Invisible Migrants. A Life History of Postwar British Emigration to Australia* (Manchester: Manchester University Press, 2005).

Harper, Marjory, *Adventurers and Exiles: The Great Scottish Exodus* (London: Profile Books, 2003).

Harper, Marjory, *Emigration from Scotland Between the Wars: Opportunity or Exile?* (Manchester: Manchester University Press, 1998).

Harper, Marjory (ed.), *Emigrant Homecomings: The Return Movement of Emigrants, 1600–2000* (Manchester: Manchester University Press, 2005).

Hart, Peter, *The I.R.A. and Its Enemies: Violence and Community in Cork, 1916–1923* (Oxford: Oxford University Press, 1998).

Hart, Peter, *The I.R.A. at War, 1916–1923* (Oxford: Oxford University Press, 2003).

Harvie, Christopher, *No Gods and Precious Few Heroes: Twentieth-Century Scotland* (Edinburgh: Edinburgh University Press, 2000, 3rd edn).

Haws, Duncan, *Merchant Fleets: Royal Mail Line, Nelson Line* (Crowborough, Sussex: TCL Publications, 1982).

Hoerder, Dirk, *Creating Societies: Immigrant Lives in Canada* (Montreal and Kingston: McGill-Queen's University Press, 1999).

Hoerder, Dirk and Leslie Page Moch (eds), *European Migrants: Global and Local Perspectives* (Boston: Northeastern University Press, 1996).

Hoerder, Dirk and Horst Rössler (eds), *Distant Magnets: Expectations and Realities in the Immigrant Experience, 1840–1930* (New York: Holmes and Meier 1993).

Hutching, Megan, *Long Journey for Sevenpence: Assisted Immigration to New Zealand from the United Kingdom, 1947–1975* (Wellington: Victoria University Press, 1999).

Jupp, James (ed.), *The Australian People: An Encyclopedia of the Nation, Its People and Their Origins* (Cambridge: Cambridge University Press, 2001).

Kalra, Virinder S., Raminder Kaur, and John Hutnyk, *Diaspora and Hybridity* (London: Sage Publications, 2005).

Kelly, Mary C., *The Shamrock and the Lily: The New York Irish and the Creation of a Transatlantic Identity, 1845–1921* (New York: Peter Lang, 2005).

Keogh, Dermot, Finbarr O'Shea, and Carmel Quinlan (eds), *The Lost Decade: Ireland in the 1950s* (Cork: Mercier Press, 2004).

Lambert, Sharon, *Irish Women in Lancashire, 1922–1960: Their Story* (Lancaster: Centre for North-West Regional Studies, 2001).

Lines, Kenneth, *British and Canadian Immigration to the United States Since 1920* (San Francisco: R&E Research Associates, 1978).

MacDougall, Ian, (ed.), *Militant Miners: Recollections of John McArthur, Buckhaven; and Letters, 1924–26, of David Proudfoot, Methil, to G. Allen Hutt* (Edinburgh: Polygon, 1981).

McCart, Neil, *20th Century Passenger Ships of the P&O* (Wellingborough: Patrick Stephens, 1985).

McCarthy, Angela, *Irish Migrants in New Zealand, 1840–1937: 'The Desired Haven'* (Woodbridge: Boydell Press: 2005).

McCarthy, Angela (ed.), *A Global Clan: Scottish Migrant Networks and Identities Since the Eighteenth Century* (London and New York: Tauris Academic Studies, 2006).

McCourt, Frank, *Angela's Ashes: A Memoir of a Childhood* (London: Flamingo, 1997).

McCourt, Frank, *'Tis* (London: Flamingo, 2000).

McCourt, Malachy, *A Monk Swimming* (London: Harper Collins, 1999).

McLellan, R. S., *Anchor Line, 1856–1956* (Glasgow: Anchor Line, 1956).

Meagher, Timothy J., *Inventing Irish America: Generation, Class, and Ethnic Identity in a New England City, 1880–1928* (Notre Dame: University of Notre Dame, 2001).

Mitchison, Rosalind, and Peter Roebuck (eds), *Economy and Society in Scotland and Ireland, 1500–1939* (Edinburgh: John Donald, 1988).

Osofsky, Gilbert, *Harlem: The Making of a Ghetto. Negro New York, 1890–1930* (New York: Harper & Row, 1971, 2nd edn; 1st pub. 1963).

Perks, Robert, and Alistair Thomson (eds), *The Oral History Reader* (London and New York: Routledge, 1998).

Pillemer, David B., *Momentous Events, Vivid Memories* (Cambridge and London: Harvard University Press, 1998).

Ray, Celeste, *Highland Heritage: Scottish Americans in the American South* (Chapel Hill and London: University of North Carolina Press, 2001).

Richards, Eric, *Britannia's Children: Emigration from England, Scotland, Wales, and Ireland*

Since 1600 (London and New York: Hambledon and London, 2004).

Roe, Michael, *Australia, Britain, and Migration, 1915–1940: A Study of Desperate Hopes* (Cambridge and New York: Cambridge University Press, 1995).

Schrier, Arnold, *Ireland and the American Emigration, 1850–1900* (Chester Springs: Dufour Editions, 1997; 1st edn 1958).

Sherington, Geoffrey, *Australia's Immigrants, 1788–1978* (Sydney: Allen and Unwin, 1980).

Wagner, Gillian, *Children of the Empire* (London: Weidenfeld and Nicolson, 1982).

Walshaw, R. S., *Migration to and from the British Isles: Problems and Policies* (London: Jonathan Cape, 1941).

Walter, Bronwen, *Outsiders Inside: Whiteness, Place, and Irish Women* (London and New York: Routledge, 2001).

White, Richard, *Remembering Ahanagran: Storytelling in a Family's Past* (New York: Hill and Wang, 1998).

Wilkie, Jim, *Metagama: A Journey from Lewis to the New World* (Edinburgh: Birlinn, 1987 and 2001).

Withers, Charles W. J., *Urban Highlanders: Highland-Lowland Migration and Urban Gaelic Culture, 1700–1900* (East Linton: Tuckwell Press, 1998).

Wyman, Mark, *Round-trip to America: The Immigrants Return to Europe, 1880–1930* (Ithaca and London: Cornell University Press, 1993).

Chapters and articles

Almeida, Linda Dowling, 'A great time to be in America: the Irish in post-Second World War New York City', in Dermot Keogh, Finbarr O'Shea, and Carmel Quinlan (eds), *The Lost Decade: Ireland in the 1950s* (Cork: Mercier Press, 2004), pp. 206–20.

Anderson, M., 'Population and family life', in T. Dickson and J. H. Treble (eds), *People and Society in Scotland*, Vol. 3: *1914–1990* (Edinburgh: John Donald Publishers, 1992), pp. 12–47.

Baily, Samuel L., 'Cross-cultural comparison and the writing of migration history: some thoughts on how to study Italians in the New World', in Virginia Yans-McLaughlin (ed.), *Immigration Reconsidered: History, Sociology, and Politics* (New York and Oxford: Oxford University Press, 1990), pp. 241–53.

Bain, Irene, 'Post-war Scottish immigration', in James Jupp (ed.), *The Australian People: An Encyclopedia of the Nation, Its People and Their Origins* (Cambridge: Cambridge University Press, 2001), pp. 668–74.

Benmayor, Rina and Andor Skotnes, 'Some reflections on migration and identity', in Rina Benmayor and Andor Skotnes (eds), *International Yearbook of Oral History and Life Stories*, Vol. 3: *Migration and Identity* (Oxford: Oxford University Press, 1994), pp. 1–18.

Berthoff, Rowland, 'Under the kilt: variations on the Scottish-American ground', *Journal of American Ethnic History*, 1:2 (1982), pp. 5–34.

Bodnar, John, 'Generational memory in an American town', *Journal of Interdisciplinary History*, 26:4 (1996), pp. 619–37.

Bourke, Joanna, 'Introduction: "remembering" war', *Journal of Contemporary History*, 39:4 (2004), pp. 473–85.

Boyd, Monica, 'Family and personal networks in international migration: recent developments and new agendas', *International Migration Review*, 23:3 (1989), pp. 638–70.

Brubaker, Rogers, 'The "diaspora" diaspora', *Ethnic and Racial Studies*, 28:1 (2005), pp. 1–19.

Bumsted, J. M., 'Scottishness and Britishness in Canada, 1790–1914', in Marjory Harper and Michael E. Vance (eds), *Myth, Migration and the Making of Memory: Scotia and Nova Scotia, c.1700–1990* (Halifax and Edinburgh: Fernwood Publishing and John Donald Publishers, 1999), pp. 89–104.

Cameron, Ewen A., 'The Scottish highlands: from congested district to objective one', in T. M. Devine and R. J. Finlay (eds), *Scotland in the Twentieth Century* (Edinburgh: Edinburgh University Press, 1996), pp. 153–69.

Campbell, Malcolm, 'Emigrant responses to war and revolution, 1914–21: Irish opinion in the United States and Australia', *Irish Historical Studies*, 32:125 (2000), pp. 75–92.

Campbell, Malcolm, 'Immigrants on the land: a comparative study of Irish rural settlement in nineteenth-century Minnesota and New South Wales', in Andy Bielenberg (ed.), *The Irish Diaspora* (Harlow: Longman, 2000), pp. 176–94.

Campbell, Malcolm, 'Ireland's furthest shores: Irish immigrant settlement in nineteenth-century California and Eastern Australia', *Pacific Historical Review*, 71:1 (2002), pp. 59–90.

Campbell, Malcolm, 'Irish nationalism and immigrant assimilation: comparing the United States and Australia', *Australasian Journal of American Studies*, 16:2 (1996), pp. 24–43.

Campbell, Malcolm, 'The other immigrants: comparing the Irish in Australia and the United States', *Journal of American Ethnic History*, 14:3 (1995), pp. 3–22.

Casey, Marion R., '"From the east side to the seaside": Irish Americans on the move in New York city', in Ronald H. Bayor and Timothy J. Meagher (eds), *The New York Irish* (Baltimore and London: Johns Hopkins University Press, 1996), pp. 395–418.

Cattell, Maria G. and Jacob J. Climo, 'Meaning in social memory and history: anthropological perspectives', in Jacob J. Climo and Maria G. Cattell (eds), *Social Memory and History: Anthropological Perspectives* (Walnut Creek: Altamira Press, 2002), pp. 1–36.

Cohen, Anthony P., 'Culture as identity: an anthropologist's view', *New Literary History*, 24 (1993), pp. 195–209.

Confino, Alon, 'Collective memory and cultural history: problems of method', *American Historical Review*, 105:5 (1997), pp. 1386–403.

Constantine, Stephen, 'British emigration to the Empire-Commonwealth since 1880: from overseas settlement to diaspora?', *Journal of Imperial and Commonwealth History*, 31:2 (2003), pp. 16–35.

Constantine, Stephen, 'The British government, child welfare, and child migration to Australia after 1945', *Journal of Imperial and Commonwealth History*, 30:1 (2002), pp. 99–132.

Constantine, Stephen, 'Children as ancestors: child migrants and identity in Canada', *British Journal of Canadian Studies*, 16:1 (2003), pp. 150–9.

Conzen, Kathleen Neils, David A. Gerber, Ewa Morawska, George E. Pozzetta and Rudolph J. Vecoli, 'The invention of ethnicity: a perspective from the U.S.A.', *Journal of American Ethnic History*, 12:1 (1992), pp. 3–41.

Corcoran, Mary P., 'The process of migration and the reinvention of self: the experiences of returning Irish emigrants', *Éire-Ireland*, 37:1 (2002), pp. 175–91.

Cowan, E. J., 'From the Southern Uplands to Southern Ontario', in T. M. Devine (ed.), *Scottish Emigration and Scottish Society* (Edinburgh: John Donald Publishers, 1992), pp. 61–83.

Cowan, Edward J., 'The myth of Scotch Canada', in Marjory Harper and Michael E. Vance (eds), *Myth, Migration and the Making of Memory: Scotia and Nova Scotia, c.1700–1990* (Halifax and Edinburgh: Fernwood Publishing and John Donald Publishers, 1999), pp. 49–72.

Delaney, Enda, 'Placing postwar Irish migration to Britain in a comparative European perspective, 1945–1981', in Andy Bielenberg (ed.), *The Irish Diaspora* (London: Longman, 2000), pp. 331–56.

Devine, T. M., 'The invention of Scotland', in David Dickson, Seán Duffy, Cathal Ó Háinle and Ian Campbell Ross (eds), *Ireland and Scotland: Nation, Region, Identity. A Record of the TCD Conference September 2000* (Dublin: A. & A. Farmar, 2001), pp. 18–24.

Devine, T. M., 'Irish and Scottish development revisited', in David Dickson and Cormac Ó Gráda (eds), *Refiguring Ireland: Essays in Honour of L. M. Cullen* (Dublin: Lilliput Press, 2003), pp. 37–51.

Devine, T. M., 'Making the Caledonian connection: the development of Irish and Scottish Studies', in Liam McIlvanney and Ray Ryan (eds), *Ireland and Scotland: Culture and Society, 1700–2000* (Dublin: Four Courts Press, 2005), pp. 248–57.

Devine, T. M., 'The paradox of Scottish emigration', in T. M. Devine (ed.), *Scottish Emigration and Scottish Society*, (Edinburgh: John Donald Publishers, 1992), pp. 1–15.

Dickson, Tony, and Jim Treble, 'Scotland, 1914–1990', in Tony Dickson and James H. Treble (eds), *People and Society in Scotland*, Vol. 3: *1914–1990* (Edinburgh: John Donald, 1992), pp. 1–11.

Doyle, David Noel, 'The Irish in Australia and the United States: some comparisons, 1800–1939', *Irish Economic and Social History*, 16 (1989), pp. 73–94.

Finlay, Richard J., 'Continuity and change: Scottish politics, 1900–45', in T. M. Devine and R. J. Finlay (eds), *Scotland in the Twentieth Century* (Edinburgh: Edinburgh University Press, 1996), pp. 64–84.

Fitzpatrick, David, 'Irish emigration in the later nineteenth century', *Irish Historical Studies*, 22:86 (1980), pp. 126–43.

Gans, Herbert J., 'Comment : ethnic invention and acculturation, a bumpy-line approach', *Journal of American Ethnic History*, 12:1 (1992), pp. 42–52.

Gans, Herbert J., 'Symbolic ethnicity: the future of ethnic groups and cultures in America', *Ethnic and Racial Studies*, 2:1 (1979), pp. 1–20.

Gerber, David A., 'Forming a transnational narrative: new perspectives on European migrations to the United States', *History Teacher*, 35:1 (2001), online at http://www.historycooperative.org/journals/ht/35.1/gerber.html.

Gerber, D. A., 'The immigrant letter between positivism and populism: the uses of immigrant personal correspondence in twentieth-century American scholarship', *Journal of American Ethnic History*, 16:4 (1997), pp. 3–34.

Green, Anna, 'Individual remembering and "collective memory": theoretical presuppositions and contemporary debates', *Oral History*, 32:2 (2004), pp. 35–44.

Green, Anna, 'The shipping companies and '51', in David Grant (ed.), *The Big Blue: Snapshots of the 1951 Waterfront Lockout* (Christchurch: Canterbury University Press, 2004), pp. 109–14.

Green, Nancy L., 'The comparative method and poststructural structuralism: new perspectives for migration studies', in Jan Lucassen and Leo Lucassen (eds), *Migration, Migration History, History: Old Paradigms and New Perspectives* (Bern: Peter Lang, 1997), pp. 57–72.

Green, Nancy L., 'The modern Jewish diaspora: eastern European Jews in New York, London, and Paris', in Dirk Hoerder and Leslie Page Moch (eds), *European Migrants: Global and Local Perspectives* (Boston: Northeastern University Press, 1996), pp. 263–81.

Hammerton, A. James, '"We're not Poms": the shifting identities of post-war Scottish migrants to Australia', in Angela McCarthy (ed.), *A Global Clan: Scottish Migrant Networks and Identities Since the Eighteenth Century* (London and New York: Tauris Academic Studies, 2006), pp. 222–42.

Harper, Marjory, 'Enticing the emigrant: Canadian agents in Ireland and Scotland, c.1870–c.1920', *Scottish Historical Review*, 83:1 (2004), pp. 41–58.

Hearn, Jonathan, 'Narrative, agency, and mood: on the social construction of national history in Scotland', *Comparative Study of Society and History*, 44:4 (2002), pp. 745–69.

Hoerder, Dirk, 'Migration in the Atlantic economies: regional European origins and worldwide expansion', in Dirk Hoerder and Leslie Page Moch (eds), *European Migrants: Global and Local Perspectives* (Boston: Northeastern University Press, 1996).

Horsbroch, Dauvit, 'The Scots language: an historical and political assessment', in Ignacy Ryszard Danka and Piotr Stalmaszczyk (eds), *Studia Indogermanica Lodziensia IV. Language Contact in the Celtic World* (Łódź, 2002).

Kansteiner, Wulf, 'Finding meaning in memory: a methodological critique of collective memory studies', *History and Theory*, 41 (2002), pp. 179–97.

Kenny, Kevin, 'Diaspora and comparison: the global Irish as a case study', *The Journal of American History*, 90:1 (2003), pp. 134–62.

Keyes, Charles F., 'Towards a new formulation of the concept of ethnic group', *Ethnicity*, 3:3 (1976), pp. 202–13.

Lindsay, Isabel, 'Migration and motivation: a twentieth-century perspective', in T. M. Devine (ed.), *Scottish Emigration and Scottish Society* (Edinburgh: John Donald Publishers, 1992), pp. 154–74.

Lucas, D., 'Scottish immigration, 1861–1945', in James Jupp (ed.), *The Australian People: An Encyclopedia of the Nation, Its People and Their Origins* (Cambridge: Cambridge University Press, 2001), pp. 665–8.

MacRaild, Donald M., 'Crossing migrant frontiers: comparative reflections on Irish migrants in Britain and the United States during the nineteenth century', *Immigrants and Minorities*, 18:2&3 (1999), pp. 40–70.

Massey, Douglas S., Joaquín Arango, Graeme Hugo, Ali Kouaouci, Adela Pellegrino and J. Edward Taylor, 'Theories of international migration: a review and appraisal', *Population and Development Review*, 19:3 (1993), pp. 431–66.

McCarthy, Angela, 'Ethnic networks and identities among interwar Scottish migrants in North America', in Angela McCarthy (ed.), *A Global Clan: Scottish Migrant Networks and Identities Since the Eighteenth Century* (London and New York: Tauris Academic Studies, 2006), pp. 203–26.

McCarthy, Angela, '"For spirit and adventure": personal accounts of Scottish migration to New Zealand, 1921–1961', in Tom Brooking and Jennie Coleman (eds), *The Heather and the Fern: Scottish Migration and New Zealand Settlement* (Dunedin: Otago University Press, 2003), pp. 117–32.

McCarthy, Angela, 'National identities and twentieth-century Scottish migrants in England', in William L. Miller (ed.), *Anglo-Scottish Relations from 1900 to Devolution and Beyond* (Oxford: Oxford University Press, 2005, Proceedings of the British Academy 128), pp. 171–82.

McCarthy, Angela, 'Personal letters, oral testimony, and Scottish migration to New Zealand in the 1950s: the case of Lorna Carter', *Immigrants and Minorities*, 23:1 (2005), pp. 59–79.

McCarthy, Angela, 'Scottish national identities among inter-war migrants in North America and Australasia', *Journal of Imperial and Commonwealth History*, 34:2 (2006), pp. 201–22.

McCrone, David, 'Who do you say you are? Making sense of national identities in modern Britain', *Ethnicities*, 2:3 (2002), pp. 301–20.

McNickle, Chris, 'When New York was Irish, and after', in Ronald H. Bayor and Timothy

J. Meagher (eds), *The New York Irish* (Baltimore and London: Johns Hopkins University Press, 1996), pp. 337–56.

Moch, Leslie Page, 'Networks among Bretons? The evidence for Paris, 1875–1925', *Continuity and Change*, 18:3 (2003), pp. 431–55.

Moya, Jose C., 'Immigrants and associations: a global and historical perspective', *Journal of Ethnic and Migration Studies*, 31:5 (2005), pp. 833–64.

Nadell, Pamela S., 'United States steerage legislation: the protection of the emigrants en route to America', *Immigrants and Minorities*, 5:1 (1986), pp. 62–72.

Newlands, David, 'The regional economics of Scotland', in T. M. Devine, C. H. Lee and G. C. Peden (eds), *The Transformation of Scotland: The Economy Since 1700* (Edinburgh: Edinburgh University Press, 2005), pp. 159–83.

Nilsen, Kenneth E., 'The Irish language in New York, 1850–1900', in Ronald H. Bayor and Timothy J. Meagher (eds), *The New York Irish* (Baltimore and London: Johns Hopkins University Press, 1996), pp. 252–74.

Nora, Pierre, 'Between memory and history', in Pierre Nora (ed.), *Realms of Memory: Rethinking the French Past*, Vol. 1: *Conflicts and Divisions* (New York: Columbia University Press, 1996), pp. 1–20.

Payne, Peter L., 'The economy', in T. M. Devine and R. J. Finlay (eds), *Scotland in the Twentieth Century* (Edinburgh: Edinburgh University Press, 1996), pp. 13–45.

Richards, Eric, 'Hearing voices: an introduction', in A. James Hammerton and Eric Richards (eds), *Speaking to Immigrants: Oral Testimony and the History of Australian Migration. Visible Immigrants: Six* (Canberra: Australian National University, 2002), pp. 1–19.

Ridge, John T., 'Irish county societies in New York, 1880–1914', in Ronald H. Bayor and Timothy J. Meagher (eds), *The New York Irish* (Baltimore and London: Johns Hopkins University Press, 1996), pp. 275–300.

Ryan, Louise, 'Moving spaces and changing places: Irish women's memories of emigration to Britain in the 1930s', *Journal of Ethnic and Migration Studies*, 29:1 (2003), pp. 67–82.

Schiller, Nina Glick, Linda Basch, and Cristina Blanc-Szanton, 'Transnationalism: a new analytic framework for understanding migration', in Nina Glick Schiller, Linda Basch, and Cristina Blanc-Szanton (eds), *Towards a Transnational Perspective on Migration: Race, Class, Ethnicity, and Nationalism Reconsidered. Annals of the New York Academy of Sciences*, 645 (New York: New York Academy of Sciences, 1992), pp. 1–24.

Schrover, Marlou and Floris Vermeulen, 'Immigrant organisations', *Journal of Ethnic and Migration Studies*, 31:5 (2005), pp. 823–32.

Schuetz, Alfred 'The homecomer', *American Journal of Sociology*, 50:5 (1945), pp. 369–76.

Sherington, Geoffrey, '"A better class of boy": the Big Brother movement, youth migration and citizenship of empire', *Australian Historical Studies*, 33:120 (2002), pp. 267–85.

Summerfield, Penny, 'Culture and composure: creating narratives of the gendered self in oral history interviews', *Cultural and Social History*, 1:1 (2004), pp. 65–93.

Thomson, Alistair, '"I live on my memories": British return migrants and the possession of the past', *Oral History*, 31:2 (2003), pp. 55–65.

Thomson, Alistair, 'Moving stories: oral history and migration studies', *Oral History*, 27:1 (1999), pp. 24–37.

Tilly, Charles, 'Transplanted networks', in Virginia Yans-McLaughlin (ed.), *Immigration Reconsidered: History, Sociology, and Politics* (New York and Oxford: Oxford University Press, 1990), pp. 79–95.

Vertovec, Steven, 'Conceiving and researching transnationalism', *Ethnic and Racial Studies*, 22:2 (1999), p. 447–62.

Vertovec, Steven, 'Transnationalism and identity', *Journal of Ethnic and Migration Studies*, 27:4 (2001), pp. 573–82.

Wyman, Mark, 'Emigrants returning: the evolution of a tradition', in Marjory Harper (ed.), *Emigrant Homecomings: The Return Movement of Emigrants, 1600–2000* (Manchester: Manchester University Press, 2005), pp. 16–31.

Yans-McLaughlin, Virginia, 'Metaphors of self in history: subjectivity, oral narrative, and immigration studies', in Virginia Yans-McLaughlin (ed.), *Immigration Reconsidered: History, Sociology, and Politics* (New York and Oxford: Oxford University Press, 1990), pp. 254–92.

Index

Lightning Source UK Ltd.
Milton Keynes UK
UKOW050253240113

205284UK00002B/47/P